W9-CIB-475

SPIRITUALITY, GENDER,
AND THE SELF
IN RENAISSANCE ITALY

Querciolo Mazzonis

Spirituality, Gender, and the Self in Renaissance Italy

*Angela Merici and the
Company of St. Ursula (1474–1540)*

THE CATHOLIC UNIVERSITY OF AMERICA PRESS
Washington, D.C.

Copyright © 2007
The Catholic University of America Press
All rights reserved
The paper used in this publication meets the minimum requirements
of American National Standards for Information Science—Permanence
of Paper for Printed Library Materials, ANSI Z39.48-1984.

∞

LIBRARY OF CONGRESS CATALOGING-IN-PUBLICATION DATA
Mazzonis, Querciolo, 1965–
Spirituality, gender, and the self in Renaissance Italy : Angela Merici and
the Company of St. Ursula (1474–1540) / Querciolo Mazzonis.
p. cm.
Includes bibliographical references and (p.   ) index.
ISBN-13: 978-0-8132-1490-0 (pbk. : alk. paper)
ISBN-10: 0-8132-1490-4 (pbk. : alk. paper)
1. Angela Merici, Saint, 1474–1540.   2. Christian saints—
Italy—Brescia—Biography.   3. Ursulines—Italy—History.
4. Brescia (Italy)—Church history.   I. Title.
BX4700.A45M39 2007
271'.97402—dc22
2006006977
[B]

Contents

Acknowledgments

As often occurs with first books, *Spirituality, Gender, and the Self in Renaissance Italy* has distant roots. My interest in St. Angela Merici, spirituality, gender, the Renaissance, and the concept of the "self" goes back to my university years in Rome in the late 1980s. The intellectual evolution of my research took shape across three countries, as its bibliographical references, both Italian and Anglo-American, show. In Italy I was first inspired by the lectures and early pioneering essays on gender and medieval piety (published in the 1970s) by the controversial Italian anthropologist Ida Magli. The works of Italian scholars such as Gabriella Zarri helped me focus on Italian religious women. My research developed at Royal Holloway College, University of London, where I did a Ph.D. on this subject. I am indebted to my supervisors, Lyndal Roper and Sandra Cavallo, as this book represents a substantial revision of my thesis. Finally, American studies on female spirituality, medieval culture, and gender have shaped many aspects of my work.

Spirituality, Gender, and the Self is a study of Angela Merici and some traits of female spirituality and early modern Catholicism, all within their social and cultural contexts. I chose Angela Merici as my primary focus because, as I demonstrate in this book, she is a particularly rich figure, both as a thinker in her own right and as a locus of Renaissance spirituality. If female religiosity has been recently recognized as a subject of historical inquiry, the importance and significance of Angela Merici still has to be fully acknowledged. Her writings, in my opinion, mirror the female approach to the sacred and the complexity of the religious transition of the period. They put forward an original spiritual ideal and are

vii

particularly rich from a human perspective. For these reasons the heirs of Angela—diversified in a variety of organizations all over the world—still feel a very strong attachment to the Brescian saint today. I would like to remember two of them here: Luciana Mariani and Elisa Tarolli, coauthors of the most recent and accurate work on Angela. For many years they helped and advised me with absolute respect for my lay interpretation of "their" saint. I am very sorry that they did not live to see this book published.

I would like to thank all my colleagues, former teachers, and friends who influenced me and helped me to shape this book. I am especially grateful to Tom Cohen and Alison Frazier who, with extraordinary generosity, offered me their intellectual and linguistic suggestions. I would like to thank Caroline Bynum, Sara Cabibbo, Francesca Cantù, David D'Avray, Claudia Di Filippo Bareggi, Maria Rosa Di Simone, Simon Ditchfield, Robin DuBlanc, Silvia Evangelisti, Maria Paola Guarducci, Raymond Gillespie, Colm Lennon, Linda Lierheimer, Jehanne Marchesi, John Martin, Chiara Orelli, and Mario Rosa for their contributions and support. Errors that remain are, of course, my own. I am also grateful to the Institute of Historical Research of London and the Italian Ministry of Education, which funded this project at crucial stages, and to the Università degli Studi di Siena for allowing me the time and tranquility to write. This book is dedicated to the memory of my father, Filippo Mazzonis.

Introduction

Angela Merici was born circa 1474 in Desenzano del Garda, a small town in the province of Brescia, to an impoverished family of the lower nobility. Drawn to a spiritual life of prayer and penitence from early childhood, Angela became a tertiary of the Franciscan order in her twenties, pursuing a spiritual life while remaining out in the world. In 1516 Angela moved to Brescia, where she established her reputation as a spiritual leader and became a religious focal point for the citizens. She died there in 1540. The name of Angela Merici is known in particular in connection with the Company of St. Ursula (founded in 1535), which allowed women to live a spiritual life outside the convent. Already very popular during Angela's lifetime, the company expanded greatly toward the end of the sixteenth century and into the seventeenth, becoming famous especially for the teaching activities it provided for women.

We still lack a full modern study of Angela Merici, one that would explain her significance and originality. So far, the Brescian saint's importance has been acknowledged in several studies of female religiosity and of the so-called Catholic Reformation. Most of the historiography regarding Merici has assumed that the company was a charitable institute devoted to work in hospitals and to religious education and protection of poor girls.[1] This interpretation, however, not only lacks historical evidence, it also fails to

---

1. See, in particular, Monica, *Angela Merici;* Guerrini, *La Compagnia di S.Orsola;* Cistellini, *Figure della riforma pretridentina;* Caraman, *St. Angela;* Ledòchowska, *Angèle Merici;* Blaisdell, "Angela Merici and the Ursulines"; Liebowitz, "Virgins in the Service of Christ." This theory was also adopted in broader studies on women's religiosity and on the Catholic Reformation.

capture the most original aspects of Merici's foundation, the logic of her spirituality, its religious roots, and its overall historical meaning.

The most reliable source of information on the life of Angela and the history of the Company of St. Ursula is the substantial research by three exponents of Merici's institute: Luciana Mariani, Elisa Tarolli, and Marie Seynaeve. *Angela Merici. Contributo per una biografia* (1986) has clarified many aspects of Angela's life and of the people around her, and brought to light new important documents. A few other studies have proposed interpretations of Merici's religious ideals and these will be discussed in my work.[2]

Spirituality, Gender, and the Self builds on the *Contributo* to place Angela Merici and the Company of St. Ursula in historical and religious context and to analyze them from a variety of perspectives: institutional, social, spiritual, and cultural. If Angela's work and figure represent the core of my research, this book also intends to contribute to the understanding of the wider historical-religious context, of which Merici represents one of the most significant interpreters. This work offers broad historical reconstructions in which Angela Merici's contribution and significance are evaluated. Nonspecialist readers might particularly benefit from some of these reconstructions as they provide them with a useful framework.

To begin with, this book sheds lights on Angela Merici's life and her writings for the company. Angela, like other mystic women such as Angela of Foligno and Catherine of Siena, was considered a *santa viva*, a living saint. Angela's social recognition derives from her mysticism, sacred knowledge, humanity, and participation in civic life. Angela's originality and genius, however, reside above all in the foundation of the Company of St. Ursula, because there she put her theology into practice: she translated her spiritual ideas and experience into a defined model of religious life for other women. The

2. Prodi, "Vita religiosa"; Zarri, "Orsola e Caterina"; Naro, *Angela Merici.*

company proposed a form of consecration for women outside the convent, in the midst of the secular world, as an alternative to monasticism. Merici's form of religious life was innovative also because it was individual, inward-looking, a-institutional, and transcendent. Although Merici's religious thought is expressed in a clear and linear form, it is in fact complex and can be truly described as a theology.

From a "women's history" perspective, Angela's company had important consequences. Although rooted in the mainstream gender ideology of the time, the company offered the Ursulines the possibility of living beyond the limits imposed on women. In a society in which women were expected to choose between marriage and the convent, the Ursuline was an anomaly, the prototype of the lay single woman. Furthermore, Merici's model for religious life gave women independence at both spiritual and social levels: the Ursuline was free to shape her relationship with the divine, and the company was a self-sufficient organization, entirely composed of and managed by women. The Ursulines also gained opportunities for public visibility through active roles in the community. And, in Angela's rule, the Ursuline was respected as an individual and considered a full human being, with intellect, will, and emotions.

Spirituality, Gender, and the Self analyzes Angela Merici's spirituality deeply and in relation to two religious contexts: the tradition of medieval female spirituality and pre-Tridentine Catholicism. The book argues that the most significant context for understanding Angela Merici, her company, and her religious thought is that of the experience of late medieval religious women. Angela's way of perceiving the relationship with the "sacred" exhibits significant continuities with that expressed by late medieval spiritual women who lived outside conventual institutions, namely the beguines, the tertiaries, the *pinzochere,* and the recluses. Angela's most original contribution to the history of female religiosity is that for the first time she codified its most radical traits into a "proper" religious rule. Angela Merici's rule also helps us to clarify significant traits of the female approach to the sacred (so much debated by historians) and to evaluate the development of female spirituality from the late Middle Ages to the early modern period. Angela's rule is particularly apt for studying female spirituality because it represents an excellent example not only of a document written by a woman but also of a model of relationship with God conceived by a woman for other women. Angela's rule, for instance, provides an example of how spiritual women conceived their relationship with the transcendent and with society, of how they viewed their religious identity, their attitude toward institutional aspects of religion, and it reveals a new approach toward penitential practices.

My second task is to set Merici amid the spiritual currents in Italy on the eve of the Council of Trent. Merici lived and conceived her company in one of the most complex periods in the history of Christianity, one that still allowed a variety of religious experiences. My work reinforces recent criticism of the depiction of pre-Tridentine Catholic spirituality as dominated by the need to reform the church and by charitable awakening.[3] I, too, will propose that the period was more complex than that traditional model allows. In particular, I explore Catholic spirituality of the period, analyzing the emphasis on individuality, interiority, and morality. Though these themes are known, I discuss them here in a vast array of religious traits, such as prayer, penance, charity, will, vows, and codes of behavior. I consider these aspects in some of the most representative individuals and religious associations of the period: in humanists such as Erasmus of Rotterdam, in exponents of reformed religious orders such as the Dominican Battista Carioni da Crema and the Lateran Canon Serafino Aceti de' Porti da Fermo, in religious orders and confraternities founded at that time such as the Barnabites, the Jesuits, the Company of Divine Love, and the Company of Buon Gesù, as well as one earlier confraternity, the Battuti of S. Domenico of Bologna. Merici's work represented an institutional outcome

<hr />

3. O'Malley, "Was Ignatius Loyola a Church Reformer?" and *Trent and All That;* Bonora, *I conflitti della Controriforma;* Solfaroli Camillocci, *I Devoti della Carità.*

of this spiritual trend. At the same time, however, compared to her male contemporaries, she shows significant differences that reflect the diversity of the female and the male approach to the sacred.

This work also investigates the reaction of Brescian society to Merici's ideal. I have reconstructed the social background of the Ursulines, both in Angela's times and later, through analysis of the archival material found in Brescia and in published sources. I suggest that the reasons for the social outlook of the company lies in the way this coincided with the social dynamics of Brescia and, in particular, its class and gender ideals. Finally, my work discusses the reshaping of Merici's company after the founder's death and within the context of the Tridentine reformation.

This book stresses the analysis of spirituality. By spirituality I do not mean something personal, ineffable, and opposed to materiality. I intend the ideals of religious perfection and of relationship with God that emerge, for instance, from the manners of praying and of doing penance, from the meanings held by concepts such as "poverty" and "charity," and from the ways in which "God" and "Christ" are represented. The sources privileged here for studying spirituality are the religious rules and statutes, devout vernacular manuals, and private letters. The analysis of spirituality is important because the relationship with God and the ideals of religious perfection are part of the experience of individuals and are ingrained in institutions—especially in periods, such as the one here considered, in which society was largely permeated by a sacred view of reality. My work, therefore, takes the view that spirituality represents a way to perceive reality, is historical, and changes over time. It is for this reason that it is essential to study spirituality as any other historical phenomenon, by investigating the traits that a religious concept or practice takes on in a given period and context. I have thoroughly examined what Angela wrote for the Company of St. Ursula (*Rule, Advice,* and *Testament*), showing her ideal of the relationship with God and with the sacred in general. I have made a linguistic analysis of her writings, compiling the frequency with which significant words of her religious ideal recur (for example, *Christ, charity,* and *will*) and the context in which she used them. I have approached the spiritual contexts that influenced Angela Merici with the same attitude.

Spirituality, Gender, and the Self tries to understand the "historical significance" of spirituality. I do not explain the presence of a given religious trait in a sixteenth-century spiritual author—such as interiority or morality in Battista da Crema—with reference to an earlier writer—such as Augustine, Cassian, or Thomas à Kempis. Spiritual forms are here explained within a historical context, in relation to those aspects that contributed to shape them. My approach takes the view that ways of relating to the supernatural and the ideals that every age has of religious perfection are connected in a complex manner to the system of values in a culture—to its particular mentality, its social, economic, and political context. Thus, a first type of analysis proposed here considers the relationship between spirituality and "politics," as in this way we can explain some changes that took place in the Company of St. Ursula after Trent. A second approach seeks, instead, the "social" significance of spirituality, the "function" held by a religious trait within the social dynamics. I have thus discussed the form of life offered by the company in relation to the issues of honor in different social groups in Brescia. A third type of analysis—particularly relevant to this work—consists in a "cultural"—or anthropological—evaluation of spirituality, one that seeks to link spiritual forms to society through a "conceptual" connection.[4] This methodology examines spirituality in parallel with other disciplines, social behavior, and mental attitudes and seeks to establish a relationship not in terms of direct influence but of meaningful correspondence. Considered

---

4. This historical approach is exemplified in works of anthropology such as Kroeber, *The Nature of Culture,* and Geertz, *The Interpretation of Cultures.* Caroline Bynum has explained medieval women's extreme penitential activity through the concepts of food, body, and the meanings associated with "woman" that were endorsed in other fields of society. See *Jesus as Mother; Holy Feast and Holy Fast,* and *Fragmentation and Redemption.*

thus, spirituality becomes part of cultural development and in turn can help us to understand the society that expresses it—in the same way that literature and philosophy do.

The concepts through which I examine the relationship between Angela's spirituality and Italian Renaissance culture are perceptions of gender and the notion of the self—and, to a lesser extent, attitudes toward poverty. In my analysis of gender—here considered as a cultural construction, not the result of biological differences—I investigate the continuities and differences between Angela Merici's spirituality and the meanings attached to being a woman in that period. From this perspective I also discuss some characteristics of the female approach to the sacred, and I put forward some reflections for considering women's opportunities and limits within medieval and Renaissance religion. The case of Angela Merici suggests that women assimilated male culturally dominating perceptions of femininity through a process of adaptation and selection.

The concept of the "self" (like that of "time") is not a constant, but a historical variable crucial to decoding culture. Historiography has debated its forms and modernity in relation to several contexts, such as medieval theology, Renaissance society, and the Protestant Reformation. My study aims to demonstrate that pre-Tridentine Catholic spirituality reflected contemporary perceptions of individuality, interiority, and human agency. From this perspective, Angela's case offers a significant opportunity for discussing the "modern" aspects of women's subjective representations of themselves within religion.

At the end of my cultural analysis I have concluded that Angela Merici's spirituality (in particular its most audacious traits) emerges as a product of a developing idea of the self and of certain gender perceptions about women that she adapted within a religious model that offered new opportunities for active roles and self-expression to individuals.

In this book, thus, I have tried to tell a story about Angela Merici, the Ursulines, and the society in which they lived. The main character is spirituality—mainly Angela Merici's spirituality—which, while it speaks to us about models of perfection and ways of relationship with God, also reveals notions concerning women's lives and people's worldviews in the Renaissance. To be sure, in this story there are many faults, as there are aspects of the Brescian saint that I have not investigated—her idea of pilgrimage and her significance in relation to contemporary pedagogical models are only two examples—and some cultural considerations are more suggestive than conclusive. My hope is that—despite this—readers will find this story meaningful.

Spirituality, Gender, and the Self is organized as follows. Chapter 1 examines Angela's figure and her company's main organizational features within the context of medieval female religiosity. At the end it discusses the supposed charitable and educational nature of the company promoted by Merici's historiography. Chapter 2 compares Angela's rule with mainstream didactic literature directed to women. Then it investigates the social background of those involved in the company, connecting this to the political and economic transformation of Brescia. Finally, it establishes the authorship of the rule. Chapter 3 examines Angela's ideal of experience of the "sacred" in relation to that expressed by late medieval spiritual women and to cultural conceptions about gender. Chapter 4 situates Merici's spirituality within the multifaceted spiritual expressions that preceded the Council of Trent. Chapter 5 is divided into two parts. The first proposes a cultural analysis of the spiritual models discussed in chapters 3 and 4. The second forms an epilogue to the story of Angela's company, as it deals with the transformations of the institute in the post-Tridentine era.

Abbreviations

MTS   Mariani, Tarolli, Seynaeve, *Angela Merici: Contributo per una biografia*

PE   *Polizze d'Estimo in ordine cronologico e in ordine alfabetico dall'anno 1517 all'anno 1687*

PN   *Processo Nazari,* i.e., Nazari De Sayani, *Le justificazioni della vita della Reverenda Madre suor Angela Terzebita*

Reg.   Merici, *Regula della Compagnia de Santa Orsola*

Ric.   Merici, *Arricordi che vanno alli Colonelli*

Tes.   Merici, *Testamento della Madre suor Angela lassato alle Matrone*

Spirituality, Gender, and the Self in Renaissance Italy

CHAPTER I

Angela Merici and the Company of St. Ursula

Angela Merici's religious experience and the historical significance of the Company of St. Ursula should be viewed within the context of late medieval female religiosity. From the twelfth to the sixteenth century a significant number of laywomen, called *pinzochere,* tertiaries, recluses, beguines, and *beatas,* followed a religious life outside the convent, either in their own homes or in small, informal communities. They pursued a religiosity based on penitential asceticism, charity, poverty, chastity, and mysticism, eschewing male clerical authority. This kind of religious life represented a cultural possibility available in many parts of Europe (Mediterranean Europe, the Low Countries, the Rhineland, the north of France, and England) and especially in central and northern Italy. In Italy in the first half of the sixteenth century, this type of spirituality reached a turning point: it achieved its maximum popularity and began its decline. Angela Merici (1474–1540) fits within this history since she herself lived her spiritual life outside the convent and was considered a santa viva, a living saint. Through the Company of St. Ursula Angela was confident enough to convert her personal experience into a new religious model for women. The company mirrored medieval women's approach to the sacred as it codified their living arrangements and spirituality at an institutional level. After Angela's death, at least in Italy, the development of the company reflected the gradual decline of women's religious opportunities.

This chapter examines Angela's personality and religious life in connection with the experience of late medieval spiritual women. Furthermore, the chapter highlights the originality of Angela's company among the existing religious and lay associations for women. The chapter challenges the prevalent views that the company was established to protect imperiled women and characterized by charitable and educational purposes.

WOMEN'S RELIGIOUS LIFE,
TWELFTH TO SIXTEENTH CENTURIES

Spiritual Women's Forms of Life

The roots of Merici's religious life lay in the Middle Ages with the birth of the penitential movement and of new forms of spirituality, of which Francis of Assisi was one of the most significant expressions. Between the eleventh and the thirteenth century religious life underwent a dramatic change: the proliferation of itinerant preachers and hermits; the rise of the Mendicant orders, confraternities, and solitary reclusion; the diffusion of heresies; the reform of existing monastic orders and the foundation of new ones. Monastic life ceased to be the only form of religious perfection as other new forms emerged, such as apostolic poverty, mendicancy, and evangelical preaching. In this period a new type of spirituality, affective and Christocentric, based on a more personal relationship with God, was spreading both in convents and among devout lay-folk.[1] However, it was pursued especially by the laity in the cities of many parts of Europe—in particular in northern and central Italy. This religious movement expressed new needs for contact with the transcendent and elaborated new forms of salvation. Despite the church's attempt to place the penitential movement under the obedience of the Franciscans and Dominican third orders, the laity was never completely controlled.

---

1. See, for example, Vauchez, *The Laity in the Middle Ages*.

Women participated in the new religious movements in different ways, and their opportunities for religious activism increased.[2] The number of women increased in convents, where they held positions of responsibility;[3] they were well represented in the leading heresies of the Middle Ages;[4] and they were active in the confraternities.[5] Women became an enthusiastic audience for preachers and reformers and participated in the apostolic life of charity, poverty, and penance.[6] Women were particularly attracted by the lay model of religious life and in some instances they outnumbered men in their participation in religious movements.[7]

Though many women experienced their religious creativity as nuns,[8] spiritual women more often pursued their life of the spirit

2. For an overview of the phenomenon, the pioneering work of Herbert Grundmann is still valid. A recent English translation is *Religious Movements in the Middle Ages.* See also Bynum, "Religious Women in the Later Middle Ages."

3. The proportion of monks and nuns is still not clear. Historians agree that in the tenth and eleventh centuries few female monasteries were founded. For England, France, and Belgium, see Schulenberg, "Women's Monastic Communities"; for Italy, see Barone, "Society and Women's Religiosity." Before 1500 women's houses accounted for a quarter or a fifth. In the sixteenth century the ratio was reversed, and in many parts of Europe nuns outnumbered monks (Bynum, *Holy Feast and Holy Fast,* 14). According to Zarri, between the second half of the fifteenth century and the second half of the sixteenth, female monasticism increased considerably both in the number of convents and in the actual number of nuns within individual institutions. The preaching of the Franciscan Observants sustained by the Italian princes played an important part in this process (see Zarri, "Monasteri femminili e città").

4. Heretical movements developed in the north of Italy, in France, and in northern Europe. Noblewomen (especially in France) sustained many of these movements. One-third of Lollards in the thirteenth and fourteenth centuries were women.

5. See Terpstra, "Women in Brotherhood"; Casagrande, "Confraternities and Lay Female Religiosity"; Esposito, "Men and Women in Roman Confraternities."

6. See, for example, Società Internazionale di Studi Francescani, *Movimento religioso femminile.*

7. The beguines were more numerous then the Beghards; the recluses were mainly women (Bornstein, "Women and Religion in Late Medieval Italy," 10). Herlihy found that pinzochere represented the second largest group (after servants) among the occupations involving women in fifteenth-century Florence (*Opera Muliebria,* 159, cited in Gill, "Open Monasteries for Women in Late Medieval and Early Modern Italy").

8. In northern Europe some famous nuns were Hildegard of Bingen (1089–1179),

outside the convent. Female religious life during the late Middle Ages was fluid, eschewing clear religious status. In northern Europe the most typical form of female semireligious life was that of the beguines.[9] They were laywomen who led a common life, renouncing secular values such as marriage, possessions, and family ties.[10] The beguines lived in poverty and chastity, in penance and prayer, and supported themselves through manual work.[11] They were also active in works of charity: teaching children, tending the sick, and helping old women. Although the beguines most commonly lived in small convents, frequently they lived together in groups of houses in the city, often near a church, thus forming a kind of sacred city of their own. They were loosely organized and did not practice monastic seclusion. It does not appear that they had a complex hierarchy or common dress, and they did not take vows. Although the beguines were condemned by the Council of Vienne in 1311–12, the movement continued. But the number of foundations decreased, and the beguines' life became more controlled and gradually more secluded.[12]

In Italy, like the beguines, many women conducted a life of prayer, penance, and charity outside the convent—in their own

---

Mechthild of Magdeburg (1212–94), Mechthild of Hackeborn (1241–98), and Gertrude of Helfta (1256–1301). In Italy Clare of Assisi (1193–1253) and Clare of Montefalco (1268–1308) were well known.

9. Mary of Oignies (d. 1213), Hadewijch (d. ca. 1250), Beatrice of Nazareth (1204/5–68), and Margaret Porete (d. 1310) were beguines who wrote mystical treatises and became known to their contemporaries. On the beguines, see Simons, *Cities of Ladies*. Essays on the beguines' spirituality are in Dor, Johnson, and Wogan-Brown, *New Trends in Feminine Spirituality*.

10. The beguines, however, could keep possessions and return to the world to get married. Some beguines came back to the beguinages and brought their children with them.

11. The majority of the beguine workers were employed in the textile industry. What they earned served for their subsistence and to help the needy. Sometimes they received financial assistance from pious foundations.

12. Simons, *Cities of Ladies*, 118–37. On the development of active forms of life for women, see also Harline, "Actives and Contemplatives."

homes.[13] They were known as *bizzoche* or pinzochere and often were affiliated with a third order (Franciscan or Dominican).[14] Their main difference from the beguines was that their communal dimension was less central. Although informal communities of bizzoche and tertiaries existed, Italian penitents more often lived either individually in their own homes or in small groups. Italian penitents (like the beguines) were often middle class (while nuns were normally aristocratic). Generally they were widows or unmarried, but they could also be married and lead a spiritual life with their husbands.

Sometimes spiritual women pursued urban or suburban hermitic seclusion in a room in their own home or in a cell next to a church or the city walls. They were called *cellane,* or recluses.[15] Another semireligious form of life embraced by women across Europe was that of the lay convert. In Italy these women were called *oblate* and worked in monasteries or hospitals affiliated with monasteries or with a civic institution. Finally, before the Council of Trent convents were not synonymous with *clausura* since women could easily get dispensations to leave their convent.[16] These kinds of living arrangements were also widespread in Spain, where women visionaries were called beatas.[17]

13. A selection of essays on the subject is Bornstein and Rusconi, *Women and Religion in Medieval and Renaissance Italy.*

14. Umiltà of Faenza (1226–1310), Margherita da Cortona (1247–97), Angela of Foligno (1248–1309), Catherine of Siena (1347–80), and Francesca Romana (1384–1440) were some of the famous Italian laywomen who lived in this condition. An introduction to the secular third orders is Emanuele Boaga, "Terz'Ordine secolare," in *Dizionario degli instituti di Perfezione,* vol. 9 (1997).

15. Umiliana de Cerchi (1219–46) was a famous Italian woman who led a hermit's life. Solitary reclusion was also common in England. Julian of Norwich (1343–1413) was a famous English recluse.

16. See, for example, Laven, *Sisters of Venice.*

17. They generally lived alone without formal vows and with informal ties to the church through a confessor. Prophetic authority was recognized by their followers. See Bilinkoff, *The Avila of Saint Teresa;* Weber, "Recent Studies on Women and Early Modern Religion in Spanish"; Ahlgren, *The Inquisition of Francisca.*

As will be discussed in chapter 3 in greater detail, one of the main characteristics of female spirituality was the mystical relationship with the divine. Building on religious models that were increasingly individual, Christocentric, and affective, many spiritual women expressed their relationship with the sacred through the figure of the Bride of Christ, achieving a profound fusion with the divine. Within this spiritual approach, visions, ecstatic raptures, and prophecies often enriched women's experience of the divine. Furthermore, within a religiosity that stressed Christ's suffering on the cross as central to the *Imitatio Christi* and gave spiritual significance to physical penitence, women brought the practice of the suffering of the body to an extreme.

Spiritual Women and Society

Through this religious figure women succeeded in overcoming some of the constraints late medieval society put on them. Women were often confined within the family or the convent; they were excluded from politics, ecclesiastic roles, and public offices; they were deemed inferior to men in law, philosophy, and medicine; they were not allowed to study in universities and suffered restrictions in the world of work and in access to property. Although spiritual women often encountered the opposition of society, the mystic model could offer a woman an independent life, public visibility, religious knowledge, and the possibility of social action. Considered privileged channels of the voice of God, mystic women could exercise significant influence within society, which allocated a space of social action to the intervention of the supernatural. Their deep identification with Christ allowed them to exercise some of his roles, such as apotropaic (protective) and thaumaturgic (healing) powers. Thanks to their mystical and prophetic gifts they attracted the attention of secular and religious authorities and were at the center of popular devotion. These spiritual women, often coming from poor families and often illiterate, had theologians and clergymen visiting them and listening to their interpretations of the Holy

Scriptures and sermons. In some cases they had a circle of devoted followers, both lay and religious, who believed in their prophecies. Many of them had a confessor or biographer who recorded the events of their lives. Spiritual women exercised an active apostolate in the secular world in a variety of ways, such as practicing charitable works, preaching, advising princes and common people, acting as peacemakers, and promoting the reform of the church and of religious mores.[18] Spiritual women found a means to have their identity recognized by society because they were able to assert their will in their communities and families and in their mystical relationship with Christ.

Women pursued this spirituality outside or alongside of ecclesiastical institutions. The increasing number of canonized women and the cult accorded to them testify that, to some extent at least, the church officially accepted women's religiosity. The number of women canonized by the church increased from 11.8 percent in the twelfth century to 22.6 percent in the thirteenth and to 27.7 percent in the fifteenth.[19] Furthermore, more laywomen than laymen were canonized: after the middle of the fourteenth century three quarters of lay saints were women.[20]

For all its high recognition among both lay and religious people, this figure of the spiritual woman living in the world was in many respects disturbing. It was a dangerous alternative to the church's monopoly of religiosity. By allowing women a public role, the Bride of Christ paradigm put them outside the traditional classification of wife or nun and outside male control. The church tried to control these aspects of female religiosity through the figure of the confessor or to impose conventual life. The relationship between spiritual fathers and holy women was very complex, and the for-

---

18. The most famous spiritual women who exercised political roles in their societies include Bridget of Sweden and Catherine of Siena, who played an important part in the return of Pope Gregory XI from Avignon to Rome.

19. Weinstein and Bell, *Saints and Society,* 220–21.

20. Vauchez, *La sainteté en Occident aux derniers siècles du Moyen Age,* 216–18.

mer often became devout followers of those they were supposed to guide.[21] With the bull *Periculoso* in 1298, the church tried to impose enclosure on informal communities of women (with little success) and condemned the beguine movement, curtailing it somewhat. Furthermore, from the fifteenth century on, recluses were forced to join communities of tertiaries, and spontaneous groups of penitents often fell under the jurisdiction of the mendicant orders, which pushed toward regularization.[22] In the late fifteenth century the regular third orders were also founded, and the church tried to cloister them, too. Spiritual fathers and hagiographers composed tame portraits of female saints in order to promote more conventional models of sainthood for women, suitable for the inspiration of the female public.[23]

In the period when Angela Merici lived, the number of Italian women reputed to be saints during their lifetimes reached its peak.[24] Women found new possibilities in the cities and courts of northern Italy: spiritual women could more readily exercise the role of "divine mothers" and be seen as "living saints," *sante vive*.[25] In the Italian peninsula, the first three decades of the sixteenth century were characterized by social crisis and spiritual tension. The eco-

21. See Prosperi, "Dalle 'divine madri' ai 'padri spirituali,'" and the recent work by Bilinkoff, *Related Lives.*

22. Despite the high number of recluses, there are few hagiographical legends proposing their lives as a model (one notable exception is Margherita da Cortona, who lived as a *reclusa,* ignoring the opposition of the Franciscans). The mendicant orders always gave preference to communal forms of life, in which it was easier to control women's religious movements. See Benvenuti Papi, "'Velut in Sepulchro'" and "Frati mendicanti e pinzochere in Toscana." See also Rigon, "A Community of Female Penitents in Thirteenth-Century Padua"; Gill, "Open Monasteries for Women in Late Medieval and Early Modern Italy."

23. See, for example, Scattigno, "Maria Maddalena de' Pazzi."

24. According to a list of 261 famous Italian religious women who died between 1206 and 1934, it emerges that 55 spiritual women died between 1250 and 1350, 26 between 1350 and 1450, 78 in the period from 1450 to 1550, and only 12 between 1550 and 1650 (Bell, *Holy Anorexia,* 247–72). This data is partial as it considers only those of whom we have written records.

25. Zarri, *Le sante vive.*

nomic expansion of the fifteenth century was over, and the wars of Italy caused famine and epidemics, contributing to widespread social tension and political instability. The clergy were often absent from their pastoral duties and distant from the spiritual needs of the people. Within this context the number of women with charismatic gifts and, in particular, prophetic power, increased. A number of secular rulers, seeking protection for their cities, courted the presence of these women.[26] Mystic women, with their prophecies and revelations, were often at the center of debates concerning the reformation of the church[27] and the devotion of common people. The life and spirituality of Angela Merici fits well into this context.

LIFE OF ANGELA MERICI

Sources

The aim of my brief reconstruction of Angela's life is to present the saint's personality and deeds through the perspective of women's spiritual life that we have discussed so far. The sources regarding Angela's life do not match her fame. Very little is known, especially about the period prior to her arrival in Brescia. The main source of information concerning her life is the so-called *Processo Nazari*, which is not a hagiographical account but a recollection of testimonies given by four witnesses and recorded by Brescian notary Giovan Battista Nazari in 1568.[28] The *Processo Nazari* was carried

---

26. Osanna Andreasi held a political a role at the court of the Gonzaga in Mantua, and Stefana Quinzani replaced her after her death (as an advisor) and was in contact with Ercole d'Este. Caterina da Racconigi was consulted by Claudio di Savoia, Lucia da Narni advised Ercole d'Este, Colomba da Rieti was in contact with the Baglioni and Borgia, Arcangela Panigarola was venerated by the governor of Milan, Elena Duglioli was hosted in the court of Monferrato, Caterina de Ricci was visited by the mother of the Duke of Florence (Zarri, *Le sante vive*).

27. For example, Catherine of Genoa (d. 1510), Arcangela Panigarola (d. 1525), and Antonia Negri (d. 1555).

28. *Le justificationi della vita della Reverenda Madre suor Angela Terzebita.* The original is missing, but there are two transcriptions, one in the *Secondo Libro Generale* of the company, and one in the *Sacra Rituum Congregationis, Processus* 341, ff. 936v–45v.

out with the intent of promoting Angela's sanctification process. The two main witnesses, Agostino Gallo and Antonio Romano, knew Angela well because she had lived in their houses, while Giacomo Chizzola and Bertolino Boscoli had met her occasionally. All were laypeople (two merchants, one worker, and one nobleman) who shared a sincere friendship or admiration for her and, in agreement with the leaders of the Company of St. Ursula, wished to initiate Angela's canonization process. As we will see later, the person closer to Angela Merici was the Brescian notary Gabriele Cozzano, who is closely linked to her foundation of the Company of St. Ursula and who left some letters providing information about the company and Angela's life.[29] At the time of the *Processo Nazari,* however, Cozzano was probably already dead. At the *Processo,* unfortunately, no Ursuline was asked to testify.

Although Angela was a famous spiritual woman during her time, she had no hagiographer or group of devotees who registered the deeds of her life. Hagiographical accounts written after her death add little to what the witnesses declared at the *Processo.*[30] Apart

---

The *Processo Nazari* is also published in Mariani, Tarolli, and Seynaeve, *Angela Merici,* 533–40. From now on I will refer to this text as MTS and to the *Processo Nazari* as *PN.*

29. Cozzano, *Epistola confortatoria,* in MTS, 556–64; *Risposta,* in MTS, 564–82; *Dichiarazione,* in MTS, 582–95.

30. Angela's first biography is a manuscript commissioned by the mother general of the company and composed in the mid-sixteenth century by the Capuchin friar Maria Bellintani da Salò, *Vita della B. Angela da Desenzano.* The first printed hagiography was written by the Florentine Jesuit Ottavio Gondi, *Vita della Beata Angela Bresciana, prima fondatrice della Compagnia di S. Orsola.* Gondi was the confessor of the famous Florentine mystic Maria Maddalena de' Pazzi. This biography, largely based on Bellintani's *Vita,* was commissioned by Alessandro Luzzago, a well-known religious reformer in Brescia who was " protettore" of the company and the nephew of one of the first governors. Gondi's *Vita* was a "best seller," as it had six editions between 1600 and 1638. The biography written in 1648 by the Jansenist Jean Hugues Quarré (*La vie de la Bienheureuse Mère Angèle*), possibly for the Ursulines in Mons (Flandres), as I will discuss later, promoted the image of Angela and her company as devoted to charitable activities, thus influencing successive interpretations of the Brescian saint. The work of the General Superior of the Brescian company, Bernardino Faino (*Vita della Serva di Dio di beata memoria la Madre Angela Merici da Desenzano*), although

from a few scattered letters containing some information on Angela, there is not much else.[31] Therefore, my main body of information concerning Merici's life comes from the *Processo Nazari* rather
than from the *Lives* composed by the hagiographers. Furthermore,
I will also refer to the *Contributo,* especially where a controversial
aspect of Merici's life arises. Although the *Processo Nazari* does not
present the problems of reliability characteristic of hagiographical
sources, in reporting the events of Merici's life, it is important to
consider the issue of the expectations and ideas of the witnesses
with regard to female sanctity and to try to dig out aspects that
were mentioned but not emphasized.

Childhood and Adolescence

Angela Merici was born in Desenzano del Garda in northern
Italy between 1470 and 1475.[32] Desenzano was a small town in the
province of Brescia situated on the southwestern shore of Lake
Garda. Angela's father, Giovanni Merici, belonged to a family of
impoverished minor nobility with urban and commercial roots.
He was originally Brescian but took citizenship in Salò after Angela was born. His family belonged to the urban merchant stratum,
which was involved in the trade of wool and leather and which

---

based on fresh archival research, still presents the events of Angela's life without scientific rigor and through an apologetic perspective. The most comprehensive and rigorous study of Merici's life is Carlo Doneda's *Vita della B. Angela Merici da Desenzano.*
Doneda was a Brescian priest and librarian at the Queriniana who had been asked by
the mother general of the company to find material to support the cause of Angela in
her beatification process. His work presents or refers to important documents regarding the company, some of which subsequently were lost. The life by the Jesuit Girolamo Lombardi, *Vita della B. Angela Merici,* is also rich in documentation (but not as
accurate as Doneda's).

31. *Estratto d'una lettera del P. Francesco Landini,* in MTS, 531–32; Nassino, *Registro,*
in MTS, 520; Tribesco, *Gionta alle cose sopradette,* in MTS, 594–95.

32. The date is established on the basis of the testimony of Brescian nobleman Pandolfo Nassino, who stated that when Angela died she was between sixty-five and sev-
enty years old (*Registro,* 574–75). Bernardino Faino established Angela's birth as 1474.
However, he did not quote his source for this date (*Vita della Serva di Dio,* 9).

transferred part of the wealth in the countryside.[33] Desenzano had a very important market of cereals, and it is likely that Angela's father had a trade. Angela's mother's family (Biancoso) was based in Salò and seems to have been of a higher status. Caterina Merici's brother (ser Biancoso di Salò) was a lawyer and member of the city council. Angela had one or two older brothers, one older sister, and one younger brother. The economic situation of the Merici family is not certain. The Capuchin friar Francesco da Desenzano, who examined the tax records during the canonization process (which subsequently went missing), said that their economic situation was not bad: "at that time the income the family drew from Desenzano was not tenuous."[34] We know from the book of the "rasse"[35] that in 1489 her family had property in livestock and land in Desenzano. We also know that in 1523 Angela declared a piece of land cultivated with a vineyard.[36]

According to witnesses and hagiographical accounts, Angela pursued a devout life from her childhood, and she developed it in harmony with her family. It seems that her family did not try to oppose her devotion by forcing her to consider marriage or the convent.[37] Angela told her friends that she received religious education from her father, who used to read the lives of the saints to the family, and that she was influenced by these readings: "At the age of five or six she began to practice abstinence (following the good education provided by her father) and to live in retirement from people, so that she might give herself wholly to prayer and devotions. And the

33. Belotti, "Umanesimo cristiano," in *Angela Merici,* 36–52.

34. Lombardi (*Vita,* 3) affirms that the friar saw the tax records for the years 1517, 1526, 1529, 1530, and 1556, containing the payments made by Angela and her family.

35. The book of the "rasse" is the register of accusations for damages caused by people to property. They are in the Archivio Antico Comunale di Desenzano, reg. 40 (see MTS, 4–5, 74).

36. "Sur Merizi habet petiam terrae aratoriae vidatae in contrata Caser a Zorzo Monte, a sero Petrus Domigo: Lire 5" (Archivio Antico Comunale di Desenzano, *Libro d'Estimo,* reg. 56, in MTS, 530).

37. Like Angela, her elder sister was not married.

more she grew in age, the more she devoted herself to these, and to contemplative life."[38] The fact that she asked the Ursulines to pray for their parents and the expressions of motherly affection in Angela's pedagogical advice *(Arricordi* and *Testamento)* do suggest that Angela's relationship with her family was good.

A Period of Transition

When Angela was about eighteen, her father, mother, and sister all died of unknown causes.[39] As in the case of other saintly women, hagiographers interpreted this as a divine sign.[40] For Angela this event represented a further urge toward the spiritual life she had undertaken. It was during this period that she had her first vision. While praying for the salvation of her sister, she saw her in the sky among a group of angels:[41] "Where, one day, finding herself in a small field of her own near Desenzano, and there praying for her sister with the usual prayers, at midday she saw a host of angels in the air, in the midst of whom was the soul of her beloved sister, joyful and triumphant."[42]

Now an orphan, Angela went with her younger brother to live in Salò in their uncle's house. Salò was quite a rich city, and the life it offered her was different from the rural life she had known. From the anecdotes reported in the hagiographical accounts, it seems that this was a difficult period and that her devotional choice may have been at risk, due either to external pressure (the new family wanting her to marry) or to her inner uncertainty. In accounts of

---

38. As referred to by Gallo in the *PN,* f. 942r, in MTS, 537; *Reg.,* V.

39. The name of Giovanni Merici appears for the last time in Desenzano's documents in 1492 (MTS, 89).

40. Bellintani affirms: "and so that . . . [Angela] be entirely of God, she remained at her age an orphan" *(Vita).*

41. The sources state that Angela was worried about her sister's salvation. It is possible that the latter had a more rebellious nature: according to the "rasse," she was responsible for some damage to the property of the Merici's neighbors (see MTS, 80–83).

42. Romano: *PN,* ff. 937r–v, in MTS, 533.

her life, this period is characterized by an emphasis on her penitential asceticism and her fight against the devil and temptations. Gallo reports that Satan appeared to Angela in the form of an angel "who was so beautiful, that no person could believe or imagine it . . . [Angela] immediately lay down on her face crying out: go to hell, enemy of the cross . . . and so it disappeared immediately."[43]

Angela, Franciscan Tertiary

After a few years (she may have been in her early twenties), during which she attended the church of the Observantist Franciscan order of Salò, Angela became a tertiary of that order. Angela's friend, Agostino Gallo, affirmed that she entered the third order because she wanted to continue her devotional life and worship: "And the more she grew in age, the more she practiced those [penances], and contemplative life, so that she took the habit known as that of the third order, so that she would more easily be able to go to masses, confessions and communions, since at that time frequent communion was not conceded to lay persons."[44] Entry into the third order was also a way of acquiring an acceptable social status that made it possible to resist family and social pressure to marry. Angela's choice of the third order testifies to her preference for a religious life lived in the world rather than in a convent. Her future foundation of the Company of St. Ursula developed further this ideal.

According to a Lateran Canon preacher, Giacomo Tribesco, who met Angela toward the end of her life, at that time she was working in her relatives' house while living a penitential life. This was the type of life she was to lead later in Brescia and that her rule would subsequently allow the Ursulines to live: "in her youth, living in

---

43. *PN*, f. 945r, in MTS, 539. The hagiographers also recount that on another occasion, she put soot on her hair because some young girls told her that she would not have problems in finding a husband, and that once she threw dust on a luxurious salad prepared for her (Bellintani, *Vita*, f. 5v).

44. *PN*, 942r, in MTS, 537.

the house of relatives, she performed all the tasks women are used to carry out in a house, such as make butter, bake bread, carry water and many other labours . . . throughout the week, she ate nothing other than on Thursday and as much bread as covers the half of the palm of a hand, she showed me on her left hand with her right the quantity of bread that she ate."[45]

Angela returned to Desenzano, where she owned some land and where she pursued, in accordance to the Franciscan third order, a life of prayer, penance, and, possibly, works of mercy such as visiting the sick and comforting the dying.[46] During this period, she experienced a second vision in which she saw pairs of virgins and angels going up a stairway that connected the earth and the sky. This vision became one of Angela's distinctive hallmarks in the hagiographical accounts (often shown in pictorial representations). It was invested with particular significance since it was interpreted as the divine inspiration of the future foundation of the Company of St. Ursula.[47]

Angela, Santa Viva

Angela—at about forty years of age—arrived in Brescia in 1516. There she established her reputation as a "living saint." Brescia was the most important city of the Venetian dominion, a major source of income and a strategic center for the defense of its commercial routes.[48] At that time it had a population of about forty thousand

45. In *Di vari santi Bresciani,* ff. 15v–16r, in MTS, 594–95.

46. MTS, 107. See Nicholas IV's bull *Supra Montem* of 1289, in Gilles Gérard Meersseman, *Ordo fraternitatis,* 1:394–400. It is possible that Angela followed *Questo sia el modo che hanno revere quelli del Terzo Ordine del glorioso Sancto Francesco.*

47. However, it is not clear whether she really had two visions, or whether the first was later embellished and given a different interpretation. The image of the stairways was modeled on Jacob's dream, which was very popular in late medieval ascetic literature.

48. Brescia was a free commune in the twelfth century, but because of its geographical position and because it lacked a strong local authority, it was always subject to the interests of Milan and Venice. The definitive Venetian annexation of Brescia took place in 1426 and lasted for four centuries, except for the period between

inhabitants. In the late fifteenth century and in the early decades of the sixteenth, the Brescian economy had suffered several overlapping crises caused by war, famine, and epidemics. When Angela arrived, the city was still recovering from the devastation caused by the French troops led by Gaston de Foix in 1512.

From a religious perspective Brescia reproduced the dynamics of many early-sixteenth-century Italian cities: the pastoral service of the clergy was lacking; there were attempts to reform the religious orders; the council and the laity in general actively promoted religious initiatives, such as public celebrations and founding hospitals; popular preaching was made by external preachers (Savonarola preached in Brescia in 1494) and hermits. In Brescia there also was a tradition of female mysticism. The most famous mystic woman was Laura Mignani (1480–1525), a nun in the convent of St. Croce and a point of reference for several aristocrats and prominent religious individuals. Several other mystic women lived in the city under a variety of conditions or in the local monasteries. This same convent of St. Croce was the home of Laura Paratico (1467–91), suor Candida (d. 1515), and Elisabetta Ardesi (d. 1525?). Giulia Tiberi (d. 1512), Elisabetta Marini di Adro (d. 1524), Agnese Benzoni (d. 1527), and Pace Migliorati (d. 1529) lived in the Dominican convent of St. Caterina. Lucia da Bagnolino (early 1500s) lived as an Augustinian hermit with a companion, suor Domenica (1470–1533) was a wandering penitent, and Benedetta Moreschi (1500–50) was a Dominican tertiary.[49]

1509 and 1516 when Brescia was under French (1509–12) and then Spanish rule (1512–16)—and this was not without consequences. Unlike other Italian states (Milan and Florence, for example), Venice respected local statutes and used local administrative structures. The Brescian Council was responsible for the administration of direct and indirect taxes and for the promulgation of municipal laws concerning economic, political, and religious problems. Venetian patricians could not participate in these municipal governments, nor could the Brescian elite take part in the legislative and executive decisions that emanated from the center. Venice controlled Brescia through two rectors: a *podestà*, who supervised civil and judicial affairs; and a *capitano*, in charge of military affairs and finance.

49. See Cistellini, "La vita religiosa," 451.

From both the few testimonies of Angela's friends and her own
writings, Angela emerges as a rather complex figure. She was both
contemplative and active, mystical and practical, learned and aware
of the matters of everyday life. Her personality was human, independent, and determined. She was in contact with many people
from every kind of social background. Angela attracted the attention of merchants, professionals, and nobles who remained in contact with her throughout her life, even though they did not form
a stable circle. It was with women from artisan backgrounds, however, with whom Angela shared the last ten years of her life and
founded a company. She showed a strong attachment to Brescia,
rejecting invitations from important people to stay in other cities.
Angela made several pilgrimages, even as far as Jerusalem. Like other female saints, Angela Merici established her reputation as a spiritual leader and became a religious focal point for her fellow citizens. She spent her days with all sorts of people who visited her
pleading for inspired favors. Although it does not seem that Angela was famous for miraculous phenomena and for extreme pen-
ances,[50] she was perceived as a mystic woman in contact with God
and was considered more divine than human.

In 1516 Angela was sent by the superiors of the third order in
Brescia to the house of the aristocratic family Patengola to assist
Caterina, a forty-six-year-old widow who had recently lost her three
children. There she was introduced to some young nobles and merchants who remained in contact with her. Soon after her arrival she
met Girolamo Patengola and Antonio Romano, and a few years lat-

---

50. According to Agostino Gallo's testimony, visions and other miraculous phenomena were not prominent in Angela's type of sanctity. Gallo testified that "this Rev-
erend Mother was always very distant from visions, and very much against those who
on the other hand boasted that they saw some" (*PN*, f. 944v, in MTS, 539). However,
this testimony seems extreme and not completely true. Gallo's ideal of sanctity is one
of moral virtue, and this raises doubts concerning his peremptory statement. Hagiographers and witnesses (including Gallo) reported episodes of visions and of supernatural phenomena in Angela's life. Furthermore, she admired contemporary spiritual
women who were known for their mystical and paramystical experiences (see below).

er Agostino Gallo, while Elisabetta Prato, Giacomo Chizzola, and Gabriele Cozzano probably came into her life in the early 1530s.[51] Romano and Gallo offered Angela accommodation from 1517 to 1529 and from 1529 to 1530 respectively. It is through their testimonies that we can reconstruct some important aspects of Merici's life and spirituality.

To begin with, Angela presents a strong mystical and contemplative aspect. Like many other contemporary mystic women, Angela practiced penitential life, although less harshly than many: "While she lived in my houses (which was for about fourteen years) she slept on a mat keeping a piece of wood under her head for a cushion, and I cannot remember having ever seen her eat meat, but only fruit and vegetables, drinking only water."[52] "Her way of life was constantly harsh, bearing with great heat, extreme cold, and relentless hunger."[53] Furthermore, we know that Angela wore a cilice (a hard cincture made of horse's hair) and flagellated herself with a scourge (a metal chain with many thongs).

According to Gallo, Angela spent her mornings attending mass, where she showed great devotion for the sacrament. During the

51. Girolamo Patengola was a twenty-two-year-old nobleman, Caterina's nephew. Antonio Romano was a fur merchant, originally from Ghedi, who in 1517 was between twenty-three and thirty years of age. He belongs to the category of wealthy foreign merchants who were denied Brescian citizenship despite their economic power. Agostino Gallo was an influential Brescian citizen who was actively involved in the city's political, religious, and economic life. Agostino knew Angela through his sister Ippolita who remained a widow. Agostino came from a family of the lower nobility (his father was a rich textile merchant), and his wife's family was involved in the production of bells. Agostino left the textile trade and retired to the countryside. He embodies the image of the landlord (either noble or middle class) who lived in the city but took care of his land, introduced new cultivation techniques, and wrote essays on agronomy. Gallo wrote a very successful book (it was reprinted many times and translated into French) about the advantages of the country lifestyle. Giacomo Chizzola was a representative of the high aristocracy and a well-known politician who worked for the council until 1588. He knew Angela in the last years of her life. He also had a virgin of the company in his house as servant, and he was agent of the company for many years. I will give details about the wealthy widow Elisabetta Prato and the notary Gabriele Cozzano in chapter 2.

52. Romano: *PN*, f. 937v, in MTS, 533.

53. Gallo: *PN*, f. 943r, in MTS, 538.

night she prayed, contemplated, possibly had mystical experiences, and reflected on theological problems: "She took communion every day that she could, remaining in front of the Sacrament many hours of the morning to hear the masses; and also, since she slept very little, it is to be believed that she spent the greater part of the night praying, contemplating, speculating on those divine matters which are granted to the few."[54]

At the *Processo Nazari* Bertolino de Boscolis affirmed that in 1534, while Angela was praying in a church, she was seen to levitate: "finding myself in my neighbourhood church of Saint Barnabas . . . there I saw the Mother Sister Angela who, if I remember well, while the Friar was saying the Gospel, not only I (but many of those who were attending that mass) saw the said Mother Sister Angela standing, and raised almost a span from earth, and thus she remained for a while with great wonder, and it seemed to me a miracle to see such a thing."[55]

Another important aspect of Angela's life was her theological and preaching activity. Angela was able to read both in Latin and in the vernacular, and according to her friends she used to read and study holy books. Her interpretation of the Holy Scriptures attracted many people, especially preachers and theologians. As with other female saints, this ability was viewed not as the result of individual intellectual capacity but, above all, as another indication of transcendent inspiration: "Though she was never taught even the alphabet, nevertheless she not only read a quantity of holy books, but many times I have also seen religious men, and in particular preachers and theologians, ask her to expound concerning many passages in the Psalms, the Prophets, the Apocalypse, and all of the New and the Old Testament, and hear from her such expounding

---

54. Ibid., f. 944v, in MTS, 539.

55. Bertolino de Boscolis, *PN*, ff. 940r–v, in MTS, 536. This event was also mentioned by Francesco Landini, two years before the Processo Nazari, in 1566: "and she was seen during the time of prayer with her body lifted up in the air" (*Estrato d'una lettera del P. Francesco Landini* in MTS, 531).

that they remained amazed, so that one might say that this woman had more of the divine than the human."[56] "It also appeared very remarkable to me that, not having studied Latin letters, she understood so well the workings of Latin; and moreover, not having studied the Holy Scriptures, she gave such beautiful, learned, and spiritual sermons, which at times lasted one hour."[57]

What books did Angela read? This testimony indicates the Old and New Testament, with particular reference to the Apocalypse, the Psalms, and the books of the Prophets. Angela's father read her Jacopo da Varagine's *Golden Legend* (printed eleven times in Venice from 1474 to 1500) when she was a child, and she may also have read the collections of the lives of famous virgins and martyrs (such as the *Leggendario delle santissime vergini*) together with Catherine of Siena's letters, *Dialogo della Divina Provvidenza*, and Domenico Cavalca's *Specchio della Croce*, a popular guide to spiritual life composed in the fourteenth century. Furthermore, as I discuss in chapter 4, Angela probably read Thomas à Kempis's *Imitation of Christ*, Erasmus of Rotterdam's *Enchiridion Militis Christiani*, and Battista da Crema's and Serafino da Fermo's vernacular ascetic writings.

Angela was thus learned and, as it appears from her writings for the Company of St. Ursula, she interpreted the sacred knowledge in a personal manner. Indeed, Angela became known for her wisdom; Gallo recalls that when she was in Cremona in 1529, she was visited by many important people: "Thus, the Mother being in our house, she was visited each day from morn till night, not only by many religious and very spiritual people, but also by gentlewomen and gentlemen . . . of whom each one marveled at the great wisdom in her, because they saw that she converted many to change their lives."[58]

According to the sources, Angela thus used to preach privately, holding long sermons. She was also known for her ability to con-

---

56. Gallo: *PN*, ff. 944r–v, in MTS, 539.
57. Chizzola: *PN*, f. 941r, in MTS, 536.
58. *PN*, f. 941v, in *MTS*, 537.

vert people and to incite others to follow a Christian life. We can see from her writings and the testimonies concerning her that Angela had excellent pedagogical skills: she had a "method" for dealing with people and the capacity to transmit ideas in tune with different personalities. One of the most important characteristics of Angela's personality seems to have been her human approach, which was interpreted as another sign of divine inspiration and an aspect of her sanctity. According to Bellintani, Angela's manner was one of the reasons she attracted people: "Therefore, both for the fame of her sanctity, for which she was celebrated, and for the gentle ways by which, conversing, she won the souls of the persons with whom she made friends . . . almost all competed as to who should welcome her in his house."[59] The Brescian hagiographer's point is confirmed by the words of Romano and Gallo, whose affection for Angela grew and who emphasized her caring way of communicating: "And so, while I sometimes went to visit the said Mother Sister Angela, I was seized with great affection";[60] "She spoke to me so lovingly . . . that I immediately remained a prisoner, so that not only did I not know how to live without her, but my wife too, and all my family."[61] Chizzola, too, exalts her human qualities, describing her as "alien to ambition, vainglory and anger."[62] As we will discuss in greater depth, through her writings Angela showed a capacity for psychological introspection and empathy. This human sensitivity emerges also in Cozzano's writings: "And the greatest sinner was the one she most cherished; and if she could not convert him, not even through the sweetness of love, she persuaded him to do some good, or not to do evil. Her words were so fiery, powerful and gentle, and spoken with such new vigor of grace, that everyone had to say: 'Here is God.'"[63]

---

59. Bellintani, in Lombardi, *Vita,* 53–54.
60. Romano: *PN,* f. 937r, in MTS, 533.
61. Gallo: *PN,* f. 941v, in MTS, 537.
62. *PN,* f. 941r, in MTS, 536.
63. Cozzano, *Dichiarazione,* ff. 974v–75r, in MTS, 587.

Thanks to her charisma, Angela became a point of reference for the city. She was called on to perform roles of public utility. She provided various kinds of help, such as counseling people on personal and civic matters and acting as peacekeeper: Gallo affirms that she spent "the entire day in good offices, either with her neighbors, or else in praying for them and for sinners. For many years she was of great benefit to a multitude of people, since they asked for her advice, either to change their way of life, or to bear with tribulations, or to draw up wills, or to take a wife, or to marry their daughters and sons, besides which she never lacked for work as peacemaker, between wives and husbands, sons and fathers, brothers and sisters, and so with many others according to their condition: advising and comforting each one insofar as she could, so that her work had more of the divine than the human."[64]

For all these reasons (devout and penitential life, mystic charisma, theological knowledge, counseling, and human qualities), Angela's fame increased in Brescia and its territory: "as day by day her holiness grew, the fame of her most spiritual life spread among the people; so that very many from the city of Brescia flocked to her";[65] "and having entered the city of Brescia, she had such great credit among the Brescians that she appeared to be another Deborah";[66] "the fame of her sanctity . . . not only with those of that place, but with many others from the Riviera."[67]

By 1524 Angela's fame had spread outside the Brescian territory, and persons of importance requested her presence. In 1524, when she was in Venice, some Venetian noblemen and clergymen visited her and wanted her to remain there to work in the Hospital of the Incurables. The following year, when she went to Rome, it was

---

64. *PN,* ff. 942v–43r, in MTS, 537.

65. Romano: *PN,* f. 937v, in MTS, 534.

66. As the confessor of the Company of St. Ursula, Francesco Landini testified twenty-six years after Angela's death (*Estratto d'una lettera del P. Francesco Landini,* in MTS, 531).

67. Bellintani, cited in Lombardi, *Vita,* 53–4.

Pope Clement VII who wanted her in his city. In 1532 Duke Francesco Sforza II pleaded with Angela to remain in Milan. She declined all these invitations, however, and remained in Brescia all her life. Angela's refusal to move elsewhere can be seen as a sign of attachment to the city, another typical trait of spiritual women.[68] We can also interpret her decision to live in a house annexed to the church of St. Afra, where the relics of the patron saints of the city were kept, in this perspective.

Angela's link with female spirituality was also apparent in her marked devotion to and affiliation with contemporary women who led a similar life. This was not unusual among spiritual women, who often looked to female models, both contemporaries and ancestral Christians.[69] Angela knew the charismatic Stefana Quinzani, who lived in a convent in the nearby town of Soncino, and she venerated the Mantuan Osanna Andreasi (whose sepulcher she visited in 1522), two famous contemporary mystic women visionaries who bore the stigmata and held a political role, in particular at the Gonzaga court. Angela probably also met Laura Mignani, another well-known mystic, who lived in the convent of St. Croce in Brescia and was advisor to several religious and secular personalities, such as the founder of the Theatines, Gaetano da Thiene; the founder of the Divino Amore in Brescia, Bartolomeo Stella; the Duchess of Ferrara, Lucrezia Borgia; and the Duchess of Urbino, Elisabetta Gonzaga.[70] Angela probably also admired the charismatic Franciscan tertiary Chiara Bugni.[71] Interestingly, a few years before Angela's arrival, another charismatic woman, Giustina (or suor Candida), who died in odor of sanctity in 1515 in the monastery of St.

---

68. Osanna Andreasi, for example, wished to be "cut into mouthfuls and roasted for the salvation of the city of Mantua" (Zarri, *Sante vive,* 111).

69. See Valerio, "L'altra rivelazione: L'esperienza profetica femminile nei secoli XIV–XVI," in *Donne, potere e profezia,* 139–62.

70. MTS, 111.

71. During her sojourn in Venice, Angela stayed in the convent of Santo Sepolcro where the Franciscan tertiary had lived and died few years earlier.

Croce, had also worked in the Patengola household. She, too, may have represented a source of inspiration for Angela. Finally, Angela shows a strong affiliation with other two women saints, St. Ursula (who gives the name to the company) and St. Catherine of Alexandria (Angela founded the company on her feast day, 25 November). Both of them were symbols of mystic marriage. Catherine was also famous for knowledge, and Ursula was a symbol of virginity. We shall return to these matters.

Independence

Between 1522 and 1532 Angela undertook a series of pilgrimages. In 1522 she went to the sepulcher of Osanna Andreasi. In 1524 she embarked on a long and dangerous pilgrimage to Jerusalem with Romano.[72] This pilgrimage was marked by a number of miraculous events: during the trip she became temporarily blind (she saw the holy places "with inner eyes as if she had seen them with her outward eyes")[73] and on the way back, according to Romano, Angela's prayers saved their ship from pirates (a strong wind suddenly blew their ship away).[74] The following year, Angela went to Rome for the holy year and met Clement VII. In 1529 and 1532 Angela went to Varallo[75] to see the "Sacro Monte" with the reproduction of scenes (with sculptures) from the life of Christ. She undertook this trip a second time with a group of women who became the first members of her company.

On the whole Angela seems to have been a rather "independent" saint. Thus she had no established spiritual circle in which to spread her revelations and doctrine and was one of the few famous women of her time whose deeds no lay or religious person registered while

72. While several holy women among her contemporaries undertook this trip spiritually, Angela was the only one who did it physically (Zarri, *Sante vive,* 156).

73. As Gallo testifies: *PN,* f. 942v, in MTS, 537.

74. *PN,* f. 939r, in MTS, 535.

75. Varallo was part of the state of Milan and was situated about 130 miles northwest of Brescia.

she still lived.[76] Her milieu lacked significant spiritual figures and, apart from Cozzano, who had a specific role in her company, none of her friends seems to have had a profound awareness of her spirituality. In her friends' testimonies in the *Processo Nazari,* Angela emerges more for charisma than for doctrine, which they rarely mention. Although Angela's confessor, Serafino da Bologna, shared some of Merici's views concerning spiritual life (as I will discuss in chapter 4), he does not occupy an important place in the sources relating to Angela's life. Moreover, it is unlikely that Serafino influenced Angela significantly because he became her confessor only after 1530, when Angela's fame was already established, and because he was about thirty years younger than she. Angela, on the whole, comes across as an individual who managed her private and public life autonomously: she rejected prestigious roles that were proposed to her, she lacked influential religious circles and spiritual father, she traveled and moved frequently. The final outcome of Angela's life, the most meaningful event in which her experience and ideas found their accomplishment, is represented by the foundation of the Company of St. Ursula.

The Foundation of the Company of St. Ursula

We do not know the exact stages that led Angela to the foundation of the company, but it is likely that she had this project in mind for some time. Cozzano affirmed that Angela hesitated until she had a vision in which Christ urged her to found it.[77] Angela devoted the last ten years of her life to her project. In 1530, after a few months spent in Cremona with Gallo (because of a threatened attack on Brescia by Charles V's troops), Angela Merici returned to Brescia and lived in one of Gallo's houses. She then moved to a small flat annexed to the church of St. Afra, belonging to the Lat-

---

76. Zarri, *Le sante vive,* 142.

77. *Epistola confortatoria,* f. 963r, in MTS, 559–60. The hagiographical tradition finds its original inspiration in her early visions.

eran Canons.[78] The fact that in 1532 she petitioned to be relieved of the obligation to be buried as a Franciscan tertiary is a sign of her intention to pave the way for a new religious organization.[79] From then on we find other women in Angela's life, the women who became the original Ursulines.[80] We know that in 1532 Angela went to Varallo's Sacro Monte with a group of women. In 1533 she shared her apartment in Sant'Afra with another virgin, Barbara Fontana.[81] The sources agree that Angela used to meet regularly with these women, at first in her house and then in a small house (later transformed into an oratory) provided by an aristocratic Brescian widow, Elisabetta Prato (a future member of the company's government).[82] As I will discuss later, the company grew out of the type of life Angela and her companions were living. It also appears that Angela founded the company with this group of women (the fu-

78. In Cremona Angela fell seriously ill. Gallo recalls that one day she seemed about to die and her friend Girolomo Patengola wrote an epitaph in her honor. Apparently Angela, having listened to the epitaph, sat up on her presumed deathbed and began to talk vehemently about the joys of the afterlife to the audience present in the room. After half an hour she realized that she had recovered her strength, and she was so disappointed that she blamed Patengola for having cheated her (*PN*, ff. 943v–44r, in MTS, 538).

79. "Indultum pro moniali," in *Diversa Sacrae Penitentiariae Clementis VII. Anno IX. 1532*, reg. 79, Archivio Segreto Vaticano, in MTS, 520–21.

80. Cozzano, *Dichiarazione*, f. 974, in MTS, 586.

81. Doneda, *Vita*, 53, 142.

82. The oratory was decorated with frescoes in 1533. The paintings are described by Faino in the mid-seventeenth century: "The crucifix in a central position, as an altar piece, between hosts of weeping angels; and then annunciation, nativity, Jesus's disputation in the temple, Mary's assumption. And besides the saints: Faustino, Giovita, and Afra, the patrons of the city and the church near which Angela lived; Paula and Eustochius on a ship at the mercy of the unleashed seas, possibly in memory of her pilgrimage to the Holy Land and the dangers of the return journey; Saint Ursula on a ship, with her banner of virginity and martyrdom; Saint Elizabeth of Hungary in two panels: in one she is assisting several virgins who are spinning and winding thread, in the other she is serving eight virgins at table" (*Miscellanea*, ff. 35r–37r, in MTS, 194). However, Faino saw the paintings after they had been restored and some changes had been introduced (the virgins are dressed in a black habit that was introduced in 1582). There is no mention of Catherine of Alexandria, who might have been represented in a section of the frescoes that was already ruined at the time Faino wrote.

ture Ursulines) rather than with the widows who later administered it or under the influence of the religious orders close to her—the Franciscans or the Lateran Canons.

The company was founded on 25 November 1535 with the admission of twenty-eight virgins. Angela dictated the rule to a Brescian notary, Gabriele Cozzano, who became her personal secretary and the company's chancellor as well as its defender and legal representative. In August 1536 Angela obtained approval of the company from the vicar-general of Brescia, Lorenzo Muzio. In 1537 Angela Merici was elected head of the company.[83] In August 1539, a few months before her death, she left two written works, the *Arricordi* and the *Testamento,* as guidelines for its government.[84] In the meantime the company grew rapidly: in 1537 it counted 75 Ursulines and by Angela Merici's death in 1540, it had reached 150 members.

Angela's Death and Cult

In 1539 Angela Merici fell ill. She died on 27 January 1540. Pandolfo Nassino wrote her obituary and reported that her funeral was celebrated with solemnity and with the participation of a great many Brescian people: "On the 27th day of January 1540 the daughter of Thomaso[85] de Merichi of Desenzano, Brescian territory, died aged between about 65 and 70. A woman with a thin body

---

83. On that occasion the Ursulines met in Angela's flat ("in coquina domus habitationis D. sur Angele . . . site in contrata Sancte Afre et iuris Sancte Afre Brixie," in MTS, 517).

84. The oldest known edition of the rule is a manuscript written between the end of 1545 and the beginning of 1546, the *Regula della Compagnia de Santa Orsola* (Milan: Biblioteca Trivulziana, codice 367, in MTS, 436–58). In my analysis of Angela's spirituality I refer to this edition of the rule. The writings for the government are the *Arricordi che vanno alli Colonelli* and the *Testamento della Madre suor Angela lassato alle Matrone* (they are transcribed in *Processus* 341, ff. 946v–58v; MTS, 507–17). The English translations of Angela's writings used in this book come from *Saint Angela Merici, Writings: Rule, Counsels, Testament.* When I quote, I will refer to the rule as *Reg.,* to the *Arricordi* as *Ric.,* and to the Testamento as *Tes.* References will be given in the text. The italics in the quotations are mine.

85. In most of the documents Angela's father name is given as Giovanni.

and normal height, dressed in grey . . . with such solemnity and so many people, as if she had been a lord. The cause, this Mother Sister Angela preached to all people faith in the supreme God, so that all fell in love with her."[86] The Brescian painter Alessandro Bonvicino, known as Moretto, represented Angela on her deathbed.[87]

In fulfillment of the medieval model of sainthood, several miracles occurred after Angela's death. Angela's body was left unburied for some time because it was desired by both the Lateran Canons and the Franciscans (the disputed ended when Angela's petition was found). During that time her body did not rot and a star shone for three nights and illuminated her body. Episodes of divine intervention were reported in the presence of doubts of Merici's holiness. Furthermore, for several centuries, numerous miraculous recoveries were associated with her.[88]

Soon after Angela's death, the Company of St. Ursula and Angela's friends fostered her cult. In the seventeenth century Angela's cult remained alive in Ursuline congregations, including those in France and Canada, which promoted hagiographies or included biographical profiles in the chronicles of the orders, celebrated her feast day, and commissioned pictures and statues. Angela's native city, Desenzano, recognized her public cult by commissioning an altar and a large picture to hang in the chambers of the city council. The official process for her beatification, however, was opened only in 1757, thanks to the efforts of a Venetian Ursuline—Natalina Schiantarelli—who created a wide network of congregations throughout the world to press for canonization. In 1768 Angela was

---

86. Nassino, *Registro,* in MTS, 520.

87. From 1572 Moretto (1498–ca. 1554) had a daughter in the Company of St. Ursula. The only existing picture of Angela Merici while she was still alive was painted around 1535 by Girolamo Romanino (1484/87–1562?). See below for further details.

88. Reported in the acts of her canonization process *(Processus* 341–44).

made blessed. Pius VII declared her a saint on 24 May 1807, and her feast day is celebrated on 27 January.[89]

THE COMPANY OF ST. URSULA, A "WOMEN'S SOCIETY" (1535–40)

The Ursulines were a spiritual company following a way of life similar to that of the beguines, pinzochere, and tertiaries. Like them they were laywomen who lived a life of prayer, penance, and other devotional acts outside the convent, without formal vows and a common habit.[90] The Ursulines' living arrangements were more similar to those of the pinzochere and tertiaries than the beguines—who lived in communities—since they mostly lived in their own homes, either alone or with their relatives, or sometimes in groups of two or three. According to Angela's rule, the Ursulines participated in social life by providing society with spiritual services such as praying for souls and doing penance for the sins of people, advising, converting, and spreading peace. The Ursulines may have practiced charitable works in hospitals and in their neighborhoods, but Angela did not prescribe it. Furthermore, it is doubtful that the original Ursulines practiced any formal teaching, but they probably informally discussed spiritual issues with relatives, friends, and others. They had no common life or activity to pursue in the world, and the Ursulines could largely decide about their worldly life autonomously. The Ursulines were not subject to strict supervision but were visited every fortnight by wiser members of the company (the *Colonelle,* discussed below). They went individually to daily mass in a church of their choice, and they attended their own parish on solemn feasts. They practiced monthly confession and com-

---

89. *Sacra Rituum Congregationis, Processus,* 339–44. The most important volumes are 340 and 341.

90. Unfortunately, there are no sources other than Angela's writings attesting the life of the Ursulines.

munion to a common spiritual father they elected. They also met every month to discuss their spiritual experience (or to attend a sermon). The Ursulines followed the rule composed by Angela Merici, which was the fundamental inspiration of their spiritual life.[91]

The original Ursulines were a mixed group, mostly coming from the middle strata of society. When they entered the company they did not pay a dowry but kept their possessions and were allowed to inherit property and earn a salary.[92] If they wished, or if they needed to, they could engage in work as lady's maids or housekeepers in the houses of the Brescian aristocracy. Like the beguines, the company was a female community, independent from church hierarchy and monastic influence, though it used the services of priests and spiritual directors. The company was democratic and meritocratic, and there was no rigid hierarchy. It was self-sufficient, catering to the needs and problems of its members in order to allow them to persevere in their religious life. Interestingly, Angela's company and the beguines shared two important patrons, Catherine of Alexandria and Elizabeth of Hungary, whose significance will be discussed later.

The Ursulines were assisted in their spiritual needs by more experienced virgins called *Colonelle,* and in more practical matters by some aristocratic widows, the *Matrone.* The Colonelle acted as spiritual guides, while the widows administered the money or possessions of the company.

In some respects the religious life proposed by the Company of St. Ursula was more radical than that lived by the beguines and the tertiaries because it required a stronger religious commitment. The beguinages and the third orders were open to widows and married women, and their members were not necessarily committed

91. The chapters of the rule were: Prologue, On the manner of receiving (I), How they should be dressed (II), On the manner of behaving in public (III), On fasting (IV), On prayer (V), On going to mass every day (VI), On confession (VII), On obedience (VIII), On virginity (VIIII), On poverty (X), On government (XI).

92. The right to inherit was confirmed in a bull of Paul III.

for life. The Company of St. Ursula, by contrast, proposed a radical break from society: it required physical virginity at the moment of entry and offered the unequivocal and permanent status of "Bride of Christ." Furthermore, as will be discussed in chapter 3, Angela's rule proposed a mystical relationship with God, one that many late medieval women lived as an exceptional spiritual experience.

Despite their differences, like the beguines, the tertiaries, and the pinzochere, the Ursulines were offered the opportunity to live beyond the limits that constrained ordinary women, since life in the company gave women a certain degree of autonomy, public visibility, and subjectivity, both in their material and spiritual life. This was the type of life that Angela Merici herself followed. Let us now discuss these traits in more detail.

A Women's Community

The Company of St. Ursula was a rare case of devout association entirely composed and managed by women. Furthermore, Angela wanted to give her institution as much autonomy as possible from external interference, both lay and ecclesiastic. Autonomy from men and from the church was also characteristic of the beguine communities.

The company was divided into two tiers: the first included the virgins and the Colonelle, who were members of the institute (virgins/Brides of Christ); and the second the Matrone, widows responsible for governance. The Colonelle visited the virgins in their own homes every two weeks to attend to any sort of problem that arose. If the Colonelle couldn't solve it, the Matrone intervened. The Colonelle had a primary role in the spiritual growth of the virgins through their personal visits. The widows met with the Colonelle twice a month to discuss the virgins' problems and were expected to respond as necessary. Initially the company had no head until, in 1537, a mother general was elected for legal reasons. With the increase in members between 1535 and 1539, Angela assigned the guidance of a number of virgins to each of the four Colonelle according to the area of the city in which they lived. It is possible that the term *Colonelle* was introduced at this time, for it does not appear in the rule and was introduced before 1539 (it is present in the *Arricordi*). In Angela Merici's hometown, Desenzano, the different areas of the city and the people responsible for them were called *Colonelli*.[93] It is also possible, however, that the term came from Brescia, where it was associated with the militia of the city.

In theory, the rule also gave a role to men as "agents" *(agenti)* who were to act as protectors of the company. The assistance of the male agents was sought in those situations in which the Matrone had failed—their role was limited to defending the company from external dangers and legal disputes.[94] However, male agents were not elected during Angela's lifetime, and not until 1555 (i.e., when the company had already began to change its structure). Angela seems eventually to have decided to manage the company without male institutional support. This is confirmed by the fact that the *Arricordi* and *Testamento* (in which Angela left her advice for the administration of the company after her death) addressed only the Colonelle and Matrone, and never mentioned the agents. The only man with a role within the company was the Brescian notary Gabriele Cozzano, "Segretario et Cancelliere" of the society. As such, he carried out notarial functions such as registering the acts of the company. After Angela's death, when the company was criticized, he filled the role of its defender, writing open letters to the Ursulines to encourage them to pursue their form of life.

The company was independent from church hierarchy. No religious orders or prelates were involved with the company at an insti-

---

93. See MTS, 242.

94. "let the four virgins . . . to visit every fortnight all the other virgins, their sisters, who are scattered through the town . . . . And if they themselves could not provide a solution, they should refer the matter to the matrons. And if these cannot things right either, let the four men also to be called in so that, all together, they can concur to find a remedy . . . [if it is necessary] to go to court and through legal proceedings . . . then let the four men, out of charity, in the manner of the fathers, take the matter in hand and assist according as there is need" (*Reg.*, XI).

tutional level.[95] Churchmen were not involved—or, it seems, even present—in either the acceptance of the virgins or the elections of the members of the government. The Ursulines elected a common confessor and chose one from their own parish.[96] The confessors, however, could exercise only a limited influence on the Ursulines' life. Indeed, Merici gave the spiritual fathers a sacramental function (freeing the individual from sin and administrating communion) rather than a significant role in the spiritual guidance of the virgins (which was left entirely to the Colonelle and the Matrone). Her intention of keeping the company independent from possible external direction is also revealed by how, in the chapters "Fasting" and "Obedience," she asks the Ursulines to listen to the advice of their personal confessor rather than the common spiritual father (Reg., VII, VIII).[97]

These characteristics of the Company of St. Ursula were unusual in the contemporary devout institutions that women could join. Women who joined third orders, for example, had to submit their intention to the approval of a male member of the order—and they could be rejected. In the third orders, a female superior was subject to a *Priore*[98] who, together with the common spiritual father, was present at her election. Furthermore, in those confraternities in which women were accepted, women were excluded from administrative and managerial offices.[99] And as far as convents are concerned, although they were managed by women and offered opportunities for female autonomy, within the convents women had

95. Although it is true that in the chapter on obedience Angela asked the Ursulines to obey the bishop, this should be understood as a general attitude toward external institutions (mentioned together with the church, civic authorities, and families) and as a spiritual ideal, which I shall discuss later.

96. The Ursulines' right to choose individual confessors was officially recognized by the Vicar Muzio in 1536.

97. See MTS, 239–40.

98. As in the case of the women in the Augustinian third order. See, for example, Tilatti, "La regola delle Terziarie Agostiniane di Udine."

99. See Casagrande, "Confraternities and Lay Female Religiosity." Women were also excluded from certain confraternal activities, especially communal flagellation.

to submit to men, both at a symbolic and an institutional level: female hierarchies were placed under male surveillance (of the bishop, the confessor, or the superior of the male branch of the order), which often interfered with the life of the community.

A Company Managed from Below

Another significant peculiarity of the Company of St. Ursula consisted in the fact that the Ursulines were responsible for and protagonists of their institutional structures. The company was democratic and meritocratic, founded and managed "from below," and its members were equal "political subjects," regardless of their social background. These traits distinguished the company from female religious orders and contemporary institutions for imperiled women. These features of the company are more consistent with late medieval women's "semireligious" associations which, as will be discussed in more depth later, did not value the establishment of hierarchical structures and questions of class.

First, the Ursulines elected all members of the government, the Colonelle, the Matrone, and the mother general, as well as the common spiritual father. Even Angela Merici herself became mother general through an election.[100] The Ursulines decided which widow and virgin to appoint among the possible candidates, and no widow could enter the company without the members' vote.[101] The Matrone were not members of the company and seem not to have had the right to vote. The decisional power of the board of governors of institutes for imperiled women was normally not subject to restrictions and control from below.[102]

---

100. See the act of Merici's election, published in MTS, 517–19. Angela was elected unanimously.

101. It is possible that Elisabetta Prato (close to the company since 1532) failed to be elected as Matrona until 1539.

102. In the 1565 Statutes of the Collegio della Guastalla, founded by Ludovica Torelli for impoverished aristocratic women, we find, for example, that the members of the government were elected by the confessor and board of governors (*Statuti del Collegio della Guastalla*, in Marcocchi, *La Riforma Cattolica*, 2:157). Similarly, in the

Second, any Ursuline could become a Colonella, a spiritual guide in charge of other Ursulines, without consideration of her social upbringing. Access to this position was exclusively meritocratic: "four of the most capable virgins of the company should be elected" (*Reg.,* XI). This meant that a virgin from a poor background could have a virgin from a higher social status under her responsibility. In convents, by contrast, the family status of nuns often shaped relationships and governed access to high positions.[103]

Third, as we will see in detail later, Angela did not impose a rigid hierarchy on the Ursulines because she deemed the individual needs of the virgins more important than respect for positions of command. At least in Merici's intentions, the Matrone's decision-making power was subject to limitations set in the rule. The widows had a specific role in taking care of the needs of individual Ursulines (as reported by the Colonelle), administering the company's finances, supervising its functioning, and defending it before Brescian society.[104] The Colonelle could refuse to obey if the Matrone did not accomplish their duties. And the members of the government could be removed if they did not do their work: "If one of them was unable to fulfil her office or behaved badly, that person should be removed from the government" (*Reg.,* XI). Finally, the fact that Angela did not ask the widows to finance the company— but rather to administer it—was probably a way of limiting the widows' influence.

Compagnia della Grazia (founded in Rome by Ignatius Loyola in the 1540s for women alone), the members of the government were not elected by the women who were the object of patronage.

103. See, for example, Zarri, "Monasteri femminili e città."

104. After Angela's death, however, some of the Matrone did change many aspects of the company and exercised an authority beyond what Angela had foreseen. This was certainly the case of Elisabetta Prato, mother general from 1572 (she prepared the ground for Borromeo's reformation of the company). The conflicts and divisions within the company after 1545 followed Lucrezia Lodrone's decision to introduce the black leather belt for the Ursulines. The Matrone's intervention was partially due to the fact that Angela specified in the *Testamento* that it was possible to update aspects of the company if necessary.

These characteristics should not come as a surprise. The Company of St. Ursula was founded by Angela with a group of virgins to persevere in an official religious manner in what they had been practicing for some time. As we know from Cozzano, Merici laid down the rule with the first group of virgins through a process of theory, practice, and discussion.[105] Cozzano recalled that Angela used to propose religious practices to the future Ursulines and ask for their opinions and reactions. During that period the only future Matrona mentioned by the hagiographers was the young widow Elisabetta Prato, who gave Angela a room for the meetings with her friends. Prato, however, was not among the first Matrone of the company (who appear in the 1537 election act) but was elected only in 1539; it is unlikely that she was much involved in its foundation. The company was founded by a group of virgins guided by Angela, who was both their charismatic leader and their "peer." That Merici saw herself in this light rather than as a Matrona emerges throughout the rule (talking to the virgins, she frequently referred to Christ as "our common lover") and in the 1537 election act; although she was elected "matrem ministram et thesaurariam," her name was still among those of the virgins. Angela appears to have used the widows' influence to give stability to the company, while for the Matrone the company was a means of sanctification. Merici affirmed that if the Matrone carried out their duty properly they would enjoy celestial reward and join the virgins whom they had cared for. Those who were protected and who enjoyed the patronage, however, preceded their patrons in sainthood. It was they who would help the Matrone gain eternal salvation, as Angela explained to the aristocratic widows: "If you faithfully carry out these and other similar things . . . See a great reward will be prepared for you. And *where the daughters are, there also will be the mothers.* Be consoled; do not doubt; *we want to see you in our midst* in heaven" (*Tes.*, Last).

---

105. *Dichiarazione*, f. 974r, in MTS, 586.

In this sense the widows' patronage of the Company of St. Ursula was an original one: it was not an initiative of protection decided from above and imposed or offered. It was the people themselves (the virgins, including the charismatic foundress) who wanted to realize a new form of religiosity and found the necessary means to achieve it.

Finally, in this ideological context, we can explain why Angela may have chosen Elizabeth of Hungary as patron saint of the company. Elizabeth (1207–31) was the daughter of King Andrew II of Hungary and the wife of the Landgrave of Thuringia, Lewis IV. After her husband's death she decided to live in poverty, serving the poor and the sick. As we have seen, she is represented serving the virgins in the frescoes of the oratory where the Company of St. Ursula used to meet.[106] While in the beguinages Elizabeth was a symbol of piety and charity for the beguines who were widows,[107] in Angela's company she most likely was a symbol for the Matrone, themselves widows and noble, who exercised their charitable duties by helping the virgins in their religious life.

Worldly Self-Sufficiency

The Company of St. Ursula was an organization that existed in the world, with its own regulations, legal representatives, and governors, and that offered its members various kinds of protection. It offered economic help for the poorer virgins, found jobs for those who wanted to work, provided legal assistance in case of disputes, and assisted those who were sick or dying. It remains clear, however, that these measures were not an aim in themselves but were established to enable the Ursulines to live the religious life offered by the company. In this way, the Ursulines became self-sufficient and independent of the world in which they lived. Again, self-sufficiency was

---

106. See note 82. It is possible, however, that the oratory was painted after Angela's death.

107. Simons, *Cities of Ladies,* 89–90.

a characteristic condition of the life of women as tertiaries and be-guines, since they earned their living and helped each other.

Financially, the company was organized as follows. On the one hand the Ursulines were supposed to support themselves, given that they could keep their possessions, inherit assets, and earn a salary. The company would find a suitable family for those Ursulines who wanted to work: "if she wanted to go to work as servant or maid, those who govern should see to it that she be placed where she can feel at home and live honestly" (*Reg.*, XI). As Cozzano explains, they "buy their bread with their own hands and live by the daily sweat of their brows."[108] We also know that in 1537 at least nine Ursulines out of seventy-five were working in the houses of the Matrone or of Angela's friends (see chapter 2).

On the other hand, however, Merici foresaw that some virgins might need financial help and devised various forms of intervention. The company (through mutual assistance, the mediation of the Matrone, and the legacies of people outside the company) solved the secular problems of the Ursulines. First, Merici ordained that the Matrone administer the goods owned by the company in favor of those sisters who needed assistance: "If, by God's will and bounty, it should happen that they have money or goods in common, let it be remembered that these must be carefully administered, and prudently distributed, especially to help the sisters and according to each need which may arise" (*Reg.*, XI). We find confirmation of the economic support accorded to the poorer virgins in the patrimo-nial declarations of the Company of St. Ursula: in the declaration of 1548 the company stated: "These goods left for the love of God are distributed to the poorest girls of this company, whom we try to help according to their needs."[109] Angela specified that no out-sider was allowed to interfere with the office of the Matrone: "In this matter I do not want you to seek outside advice; you decide,

---

108. Cozzano, *Risposta*, f. 8r, in MTS, 567.
109. *Polizze d'Estimo*, b. 153. From now on I will refer to this documentation as *PE*.

only among yourselves" (*Tes.*, 9). The Matrone, however, were not asked to finance the company, and the Ursulines were not supposed to bring a dowry. As emerges from the company's patrimonial declarations, before 1548 legacies came especially from Brescian noblemen,[110] while donations from the widows and relatives of the virgins were ample only at the end of the century.[111] In addition, Merici asked the Ursulines to contribute to the common property of the company in the form of small legacies: "And if she is near to death, she should leave a little something to the company as a sign of love and charity" (*Reg.*, XI).

As well as financial help, the company found accommodation for needy Ursulines. Angela created a network that allowed all virgins to persevere in their chosen way of life. These types of arrangements are reminiscent of those used in the beguinages:[112] "If there were at least two sisters left alone, without father and mother and other superiors, then, out of charity, a house should be rented for them (if they have none) and they should be provided for in their needs. But if there is only one, then let one of the others receive her in her house, and to be given the subsidy which seems suitable to those who govern."[113] Until 1568, however, the company declared that it was paying rent only for one flat used by poor Ursulines.[114] Either only a few Ursulines were in need, or else the most common solution adopted during the first thirty years of the company was to shelter the needy in private houses.

Besides economic assistance the company provided other types

---

110. *PE*, b. 152. Angela's friend Girolamo Patengola and Giovan Battista Gavardo (probably a relative of Tomaso Gavardo) left legacies in 1537 and in 1548. The names of the aristocratic families Nigolina, Rotengo, and Ganassoni also appear in the PE of 1548, although we do not know what connections they had with the company.

111. In 1548 there is only one legacy, of 200 lire, from a Matrona of the company, Lucrezia Lodrone. Nor are there any surnames matching those of the virgins. In 1588, by contrast, we find several names of Matrone and virgins: Ugoni, Fisogni, Bargnano, Peschera, Offlaga.

112. Simons, *Cities of Ladies*, esp. 97–98.

113. Ibid.

114. In the *PE* of 1548 they claimed paying 30 lire rent per year for an apartment.

of protection. The rule explained that the company helped the virgins in legal disputes concerning inheritance or salaries: "If it should happen that one of the sisters, being an orphan, could not get what is hers, or if, being a servant, or a maid, or the like, she could not obtain her wages, or if there should arise another such situation which would make it necessary for her to go to court and through legal proceedings . . . take the matter in hand and assist according as there is need" (*Reg.,* XI). As we will see later, the documents of the company report three cases of Ursulines who were denied their right to inherit.

The company also made sure that the virgins' spiritual development was not impeded by their parents or the superiors of the house in which they lived. This is why the Colonelle regularly visited the other Ursulines in order to check whether "their mothers or other secular superiors should want to lead them into these or similar dangers, or want to prevent them from fasting, or prayer, or confession, or any other kind of good" (*Reg.,* III). Angela was aware of the kind of problems the virgins might encounter in their own homes, especially psychological ones (such as depression and pressure to give up their way of life), or physical ones (sexual advances): the Colonelle were to "comfort them and to help them if they should happen to be in some disagreement or other trouble, of body as much as of mind; or if their superiors at home did them any wrong, or wanted to prevent them from doing something good, or to lead them into the danger of doing something wrong" (*Reg.,* XI).

Furthermore, medical assistance and human comfort were provided for sick and elderly Ursulines: "Finally, if one of the sisters is ill, it is recommended that she be visited, and assisted, and served, by day and by night, if it is necessary" (*Reg.,* XI).[115] When an Ursuline died, the company as a whole took part in the funeral ceremo-

---

115. This is confirmed by the company's patrimonial declarations, which mentioned that some money was spent for the "sick in this company" (*PE,* b. 153).

ny.[116] In this way the company gave social visibility to the deceased Ursuline: "When one of them has died, then all the others will accompany her to her grave, walking two by two, with charity, and each one with a candle in hand" (*Reg.*, XI).

In conclusion, the company responded to the problems that a young girl or an old woman might have to face: economic problems, health problems, legal problems, accommodation problems, defense of sexual and social honor. Angela created a network of relations that allowed the sisters to persevere in the form of life she envisaged in the company, as Brides of Christ in the world.

Religious Status and Commitment

To a certain extent, the type of religious life Angela proposed recalls that of the beguines and of other existing forms of devout life such as the confraternities and the third orders. Like these devout organizations, she proposed a spiritual life at home, regular confession and communion, periodical meetings, frequent or daily mass, penitential life (such as fasting during certain periods of the year), vocal prayer (such as the Office of Our Lady or, for the illiterate, the Our Father), a general charitable attitude toward the neighborhood (for example, by spreading peace), and the request that the virgins avoid secular events (such as weddings and feasts). Like many contemporary devout institutions, the company also offered its members a form of affiliation and protection—for example, reciprocal help in case of sickness.

However, Angela's company required a greater degree of religious commitment, similar or even greater than that of the religious orders. Beguinages, third orders, and confraternities proposed a more flexible form of devout life. Among the beguines a variety of situations existed, and their status was not considered as definitive: widows or married women without husbands, even with

---

116. There is no mention of whether the company also paid the expenses of the funerals and the masses for the poor Ursulines.

children, could become beguines, and they were allowed to leave the community to marry or become nuns and were accepted if they returned.[117] The Virgin Mary was the most popular patron among the beguines precisely because, as a wife, mother, and virgin, she reflected their mixed condition.[118] Similarly, the third orders, and especially the confraternities, were open to married and widowed layfolk who, while undertaking certain religious practices, continued to pursue their secular lives.[119]

In Angela's company the situation was quite different. First, according to Angela's rule, the women who entered the company had to be virgins and were expected to remain so for their entire life: "everyone who is about to enter or be admitted to this Company must be a virgin and have a firm intention to serve God in this way of life" (*Reg.*, I). The status proposed by Angela's rule was incompatible with marriage and monasticism: a condition for entering the company was that "she should not have promised herself to any monastery nor to any man of this world" (*Reg.*, I). Moreover, as with nuns, at the center of Merici's rule there was a consecrated virgin and *Bride of Christ* living in union with God. Throughout the rule the Ursulines were called "Brides of the Son of God" (or similar terms):[120] "God has granted you the grace of setting you apart from the darkness of this miserable world . . . having been thus chosen to be the *true and virginal spouses of the Son of God*" (*Reg.*, Prologue).

In Angela's rule, the bridal dimension represented a proper *status vitae*, since it involved all aspects of the Ursuline's life and was conceived as definitive. By contrast, the rules of the third orders,

117. Simons, *Cities of Ladies*, 73, 119.

118. Ibid., 87.

119. Emanuele Boaga, "Terz'Ordine secolare." Although it is true that virgins were occasionally accepted as tertiaries (like Angela herself), this possibility represented more the exception than the norm.

120. Merici's Bride of Christ, as in the case of secular wives, had to be at least twelve years old.

and possibly those of the beguines, did not ask women to identify with the figure of the virgin/Bride of Christ.[121] Famous mystic
women such as Catherine of Siena and Angela Merici herself, who
belonged to the Dominican and Franciscan third orders, were considered and did consider themselves Brides of Christ, and so did
many pinzochere and beguines. They did so, however, not because
they were induced by their rules but out of their personal, spiritual
experience. Thus Angela's company represents a rare, if not unique,
case of an association that gives official recognition to the Bride
of Christ living in the world: a woman married to Christ without
rituals, vows, and a distinctive habit.[122] This religious condition is
symbolically expressed in the choice of St. Catherine of Alexandria and St. Ursula as patrons of the company.[123] Besides virginity, learning, and martyrdom, Catherine epitomizes the Bride of
Christ, a significance explicitly revealed in Girolamo Romanino's
painting *The Mystic Marriage of St. Catherine,* where the saint is represented in the act of receiving the ring from the infant Jesus, while
Angela Merici and St. Ursula look on.[124]

The life proposed by the company was considered as parallel, or
even alternative, to conventual life. This clearly emerges in several
documents concerning the original company. An introduction to
the rule, for example, says: "since not everybody is called to a life

121. See Ziegler, *Sculpture of Compassion,* 80–84.

122. There was no formal ritual of acceptance when entering the company, but the
new Ursulines were recorded in a book. The book has not survived, but the biographer
Doneda had seen it (*Vita,* 150n). On forms of female consecration, see Andrea Boni,
"Consacrazione delle vergini," in *Dizionario degli Istituti di Perfezione,* vol. 2 (1975),
1613–28. Finally, one may notice that Angela, as a tertiary, did wear a habit. Angela remained a tertiary all her life and thus she did not get rid of it. This was not in contradiction with the requirements of the company, as the rule specified that the novices
could keep the dress they used to wear in the world (*Reg.,* III).

123. Catherine was an early Christian virgin who shunned the advances of the pagan emperor Maxentius and chose martyrdom. She also defended her faith in a famous disputation with pagan philosophers. I will discuss the significance of Ursula in
the next chapter.

124. According to Simons, the beguines chose St. Catherine especially for her
learning (*Cities of Ladies,* 88).

in a convent we have established a rule for those who want to serve God in virginity or widowhood."[125] The letters written by Cozzano, who maintained the superiority of the Ursulines' secular life over monasticism, make this clear: "The Holy Spirit now calls, and invites those who desire it, to live according to this kind of life . . . I know well that [monastic life] has been advised, and instituted by the Holy Spirit . . . but according to its own times"[126]

Furthermore, as will emerge, Angela's rule is highly spiritual and depicts a relationship with God similar to that of mystic women. It prescribes a rigorous penitential life,[127] places a particular emphasis on mental prayer and, above all, proposes a deep existential transformation in the divine. This was different from the rules of the third orders and of the majority of beguine communities, where the type of devotion prescribed was quite ordinary and the spirituality expressed by mystic beguines was atypical.[128]

Another difference between Angela's model and that of the beguines, third orders, and confraternities was that the Ursulines followed the evangelical counsels of obedience, chastity, and poverty prescribed in the rules of the conventional religious orders.[129] Furthermore, another indication that the *forma vitae* of the company was perceived as a form of consecration is represented by the progressive introduction—after Angela's death—of some of the elements characteristic of conventual life such as the ceremony of ac-

125. As reported by Doneda, *Vita,* 148n (the original document is missing).

126. Cozzano, *Riposta,* ff. 34r–v, in MTS, 576.

127. Angela establishes that the Ursulines were to fast every day during Advent, for forty days after the Epiphany, during Lent, in the three Rogation days, and a week from the Ascension to the Easter of May. Also, the Ursulines fasted three days a week (Wednesday, Friday, and Saturday) from Easter to the Rogation days and from Pentecost to Advent. Furthermore, they were to fast on the vigils established by the church. Compared to the rule of Angela's third order, the main difference was the forty days after Epiphany and the three days a week from Pentecost to the Advent.

128. Galloway, "Neither Miraculous nor Astonishing."

129. Pie Raymond Régamey, "Consacrazione religiosa," in *Dizionario degli Istituti di Perfezione,* vol. 2 (1975), 1607–13.

ceptance.[130] Finally, in the papal bull of 1546, the life proposed by the company was made equal to conventual life and marriage. This emerges from the fact that the bull specified that Ursulines were entitled to inherit, even when the will linked the inheritance to entry in a convent or to marriage.[131] This is why the Company of St. Ursula has been considered a forerunner of congregations with simple vows and of secular religious institutes.[132]

Thus, the status of the Bride of Christ in the world proposed by Angela's company did not exist among the ecclesiastical institutions available to women and was an original trait even when compared to other female forms of religious life, such as beguines, tertiaries, and pinzochere. It represented a more extreme version of the medieval female forms of religious life and identity since it codifies a spiritual experience of union with the divine that was lived by women at a personal level. Angela legitimized a religious life that was lived without official recognition.

Charity and Teaching

There is a famous but erroneous commonplace regarding Merici's institute. It is often thought that the main activities of the original Company of St. Ursula were charitable works in hospitals and teaching poor girls. It is also frequently assumed that Angela founded the company to provide religious education and economic and social protection to orphans, abandoned girls, or imperiled single females.[133] Studies of Angela Merici have put far too much empha-

---

130. As noted by Zarri, "Orsola e Caterina," 546.

131. MTS, 281–84; Dassa, *La fondazione*, 180–82.

132. I.e., Beyer, *Il diritto della vita consacrata*. This has also been recognized in the decree "Vetustum et praeclarum Institutum" by the *Sacra Congregatio de Religiosis* on 25 May 1958 (in Dassa, *La fondazione*, 301–3).

133. Cistellini, *Figure della riforma pretridentina*. After Cistellini this view of the company was maintained by Caraman, *St. Angela* and, especially, by Ledòchowska, *Angèle Merici*. The influential book by Monica, *Angela Merici and Her Teaching Idea*, emphasizes the educational nature of the Company of St. Ursula (especially among diseased and poor Brescian women). Monica's argument has recently been followed

sis on these traits, which, if present, were marginal in her model of religious life. Let us discuss these aspects in more detail.

Literature on Angela Merici has established a connection between the Brescian saint and some charitable initiatives in Brescia and in the vicinity through Angela's friends. Girolamo Patengola worked in the Hospital of the Incurables from 1521, and Giacomo Chizzola and Agostino Gallo were members of its board of governors in 1535, as was Tommaso Gavardo in 1538.[134] Giacomo Bardinello was probably a member of the Divine Love in 1538.[135] Angela's cousin, Bartolomeo Biancosi, and Stefano Bertazzoli (who became a priest after he was converted by Angela) were both members of the Confraternity of Charity of Salò in 1542. Finally, from 1532, the future Matrona of the Company of St. Ursula, Elisabetta Prato, was involved with Gambara's institute for orphan girls and repentant prostitutes. Historians have therefore argued, without real evidence, that Angela Merici, too, participated to these initiatives; that her company gathered poor and orphan girls in order to give them protection, support, and a religious education; and that the members of the company viewed charitable and teaching activities as their apostolic mission in the world.

But to begin with, the image of Angela dedicated to the care of the needy, as Mariani, Tarolli, and Seynaeve have already shown, lacks historical evidence.[136] Angela's name does not appear on the roster of those involved in charitable associations, and none of her friends referred to her activity in the Hospital of the Incurables or

---

up by Blaisdell, "Angela Merici and the Ursulines," though without bringing any evidence (110). By contrast, the work of Mariani, Tarolli, and Seynaeve, *Angela Merici*, criticizes this interpretation.

134. Cistellini, *Figure della riforma pretridentina*. As noted above, the aristocrats Patengola, Chizzola, and Gavardo knew Angela and were informally connected to the company: Patengola left some property, all had Ursulines working in their houses, and Chizzola became an agent of the company after Angela's death.

135. The only mention of Angela's friendship with the artisan Giacomo Bardinello comes from the Brescian chronicler Pandolfo Nassino in the saint's obituary.

136. MTS, 169–88.

mentioned charitable work as a characteristic of her sainthood. This silence is particularly significant in the testimonies of friends who were involved in charitable institutes—for example, Agostino Gallo and Giacomo Chizzola. That some of her friends were involved in such activities does not mean that Angela was as well.

Angela did not found her company to protect the honor of its members, to sustain them financially, or to teach them catechism. There is no doubt that Angela did care about the problems of single girls without means or alone. Herself an orphan since her adolescence, she may have been more sensitive to women with familial disruption and to social problems.[137] She showed a deep knowledge of the problems a single laywoman had to face in the secular world, and she found practical solutions to them. It is also true that the company provided needy Ursulines with some material assistance. The Company of St. Ursula, however, was not specifically directed toward girls who were poor or unable to marry or enter a convent, but was open to women from every social stratum. The documents of the company reveal that most Ursulines' fathers were craftsmen and that some were of a higher status. Furthermore, they reveal that only a small percentage of the Ursulines were orphans. Angela's protective measures and assistance, therefore, did not represent a "charitable" aim but were necessary means to allow all Ursulines, including the poor and those with an unstable family situation, to persevere in a religious life in the secular world, without the protection of cloister or husband. Furthermore, as chapter 2 demonstrates, though Angela did protect her daughters' honor with moral education (such as promoting modesty and virginity), in many respects the type of life and identity she proposed did not fit the existing pedagogical models for women and attitudes toward women's honor promoted by Catholic and lay thinkers. Angela gave the Ur-

137. It is also possible that Angela's idea to provide the Ursulines with legal protection, in case they experienced difficulties in getting their dowry or salary, came from her own experience. Angela's father took his brother Carlo to court in order to have his wife's dowry back (Belotti, "Umanesimo cristiano," 49).

sulines the responsibility for their own lives and proposed virginity in the world. Moreover, life in the company did not represent, as for many institutes protecting women's honor, a temporary situation before reinsertion in society, either in the condition of the wife or of the nun, but a new, permanent female condition—that of the Bride of Christ in the world, the prototype of the single woman.

As far as teaching activities were concerned, the image of the Company of St. Ursula as devoted to the catechization of its members cannot stand. The Colonelle were not *teachers,* and the virgins under their responsibility were not their *pupils.* Rather, the Colonelle's duty (in Angela's words) was to inspire, counsel, protect, and supervise. The supposed educational aim of the company derives from the fact that Angela left some pedagogical advice to assist the spiritual growth of the virgins (especially in the *Arricordi* and the *Testamento*).[138] The evident pedagogical dimension present in Angela's writings was not, however, one of the company's aims; it simply shows that Angela thought carefully about the transmission of her ideal of religious life, which was original and complex. To ignore her theology and focus on her teaching method is rather reductive. It is true, however, that, as we shall see, Angela's pedagogy was a direct expression of her spirituality. It is probable that the successive development of the company as a teaching order has induced historians to assume that Angela herself started the educational project.

Whether the Ursulines pursued charitable and teaching activities *outside* the company is uncertain. As in the case of beguines, the members of the third orders, and confraternities, it is probable that some Ursulines choose to live their religiosity providing help to needy people in the community, both in hospitals and in the neighborhood. And it is also likely that the Ursulines preached, taught, and discussed religious matters with friends, relatives, and

138. Monica, *Angela Merici.*

others (perhaps including poor girls). These, however, were *indi-vidual* choices made within the wider and more complex frame-work of spiritual and "apostolic" life envisaged in Merici's rule. By contrast, to claim that charitable works in hospitals and teaching girls were the main aims of the company is simply wrong. There is no reference to these duties in Merici's writings for the company. As will be discussed in chapter 4, Angela did not identify "charity" with work among the poor. This indicates that performing charita-ble work was probably not a central aspect of Merici's spirituality. Furthermore, the letter of introduction to Angela's rule *(Al lettore),* which explains the significance of the institute, and Cozzano's let-ters, which defend the life of the company, lack any such reference.

The only document referring to the Ursulines' work in hospitals and to their teaching activity is a letter written in 1566 by the con-fessor of the company, Francesco Landini, to one of Carlo Borro-meo's collaborators, Franceschino Visdomini. The Milanese arch-bishop wanted to know about the company, and Landini sent some information concerning its utility. In this letter, Landini distin-guished between teaching and charity, affirming that while the Ur-sulines had just began teaching in the schools of Christian doctrine, work in the hospitals was an activity they had carried out from the beginning: "Until this time it [the company] has been used in all the hospitals of Brescia; the school of the girls of the Christian In-stitution use it now."[139] That Landini said that the Brescian hospi-tals had used the company, however, does not mean that this was its aim, though it does indicate that some Ursulines practiced char-itable works. In addition, Landini's letter belongs to a period when the Ursulines had been placed under the supervision of the Congre-gation of the Fathers of Peace. Much had changed since the found-er's death.[140] This reference to the past may have stopped short of

---

139. *Estratto d'una lettera del P. Francesco Landini,* in MTS, 532.

140. For the evolution of the company and the changes it underwent, see chap-ter 5.

Angela's own lifetime. Furthermore, and above all, Landini's testimony should be taken with a grain of salt as, anxious to convince Visdomini of the utility of the company, he mentioned aspects of religious life that, though they perhaps real, were more conventional than others that emerge from Angela's writings (but were going out of fashion within the postTridentine church).[141]

As a matter of fact, these charitable activities are absent from the early biographies of the saint and surfaced only in the mid-seventeenth century.[142] This image, adopted uncritically by subsequent biographies,[143] found fertile ground in the more recent literature that stresses charity as a distinguishing trait of the Catholic Reformation. The Company of St. Ursula was seen as an offshoot of the Company of Divine Love, the religious association epitomizing the charitable movement.[144] The representation of Merici's company as an active charitable body was also appealing to scholars of women's history, as it provided an example of reaction to the regularization of religious women attempted by the Tridentine church.[145] Though Angela did indeed offer women an original and active model of religious life, she did not identify "apostolate" with charitable works and teaching. In order to understand the kind of interaction with society she proposed, her rule must be read carefully and between the lines.

In conclusion, both Angela's figure and her company belong to the history of women's religiosity. Angela was a "sainta viva" and

141. In the same letter Landini mentions other aspects as typical of the Ursulines that were either absent or unimportant during Angela's times (such as the role of the head of the company and the value of obedience).

142. While they do not appear in the lives written by Bellintani da Salò (*Vita della B. Angela*, composed around 1550) and by Gondi (*Vita della Beata Angela*, written in 1600), we find them for the first time in Quarré, *La vie de la Bienheureuse Mère Angèle*: see MTS, 169–71.

143. With the significant exceptions of Faino and Doneda, authors of the most reliable biographies of Merici.

144. For a discussion of the historiography of the Company of Divine Love, see Solfaroli Camillocci, *I Devoti della Carità* and "Le confraternite del Divino Amore."

145. In particular Liebowitz, "Virgins in the Service of Christ."

the Company of St. Ursula reflected many aspects of medieval spiritual women's manner of association. The company was a secular organization, profoundly spiritual, totally female, democratically organized, separated from the church, and self-sufficient. Thus the company comes across as a sort of society independent from the larger one within which it existed. Angela's model of religious life was more radical than its medieval predecessors, since it codified the identity of the Bride of Christ in the world in a religious rule. And, as we shall see in chapter 3, she also codified other aspects of women's spiritual experiences. However, before turning to this type of analysis, we must assess how Angela's proposal fit into mainstream social expectations concerning women and how society reacted to her proposal.

CHAPTER 2

The Company in Society

The aim of this chapter is to examine how the figure of the Ursuline proposed in Angela's rule fit within Brescian society. The first part investigates Ursuline identity and behavior vis-à-vis contemporary ideals regarding women and points out Angela's originality in the use of certain gender assumptions concerning femininity. Although Angela employed some mainstream ideals regarding the construction of "womanhood" (such as modesty and virginity), the significance she gave them actually empowered women. Furthermore, the emerging female ideal—a virgin living in the world without protection—anticipated the lay single woman. It is for these reasons that the company was attacked by sectors of Brescian society and that a period of turmoil began after Angela's death.

The second part situates the company within Brescian social, economic, and political dynamics. It examines the social background of the Ursulines in order to understand what categories of women were attracted by Angela's religious model. The Ursulines were not poor, orphans, or in danger of losing their honor, as historiography has often assumed. The Company of St. Ursula was therefore not oriented toward a specific category of women but was open to women of all social strata. The possible reasons for the presence or absence of certain social groups have consequently been sought within the social and ideological dynamics of Brescian society. As will appear, although the aim of the company was religious, socioeconomic considerations played a part in the ways Angela's spiritual model was received.

The chapter concludes by clarifying another delicate issue regarding Angela's company—that is, the authorship of its writings and in particular of its rule. This part is preliminary to the analysis of Angela's spirituality, which is the subject of the next two chapters.

THE COMPANY OF ST. URSULA AND IDEAS ABOUT WOMEN

Prescriptive Literature

Sixteenth-century prescriptive literature produced a bloom of both religious and lay treatises directed to and concerning women. As many scholars have recently stressed, women's pedagogical models were constructed mainly around a misogynistic ideology inherited from biblical, Greek, patristic and medieval thought.[1] Didactic literature classified women and defined their duties around the distinction between virgins, wives, and widows rather than classifying them by age, class, and work. Women's main social roles were identified within the family and the convent, as wife, mother, daughter, widow, or nun. The ideological framework on which women's pedagogy was constructed deemed women to be physically, intellectually, and morally fragile.[2]

The notion of female honor was conceived within this ideological context. According to this literature, if men's honor was measured in relation to a variety of qualities (especially wisdom, courage, and power), which also included their ability and expertise in

1. See, for example, Zarri, *Donna, disciplina, creanza cristiana* and Duby and Perrot, *History of Women in the West.*

2. Eve was the paradigmatic image of the woman who was corruptible, curious, unreliable, and sensual. The female ideal was represented by Mary, who was an example of virtue fulfilled in the refusal of her sexual nature. Between the thirteenth and fifteenth centuries a more positive attitude toward women emerged among the church's writers: the humanization of Mary and the emergence of Magdalen proposed models closer to ordinary women and offered the chance of redemption. This possibility should be viewed in connection with the coincident development of the doctrine of purgatory. See Dalarun, "The Clerical Gaze."

the various fields open to them in society, a woman's honor was above all linked to chastity, modesty, and obedience. These were seen as her main qualities in connection with the roles society offered her. An honorable position was attained only through marriage or entry into a convent. On the contrary, women who remained alone were viewed with suspicion (even when widows or when pursuing a semireligious life as bizzoche).

Women's education was above all aimed at maintaining female honor. Treatises gave instructions on how to look after daughters during the marriageable period—that is, between the ages of twelve and twenty. The preservation of a daughter's honor was an important issue for the family because through the daughter's marriage the family could improve its social standing. Women's education was repressive, aiming at physical and moral custody, reflecting its conception within a misogynistic ideology. Women's "natural" weakness and value in matrimonial arrangements between families required that women submit to men and be protected, segregated, and engaged in minor works in order to fend off idleness (regarded, especially by humanists, as the source of sin).[3] Humanists such as Erasmus and Vives wanted to educate women in order to free them from their intellectual weakness, which they viewed as the cause of social and moral disorder.[4] The education proposed by lay and religious treatises was limited to pious readings (secular readings were considered dangerous) and practical, everyday household management. As far as moral education was concerned, for women this model dictated chastity, modesty, and obedience, which aimed at controlling the supposed lustful, irrational, and weak female nature.

The places where the control and the education of women took place were the family, the convent, and the institutes for women

---

3. A discussion of the forms and reasons for female custody can be found in Casagrande, "The Protected Woman" and Vecchio, "The Good Wife."

4. Vives's view on women's education is discussed in Wayne, "Some Sad Sentence"; for Erasmus's thought, see Sowards, "Erasmus and the Education of Women."

alone. From the third decade of the sixteenth century, many institutions aimed at restoring the honor and social identity of fallen or "irregular" women. These institutions provided a dowry and religious and moral education so that women could regain their position within society in the convent or within marriage.[5] Women living alone, like beggars, were seen as a source of disorder as they did not fit into the new social order. The emergence of institutions concerned with the education of such folk should be seen within a context of social reorganization and a wider attempt at disciplining society.[6]

The Ursulines' Everyday Life

In Angela Merici's writings we find prescriptions concerning the Ursulines' worldly behavior that show similarities with the pedagogical model for women elaborated by contemporary prescriptive literature. At the beginning of her rule Angela prescribed that the Ursulines should wear unadorned, simple dress.[7] They were asked not to attend public events such as weddings, dances, and plays, not to listen to secret approaches of men or women, and not to speak with women of bad reputation (*Reg.*, III). Angela also said that they should not stand on balconies or outside their house, and that when they walked on the street they must not stop and look around but must walk quickly, looking down: "Walking along the roads or streets, they should go with their eyes lowered and be modestly covered by their shawls and walk quickly, not lingering, or stopping here and there, or standing about to gaze curiously at anything" (*Reg.*, III).[8]

These prescriptions recall the pedagogical model for women that

5. Ferrante, "L'onore ritrovato"; Cohen, "Asylums for Women" and *The Evolution of Women's Asylums.*

6. See, for example, Prodi, *Disciplina.*

7. "Let it also be recalled that their clothes and manner of wearing them should be modest and simple, as truly befits virginal modesty" (*Reg.*, II).

8. Furthermore, they should not spend too much time in churches, where they could be approached by secular people (*Reg.*, VI).

we have discussed above. A woman's honor was expressed in the
way she looked around and in her posture, as these reflected the
inclinations of her soul.[9] In particular, a woman's gaze was imbued
with meaning, since looking down was connected with modesty
and obedience, and a firm look was a sign of interior order and
peace, whereas looking around curiously was a sign of dissolute interiority. Angela's recommendations were similar to those for the
behavior expected of a "good wife" (and of a daughter) depicted in
contemporary treatises. In the absence of her husband, a wife was
advised by moralists to stay at home, avoid public events, and behave according to the notion of female honor. The Ursulines, as
Brides of Christ, were required to behave in a way worthy of their
role, which did not dishonor the name of their celestial husband:
"Not performing any act or gesture which would be unworthy, especially of those who bear the name of servants of Jesus Christ"
(*Reg.*, VIIII); "They should do honour to Jesus Christ, to whom
they have promised their virginity and their very self" (*Ric.*, 5).

In their homes Ursulines must be moderate and controlled. The
Colonelle must make sure that they behaved properly: "Remind
them to behave well in homes, with good judgement, with prudence and modesty, and to be reserved and moderate in all things"
(*Ric.*, 5).[10]

The acts of eating, drinking, sleeping, laughing, and conversing
should be sober: "Let them eat and drink, not for pleasure and to
satisfy their appetite, but only out of the need to sustain nature in
order to serve God better. Let them be moderate also in sleep, sleeping only as much as necessity requires. Similarly, in laughing, let
them be reserved and moderate. In listening, not taking pleasure
except in hearing modest, and licit, and necessary things" (*Ric.*, 5);

9. Knox, "Disciplina."

10. Angela gives the same instructions to the Matrone, who must make sure that
this behavior is carried out: "you must be especially solicitous and careful that they
keep themselves intact and chaste, and that in every action and gesture they behave
with modesty and prudence" (*Tes.*, 4).

"And let the conversation with others be reasonable and modest . . . let your moderation and prudence be clearly visible to all; and so, let every action and word be honest and moderate. Not taking God's name in vain. Not swearing, but only saying simply: Yes, yes, or No, no, as Jesus Christ teaches. Not answering haughtily" (*Reg.,* VIIII).

Finally, the Ursuline was expected to comply with the laws (divine and human) and the institutions of the society in which she lived (church, company, family, and state). In her rule Angela proposed obedience to "the commandments of God . . . what the holy mother Church commands . . . one's own bishop and pastor, and one's own spiritual father, and the . . . lady governors of the Company . . . fathers, mothers, and other superiors at home . . . the laws and statues of the lords, and the governors of the states" (*Reg.,* VIII).

Thus, in its rules, the Company of St. Ursula appears to have been in line with contemporary institutions and literature concerning the education of women and social discipline. Although Angela reiterated a set of traditional values, however, within her whole program they carried a new meaning.

Angela's prescriptions should be evaluated within her particular religious model. The absence of traditional physical forms of separation (that is, the convent) required other forms of detachment from the secular world. The most obvious reason why she advised her daughters to wear simple dress, to avoid public events, not to stay too long in church, to walk quickly in the street, not to look around, not to listen to messages from men or women of doubtful reputation, was that she wanted to separate and protect the Ursulines from the risks of the world. She justified her prohibitions with the need to avoid the dangers of the secular world: "For everywhere there are dangers and various diabolical snares and traps" (*Reg.,* III). As the Ursulines were already married to Christ but were living in society, Angela interfered in every possible situation that risked contact. Thus the prescriptions concerning their exterior life should be seen as directed toward material detachment. Furthermore, Angela's prescriptions concerning modesty and obedience can be explained in terms of separation from the world inner detachment, expressed in particular by the concepts of "poverty" and "virginity." The value of modesty in laughing, sleeping, and eating should be seen within this theological context. This kind of behavior exemplified the lack of attraction that should characterize the Ursuline's inner attitude toward secular people and things.

Furthermore, by entering the company, women became responsible for their secular life. In effect, Ursulines were no longer subject to familial authority; nor did the Colonelle or Matrone supervise their everyday life. The Colonelle visited the virgins twice a month, the spiritual father saw them once a month, while relatives and employers were external to their life and were not supposed to interfere with it. Many Ursulines (probably the older ones) lived on their own or with a fellow Ursuline (like Angela herself). Angela allowed the Ursulines to make their own decisions concerning their daily life: apart from a few recommendations (regarding the avoidance of dangerous situations such as weddings, public festivals, and so on), very little is said about what to do. The Ursulines could decide where to live and if and when to work; they did not have to ask permission when they left home. They chose whom to visit, when to be visited, and were free to judge in what church to pray and for how long. They were also free to choose the type of "service to God" in the secular world that suited them best. Most important, Angela's rule gave Ursulines a good deal of freedom in shaping their spiritual lives. Angela, unlike didactic writers who told wives to submit to their husbands' authority, let the Ursulines express their own will in their celestial affiliation. As I discuss below, the Ursuline was encouraged to take full responsibility for her relationship with God. Consequently, these prescriptions did not share the repressiveness of prescriptive literature because they did not regulate everyday life and offered a divine relationship that the

Ursuline alone controlled. The advice concerning behavior did not constitute a form of discipline but merely described an attitude toward something from which the Ursuline—as a Bride of Christ—was detached. As we will see in chapter 5, when the company was reformed by Borromeo, the Ursulines' life came under the supervision of their spiritual father. In the same way contemporary secular charitable organizations for laywomen tended to impose a regimented style of life, which translated into a "clausura de facto."[11]

Finally, the ideological context on which the prescribed secular behavior was based was also different from that of male moralists. Angela did not propose modesty and obedience in order to regulate women's weakness and inner disorder. Her writings evince no common prejudices on female psychology and interiority (she entrusted the government of the company to women without involving men) and manifest a profound respect for human beings, whose complexity she acknowledged and whom she refused to judge: "who can judge the heart and the innermost secret thoughts of any creature?"[12]

The Ursulines' Identity

To a certain extent, Angela's rule reflects the view of women's *status vitae* expounded by male moralists. Angela's company was organized according to women's sexual classification: the members of the company were virgins and wives (of Christ), and the women in the government were mothers (of the virgins) and widows. Like theologians, Angela considered virginity the highest status for women. She conceived the company as a family: within this context the mothers (the Matrone and the Colonelle) were given the responsibility of protecting the honor of their daughters. Merici's use of these mainstream ideals, however, challenged expectations concerning the social roles of women.

11. Cohen, "Asylums for Women," 177.
12. *Ric.,* esp 2, 8 (quote from 8); *Tes.* 2, 5, 6. I will develop this aspect in chapter 3.

Virginity

Although it is true that virginity represented an ideal promoted by male moralists, the way Angela used it was innovative, because she proposed virginity in the secular world: "everyone who is about to enter or be admitted to this Company must be a virgin, and have a firm intention to serve God in this way of life" (*Reg.,* I). Virginity as status vitae outside convents was not the norm:[13] in the world virginity existed as a temporary situation, before marriage. Indeed, Angela's interpretation of virginity went against the mainstream notion of female honor shared by Brescian society, as is revealed in Cozzano's report on the company after Angela's death: "What Company is it that each person mocks it? Friars, priests, especially and other wise people . . . . And that sister Angela deserves to be vituperated, for having solicited so many virgins to promise virginity, without a thought for where she was leaving them in the dangers of the world . . . . And what did she think she was doing? To herself imitate a saint Benedict, a saint Claire, a saint Francis. 'And she even wanted to go further, and thought . . . to place virgins in the midst of the world, a thing which none of the patriarchs ever dared to do.'"[14]

The company was despised, especially by priests and friars and other members of the elite, because Angela allowed the virgins to live in the secular world without protection from its dangers. She was accused of presumption because none of the greatest founders of religious orders (such as St. Benedict or St. Francis) or the church fathers dared to envisage such a model. The reasons for this criticism should be sought in the value of virginity in Brescian sixteenth-century society. As we have said, virginity represented the main aspect of female honor and was part of the value of a marriageable daughter. As Ferraro has explained, marriage in Brescia was a par-

---

13. As we have already mentioned, third orders were especially reserved for mature women and widows.

14. Cozzano, *Risposta,* f. 15r, in MTS, 569.

ticularly important means of social promotion and economic (patrimonial) reinforcement.[15] Virginity therefore had to be protected through the traditional forms of the convent and family authority.[16] By contrast, Angela let the Ursulines live in the world and gave them the responsibility of managing their virginity without male control. Thus, Angela's figure of a virgin undermined the familial system and mainstream notions of women's honor.

Merici's proposal, which associated physical virginity with the religious life, was new, since convents did not require virginity for new members (they were populated by widows or abandoned wives as well as young girls). The association between virginity and membership in the company was thus original. Why was virginity central to Merici's ideal of a Bride of Christ? Why did she not allow widows or married women to assume this status vitae?

Angela's choice may be explained by reference to the symbolic value of virginity during her time. Virginity has carried complex meanings throughout history and a different significance for men and women. Since late antiquity the church fathers had associated the term *virginity* with women. By contrast, the term *chastity* was more often used for men. Whereas male chastity indicated one of the aspects of a monk's detachment from the world, for women virginity (as renunciation of sexuality and reproduction) represented abandonment of the world itself. Female virginity represented an ideal status in itself that carried wider existential connotations.[17] Religious writers celebrated virginity as the highest status of women and associated it with the condition of the Bride of Christ,[18]

15. Ferraro, *Family and Public Life in Brecia,* esp. 101–30.

16. For a discussion of the enforcement and the meaning of clausura, see Medioli, "The Clausura."

17. For the various semantic dimensions of the concept of virginity, see John Bugge, "La verginità nel medioevo," in *Dizionario degli Istituti di Perfezione,* vol. 9 (1997), 1901–13.

18. St. Jerome proposed the scale of perfection as follows: one hundred to virginity, sixty to widowhood, thirty to marriage. Augustine emphasized the importance of marriage. In the Middle Ages religious writers gave the virginal state full credit, fol-

while humanists presented it (as chastity) as an ideal toward which women should aim within marriage or widowhood.[19] The concept of virginity, however, has always carried ambiguous meanings within the Christian tradition, and virginity was invested with supernatural power and feared by philosophers and doctors. In a society that defined women through sex and exchanged them between families in order to reinforce lineage, not recognizing them as individuals,[20] the virgin who eschewed matrimonial exchange and did not fulfill women's social roles was a potentially independent woman. A virgin was a powerful type of woman because virginity freed women from male dominance and secular links. Through virginity women refused the role of wife and childbearer, which was viewed as the symbol of human slavery. Jerome affirmed that virgins overcome their female status and become men and Aquinas said that, as nuns, virgins possess the dignity of men and are liberated from subjection to men. At a symbolic level the virgin thus overcame the female condition and represented a middle course between the male and the female—a powerful figure able to mediate between the divine and the human.[21]

Angela's choice of physical virginity handled by women themselves finds its meaning within this conceptual framework. It was, in other words, a symbol of detachment from the world and of women's empowerment. At a practical level the choice of virginity was a means of detaching Christ's Bride from the world in which she lived. Widows and ex-married women could have children and

---

lowed by widowhood and then marriage. The value of marriage emerged especially in the humanist treatises of the fifteenth century (for example, Alberti and Salutati). See De Maio, *Donna e Rinascimento.*

19. Erasmus's concept of virginity is discussed in Reese, "Learning Virginity." Reese shows how Erasmus advocated a chaste life for men and women, arguing that marriage was the best way to achieve this state. However, unlike religious writers, Erasmus valued chastity outside a sacred dimension and saw it within a human context. Chastity was a means to achieve an ordered, balanced, and deeper spiritual life, as opposed to lust, which was connected with disorder and low instincts.

20. Klapisch-Zuber, *Women, Family and Ritual.*

21. Blok, "Notes on the Concept of Virginity."

complex connections with secular people. Angela wanted to have a homogeneous group of women who had no strong ties with society and were totally devoted to their divine husband. It is in this context that we can also explain the presence of three Ursulines (one Angela's contemporary and two in the following two decades) who were not virgins but widows and mothers of virgins in the company.[22] Since they had no husbands and their daughters were Ursulines too, and since they had no commitment to the secular world, their condition was compatible with the ideal of virginity as detachment. Furthermore, these virgin-mothers were Colonelle. This is important because the figure of the Colonelle—together with her spousal dimension—enacted a maternal role regarding the daughters. In short, in exceptional cases, spiritual and concrete maternity could coincide. Furthermore, as I will discuss in more detail in chapter 4, at a spiritual level virginity was understood and proposed as interior detachment from secular values. Finally, Merici viewed virginity as a powerful status vitae. In her rule, the secular life of Christ's virgin-bride was loaded with power and replete with heroic and virile implications embodied by the figure of Judith:[23] "we are called to so *glorious life* . . . . But here we must be wary and prudent, because *the greater the value* of what is undertaken, the greater the labour and danger which can be expected; for here there is no kind of evil which will not try to stand in the way . . . . *Come then,* let us all embrace this holy Rule which God in his grace has offered us. And *armed with its sacred precepts, let us behave so bravely* that we too, like holy Judith, having courageously cut off the head

.

22. "La Piza" (we don't know her real name) was probably the mother of Marta de Pezis, Ursuline in 1537. Marta died before 1540 and we do not know if her mother outlived her (see MTS, 244). We find other two cases after Angela's death. In 1555 Peregrina Casali (who was also among the first virgins), is said to be the mother of Cecilia (she voted in place of her daughter in the elections of Veronica Buzzi as mother general of the company). We find that another Colonella, Maria, is the mother of a virgin called Angela ("Angela de Maria collonella," *Secondo Libro Generale,* f. 101v).

23. Judith, a widow in the Old Testament, in the sixteenth century was also a symbol of virginity (Ciletti, "The Enactment of Ideal Womanhood").

of Holofernes, that is of the devil, may *return gloriously to our heavenly home,* where, from everyone in heaven and earth, great *glory and triumph will burst for us"* (*Reg.,* Prologue).

We can look for one of the reasons for Angela's choice of St. Ursula as the patron of the company in connection with this meaning of heroic virginity.[24] In the early sixteenth century, the legend of Ursula was popular,[25] and Angela was probably inspired by Carpaccio's famous frescos of St. Ursula, which she saw in Venice in 1524. It is easy to see the parallel between Ursula with her army of eleven thousand virgins and Angela with her company of virgins in the world. As Angela asserted, the Ursulines must follow the example of Ursula's virgins, who faced death in order to defend their virginity: "each one should be prepared to die rather than ever consent to stain and profane such a sacred jewel" (*Reg.,* VIIII).

Widowhood

Let us now consider the reasons why Angela Merici reserved the government to widows and why they accepted it. Table 1 (facing) gives the information we have concerning those in the company during Angela's period.

Most of the Matrone came from the elite of Brescian society, and three of their families were also involved in the political life of the council. Seven Matrone out of ten were aged between thirty-two and forty-four. The number of the widows' children varied considerably, from none to seven. They all bore their children when they were young.[26]

24. The legend of St. Ursula, virgin and martyr of the third or fourth century, and the eleven thousands virgins reached its definitive version in the tenth century. Ursula, the daughter of a British king, decided to consecrate herself to Christ. She undertook a three-year pilgrimage with ten aristocratic companions, each accompanied by one thousand servants. The eleven thousand virgins were eventually killed by Attila and the Huns on their way home. Their sacrifice was rewarded with God's intervention, which freed Cologne from the Huns.

25. See Zarri, "La nave di S. Orsola."

26. This reflects the tendency among the upper classes to marry their daughters when they were still in their teens to much older men.

TABLE 1. INFORMATION ON THE MATRONE

Matrone	Age in 1537	Children	Status/wealth
Lucrezia Lodrone	50–60	At least 1 son; widowed in 1525	Husband was Count Ettore Lodrone; her family (Cattani) was not noble
Ursula de Gavardo	43	In 1534, 3 children, aged 18, 11, 7	Very rich; employed a teacher and servants
Maria de Avogadri	40	At least 1 son	Noble; rich; her family was in the council
Lucretia Luzzago	49	In 1517 she was a widow with 4 children	Noble; her family (Avogadro) was in the council; she had 3 servants and 3 housekeepers, one in the company
Ginevra Luzzago	35	7 children; widowed before 1534	Rich, with a great deal of property and income; had 3 housekeepers and a teacher
Giovanna di Monti	60?	In 1517 had 7 children aged between 15 years and 15 months; widowed in 1534	Noble
Elisabetta Prato	41–44	Widowed at 38 in 1534; children unknown	Noble; her family of birth (Bargnana) was in the council; rich
Lionella di Pedeciocchi	33	Widowed at 33; no children	Not known
Caterina Mei/Meya	32–35	No children	Not known
Veronica Buzzi/Bucci	33–36	1 daughter (later in the company); widowed after 1534	Her husband (doctor collegiato) probably was a professional

Sources: Based on the patrimonial declarations of the widows' sons or husbands (see MTS, 246–52): Ursula de Gavardo, PE, n. 65, 1534; Maria de Avogadri, PE, n. 8, 1568; Lucrezia de Luzago, PE, n. 77; Ginevra Luzzago, PE, n. 77, 1517; Giovanna di Monti, PE, n. 90; Elisabetta Prato, PE, n. 110 and 231, 1534; Lionella di Pedeciocchi, PE, n. 102, 1534; Caterina Mei/Meya, PE, n. 87, 1534; Veronica Buzzi/Bucci, PE, n. 29 and n. 257, 1517; for Lucrezia Lodrone there is no PE.

From the company's foundation the aristocracy took part in its administration. Although Angela did not explicitly reserve the government to the upper classes, she clearly tried to involve upper-class women because they could protect the company. In addition, their involvement sanctioned a life many found suspect. The aristocracy responded with enthusiasm: when in 1535 Angela Merici founded the company, she specified that four widows (Matrone) were to take charge of its government; in the first elections of the company in 1537 five Matrone were elected; and in 1539, Angela Merici dedicated her *Testamento* to nine.

The reasons why Angela reserved the government specifically to widows and why they accepted it are inextricably linked. The two main motivations reside in the widows' "maternal experience" and their greater autonomy.[27] From an economic point of view, though the autonomy of widows was often limited by supervision, widowhood could give women greater freedom in the use of money and in the administration of property.[28] From the early sixteenth century widows were receptive to charity and the needs of religious institutions, especially if they were directed to women. As has been recently shown, they often figured among the promoters of convents and female religious houses and were often their self-designated heads.[29] As founders of institutions they had particularly good opportunities to exercise their administrative skills, detailing in their wills exactly how their foundations were to be established and function. With the advent of the Counter-Reformation, widows were encouraged to participate in charitable activities; this work became a main form of religious expression pursued by both lay and reli-

---

27. It is for this reason that in the sixteenth century both widows' families and prescriptive literature attempted to control and define the behavior of widows. Vives, for example, emphasized the importance of a chaste and segregated life out of respect for the husband's memory.

28. This was especially true for upper-class widows who had young children.

29. See, for example, Valone, "Roman Matrons as Patrons"; Bilinkoff, "Elite Widows."

gious women.[30] Brescia, during Angela's lifetime, had many charitable institutes that were often financed by women's wills and donations. One important example close to Angela's milieu was Laura Gambara and Elisabetta Prato's Casa delle Convertite della Carità.

Merici's choice of widows reflected their freedom from marital duties and supervision. In this condition they could make decisions in the company's interest without external influence. Though Angela did not ask them to finance the company, she proposed that noble widows administer the company's incomes because they were used to managing money and property.[31] Merici's company let them exercise their skills in an institutional way and gain eternal salvation. Angela offered the widows a proper structure—with its regulations and defined characteristics—and invited them to manage it. In this sense Angela empowered the widows' role in society and they responded positively.

Furthermore, Merici used the widows' "maternal experience" to give the daughters affection, protection, and the necessary support to achieve their spiritual well-being. In this sense Angela draws on a female religious tradition that invested motherhood with spiritual significance.[32] For example, the widows' governance is described by Angela in terms of maternal love: "And the widows [should be] as mothers, full of concern for the good and welfare of their spiritual sisters and daughters" (*Reg.,* XI). The Matrone were to administer the company's possessions according to their motherly love ("according to your motherly discretion and love"). Angela insisted on the analogy between carnal and spiritual motherhood when she referred to the Matrone in the *Testamento:* "True and loving mothers of so noble a family, confided to your hands that you may have for

30. Cohn, "Women and the Counter-Reformation in Siena," in *Women in the Street,* 57–75.

31. As we have seen in chapter 1, Merici emphasized that they should administer benefactors' legacies without taking advice from outside (*Tes.,* 9).

32. For the concept of "spiritual motherhood," see Atkinson, *The Oldest Vocation.*

them the same care and guardianship you would have if they had
been born from your own body, and even more" (*Tes.,* Prologue).

Her use of family symbolism for the widows is not surprising,
since within Brescian aristocracy, the family, and familial strategies
were at the heart of the economic system and of social prestige. Angela transferred examples from the context of the duties of carnal
mothers to the spiritual family. In order to persuade the Matrone,
she referred to how marriages were used to improve the status of
the family. Angela is very acute in exploring the typical mechanisms of a daughter's preparation for her encounter with her secular bridegroom and the anxiety of the mother, who wants to have
her future son-in-law on her side. It followed that the celestial son-
in-law deserved an even more carefully brought-up bride. By doing
this, the "mothers" would have the favor of the father of the most
important of lords:

Now one sees temporal mothers putting a great deal of care and effort
into attiring, adorning and embellishing their daughters in many different ways, so that they may please their earthly spouses; and the more important and noble these men are, the more the mothers strive with all diligence to make their daughters more and more attractive, especially in
what they understand to be more agreeable to them. And there they have
and place all their contentment . . . for in this way they also hope, because
and by means of their daughters, to have the love and favour of their sons-
in-law. How much more must you do this for those heavenly daughters of
yours, who are spouses not of earthly, corruptible, and stinking husbands,
but of the immortal Son of the eternal God? Oh, what a new beauty and
dignity to be lady-governors and mothers of the spouses of the King of
kings and Lords of lords, and to become in a way the mothers-in-law of
the Son of God; and thus, by means of the daughters, to win the favour
and love of the Most High (*Tes.,* 4).

The use of family imagery in Angela's rule and the active role
assigned to the Colonelle and the Matrone in running the company should be connected with (and testifies to) the growing importance the affective life of the family was acquiring in sixteenth-

century society and the new role mothers were expected to play.[33] In the moral literature of the early modern period the training of a wife was still based on her submission, although it was not expressed only through negative precepts. The new didactic treatises insisted on the mother taking an active part in the education of children, because a woman's character was considered more tender and patient than paternal rigor. By giving all the responsibility to the mother figures (the Colonelle and the Matrone), Angela was in tune with a new tendency emerging in early modern Italian society. Finally, as will be discussed in chapter 3, Angela Merici gave great importance to affection and love for guiding her daughters.

Conclusions

In conclusion, we can say that Angela used women's traditional identities and social roles in an innovative way. She offered Brescian widows a complex and demanding function, that of administering an original form of consecration, articulated in terms of the roles these women already had in society. In addition, the company allowed widows to express their managerial expertise and potential independence in an institutional way. The same can be said of the members, who were brides and virgins and were expected to follow the ideals of modesty, chastity, and obedience developed by society. However, they eschewed male control, became responsible for deciding their own lives, and assumed a powerful identity. Angela combined two of the most "independent" female ideals—those of

33. In the sixteenth century marriage was still viewed as a means to create alliances among families and to reinforce the social prestige of the family's lineage. The new prescriptive literature, however, placed greater emphasis on the couple and insisted that marriage should be based on personal closeness. Until the fifteenth century, prescriptive literature, by both religious (like Cherubino da Spoleto and Giovanni di Dio) and laypeople (for example, Francesco Barbaro and Leon Battista Alberti), proposed a model of complete submission to the husband, insisting on obedience, limiting the wife's duty to the generation of children, and confining her to a private role without public responsibility. See Fubini Leuzzi, "Vita coniugale"; D'Amelia, "La presenza delle madri."

virgin and widow—exploiting to the maximum degree those aspects that offered opportunities for self-expression to women.

Finally, she also prepared the way for the development of lay single women.[34] Unlike institutions for the protection of women's honor, the Company of St. Ursula proposed a new status vitae. Rather than reinsert women within the traditional models of the convent and marriage, Angela proposed the status of Bride of Christ in the world, a condition that, as we have seen in the case of the beguines, pinzochere, and tertiaries, existed only at a more informal level. From a social perspective the Company of St. Ursula allowed women, even if within a status vitae that was not exactly a lay status, to live in the world without marrying.

THE COMPANY AND BRESCIAN SOCIETY

The forma vitae proposed by Merici must have appealed to many women from every social stratum, for it offered them a great deal of control over their spiritual and material lives. The Ursulines, however, apart from a few upper-class members, came mainly from the lower-middle stratum of society. In order to explain the Ursulines' social background we ought to take into consideration the ideological and social state of Merici's Brescia. The families of the Ursulines probably played a part in allowing or hindering their daughters' entry into the company.[35] Let us turn to the social background of the Ursulines who were in the company during Angela's time (1535–40) and then propose some explanations for it.

The Members of the Company
The Social Status of the Ursulines

The sources relating to the Ursulines consist of: (1) the book of the company *(Secondo Libro Generale della Ven. Compagnia di*

---

34. As already noted by Zarri, "Il Terzo Stato," in *Recinti,* 453–80.

35. Also in consideration of the fact that among the conditions for entering the company Angela required the approval of the family *(Reg.,* I).

S.Orsola di Brescia, che finisce l'anno 1632) recording the voters in the election acts of the members of the government and the registration of the entrance of the Ursulines in the company year by year from 1572 until 1632;[36] (2) the declarations of property of the Company of St. Ursula, as well as those of the individual Ursulines (*Polizze d'Estimo*); (3) the passages in the rule of the company that concern the social background of the Ursulines; and (4) the writings of the secretary of the company, Gabriele Cozzano, and other biographers of Angela Merici.

The most important document for an analysis of the status of the Ursulines is the act of election of Angela Merici as mother general in 1537, which lists the Ursulines present at the event and specifies the professions of many of their fathers.[37] Of the fifty-two fathers mentioned, the document qualifies thirty-five of them:[38] thirty-one as "magister" and four with the title of "ser" or "dominus." The document also specifies fifteen trades in which the fathers were involved: five jewelers, three leather workers, two bakers, one trader in perfumes, one shoemaker, one glovemaker, one hatmaker, and one barber. The majority of the Ursulines, thus, belonged to the lower-middle stratum of society. Their fathers were craftsmen, mostly masters, probably owners of workshops or commercial enterprises. The connection between members of the company and

36. Respectively at ff. 52r–68v and ff. 100r–10r, 151r–83v, and from 280r.

37. In *Secondo Libro Generale*, ff. 52r–53v, in MTS, 517–19. It reports the names of the seventy-five Ursulines in the original company, it specifies whether they were working as servants, and it lists the name, title, and profession of their fathers. The information is reported in different ways, as some virgins are identified by their name and surname, others by the city of origin ("Margherita de Brixia"), by their occupation ("Agnes ancilla D. Ursule de Gavardo"), or by varying information ("Clara que habitat in domo ser Pauli de Angolo"). The same person can be identified in different ways in the different acts of the company. Further information regarding the fathers (specification of their job and whether they were dead) is apparently consistent. I will also consider those Ursulines who were not listed in the document of 1537 but who were mentioned by Cozzano as among the first virgins of the company in 1532 (*Dichiarazione*, f. 974r, in MTS, 586) and who then appeared in the act of elections of 1545 or 1558.

38. These fathers account for forty-four Ursulines out of seventy-five. As we will see later, some of the Ursulines were sisters.

Brescian craftsmen is also evident in the social rank of the witnesses in the elections of 1537, who included the son of a weaver, the son of a porter, the son of a hatmaker, and a master shoemaker (the last was the father of Barbara Fontana, the virgin who lived with Angela in the last years of the saint's life).[39]

We also find that some Ursulines belonged to a higher status (though they may have been in economic difficulties): four fathers (who account for five Ursulines) were qualified with the titles of "ser" or "dominus," which were used for people of an elevated position (one was a jeweler, one a trader in spices, and one belonged to the professions). In addition, we find that other Ursulines came from important families, since their surnames were noble and were listed among those of the Brescian councilors of the time.[40] We also have a few of these Ursulines' later patrimonial declarations that indicate that they had a right to substantial inheritances, which were contested by their relatives. The case of Laura and Paola Peschiera is particularly interesting: they claimed the right to the inheritance of the deceased "dottor Peschiera," consisting of a 3,000 lire dowry and a 400 lire legacy.[41] This is not an insignificant amount if one

39. Giovanni Pietro Fontana must have been on good terms with Angela because she left him her prayer book, as was recorded in the frontispiece: "Office of the venerable Mother sister Angela which, since her death, is mine, Zan Pietro Fontana, received by her permission" (*Processus* 340, f. 705v, in MTS, 524).

40. This is the case of Bornati, Pedrocche, Peschera, and Gaffurri. Bornati, Pedrocche, and Peschera figured among the *cives veteres* in the council prior to 1488 (the cives veteres were long-standing citizens assimilated into the nobility from the thirteenth century). See Ferraro, *Family and Public Life*, 70–71 and 74n13. Simona Bornati's father is one of those qualified as a "dominus" in the document. And Mabilia di Bornati was Matrona of the company in the second half of the sixteenth century. Laura and Paola Peschera's father was a lawyer. In 1555 Giovan Maria Peschera was also elected as "protettore" of the company.

41. *PE*, b. 103. Furthermore, Chiara and Taddea Gaffurri (in the company since 1535) encountered problems in getting their yearly income of 2,000 lire. They declared quite consistent possessions (PE b. 152, 1588) and lived in the house of another sister who was widowed and had a servant. They paid 30 lire every year to a fourth sister who was in the convent of St. Giulia (which catered mainly to the Brescian aristocracy). They received an income every year from a total credit of about 2,000 lire, and some properties that were worth about 1,200 lire. Simona Bornati was another Ursu-

considers that in the seventeenth century, when their value was at the highest point, dowries ranged among the upper classes from 8,000 to 42,000 lire.[42] Finally, there were also other Ursulines who could be numbered among those of a higher status.[43]

We also know of some Ursulines who were poorer. As we have seen, Angela established that the company should help the more needy sisters, and between 1548 and 1588 the company declared that it paid for an apartment for this purpose.[44] We also have one declaration of property made by two Ursulines who affirmed to be poor.[45]

Finally, there are some documents from a period shortly after the founder's death that are also quite explicit on the matter of class and wealth. The company's "chancellor," Gabriele Cozzano, testified angrily in 1545 that, following the crisis and divisions after Angela's death, some Ursulines had deserted the company and either married or entered a convent.[46] Although we do not know how many women provoked Cozzano's disdain, his testimony shows

---

line who had legal disputes, declaring that she was unable to claim her maternal dowry invested in a piece of land worth 670 lire (*PE*, b. 152). Her father had illegitimately sold it to the notary Anacleto Pandino, who did not want to return it. Since these Ursulines entered the company when they were very young, the dispute with the family almost certainly took place later. It is possible that the relatives refused to deliver the dowry because they did not want to recognize the status of Ursuline as equivalent to that of wife or nun (as stated in the bull of Paul III).

42. Ferraro, *Family and Public Life*, 118. The Brescian currency, the *lira pianet* (which was flat rather than concave), was worth double the Venetian lira (Martinori, *La moneta*).

43. Another Ursuline (qualified as "Domina") was the sister of a clergyman (R. di D. ni Bernardini Grossi). In addition, Caterina (daughter of the master Andree del Mangan) might have been the relative of an upper-class woman (Domina Antonia del Mangan, who had a servant in the company). In 1545 another daughter of Andree del Mangano is qualified with the title "Domina" (Domina Gratiosa). Finally, in 1545 we also find Martha Buzzi, daughter of the Matrona Veronica Buzzi (whose deceased husband was probably a professional).

44. *PE*, b. 152, 1548.

45. Maria and Scholastica, daughters of Bertolino Zanuchini da Leno, declared they lived in an apartment (*casa*) in the Hospital of the Incurables (*PE*, b. 152, 1568). Their brother had left them 400 lire, and they had an income of 20 lire a year from a Brescian farmer (for a capital of 450 lire). Scholastica was Colonella in 1572.

46. Cozzano, *Risposta*, ff. 6r–11r, in MTS, 566–68.

that some of the virgins had sufficient means to opt for these ways of living (particularly significant was their entry into convents, which required a substantial dowry and was still the preserve of the aristocracy and merchant classes). Furthermore, another indication of some of the Ursulines' wealth is contained in a letter written in 1566 by Francesco Landini, then confessor of the company. He affirmed that rich and poor virgins coexisted in the company: "The Company of S. Ursula in Brescia contains . . . many young virgins, *both rich and poor* who, though they revere holy religion, nevertheless do not feel inclined to shut themselves up so narrowly in cloisters, or bind themselves with vows, or else they cannot enter a cloister through poverty, or for other good reasons."[47]

Family, Work, and Education

Reading the documents of the company carefully, we find other interesting information concerning the Ursulines. First, family desertion and orphanhood were not requirements for acceptance in the company. In the chapter on admission of the rule, Angela advised that the virgins have parental permission ("if she has father or mother or other superiors, she [should] first ask for their consent"), and in the chapter on obedience she requires that they obey their parents and superiors in the household ("to obey fathers and mothers and other superiors at home"). The document of 1537 indicates that five out of seventy-five Ursulines were fatherless—although it is possible that the number was higher as there were another seven whose fathers are not mentioned. Second, the Ursulines could not be redeemed women with scandalous lives behind them since virginity was a condition for entry (*Reg.,* I).

Third, it seems that many of the virgins were linked to one another or to the company by family connections.[48] In the 1537 list of virgins it appears that sixteen of them were sisters.[49] Finally, an el-

---

47. *Estratto d'una lettera,* in MTS, 531. The italics are mine.
48. Familial ties were a common phenomenon in religious institutes.
49. In a number of cases sibling relationships are spelled out in the document, in

ement that reinforced the family ties within the company was the presence of one Colonella who was a widow and mother of an Ursuline.

Though the Ursulines were predominantly young, their ages seem to have varied. The minimum age for entering the company was twelve[50] and, at least in theory, members remained in the company throughout their lives.[51] We know the age of a few Ursulines: Chiara and Taddea Gaffurri joined Angela's company when they were twenty-one and seventeen; Paola and Laura Peschera entered at twenty and eighteen; Maria and Scholastica da Leno were both probably fifteen or even younger; and Flora, the servant of Patengola, joined when she was forty-one.

We know from Cozzano that the Ursulines supported themselves with their work. In Angela's rule we also find evidence that Ursulines were working in private houses (*Reg.*, XI).[52] The act of the 1537 elections specifies that nine out of seventy-five Ursulines (one of them was a Colonella) worked as lady's maids in the houses of Angela's friends and of the Matrone of the company. Though some of them may have been servants before becoming Ursulines,[53] others found jobs thanks to the intercession of the company (as stated by Angela in the rule).

As far as the education of the virgins was concerned, we find

---

others they are suggested by the fact that the Ursulines had the same father or surname. The first virgins of the company mentioned by Cozzano (some of whom were not named in the document of 1537) included another five virgins who were sisters or had sisters who joined the company later.

50. However, it was possible to accept younger girls as external members.

51. In 1555 we find that, between the two split factions, there are at least seventeen of the seventy-five virgins who elected Angela Merici as mother general of the company in 1537.

52. In referring to the secular activities of the Ursulines, Angela uses the words *Massara* and *Donzella*. Massara corresponds to a high-status servant, a housekeeper, who organized the affairs of the household. Donzella refers to a lady's maid in an important family. Angela never used the term *Serva*, which corresponded to the lowest grade of the scale. It is possible that she used these terms deliberately to give more dignity to the daughters.

53. This was the case of Flora.

some evidence that some of them were illiterate and others not. The virgins' illiteracy is suggested by Ginevra Luzzago's will, which specifies a sum devoted to the Canonici Lateranensi for a priest to read the rule to the Ursulines in the church of St. Afra.[54] Angela's prescription of practicing the Office, however, indicates that she expected at least some of them to be able to read (as we have seen she also prescribed the Our Father and Hail Mary to the illiterate).[55]

Finally, another significant aspect of the Ursulines' background in 1537 is that it is very likely that sixteen of them were originally from other cities and from the Brescian countryside.[56]

In conclusion, during Angela's lifetime the majority of Ursulines belonged to the lower-middle class and especially the craftsman's strata of society. However, the company was open to all women who wanted to live a religious life in the secular world, as the presence of a number of women with a higher social background shows. The explanation for the high presence of women from a specific level of society should be sought, therefore, in the attitude of Brescian society toward the company rather than in the foundress's intentions.[57] This is why it is necessary to investigate the social dynamics of Brescia during Merici's time.

The Company in the Brescian Economic, Social, and Political Contexts

The period between the second half of the fifteenth century and the first half of the sixteenth century was very eventful for Brescia.[58]

54. In MTS, 606.

55. "And those who know how to read will say the Office of the Dead; and those who cannot read will say thirty-three Pater Nosters and as many Ave Marias" (*Reg.*, XI).

56. Many of the virgins' surnames in the 1537 document correspond to places, which were probably the cities of origin of their families (such as Isabette q. Beltrami Fachere de Martinengo and Honoria filia magistri Marcolini de Castiono).

57. We must also consider that Angela required the approval of the family among the conditions for entering the company (*Reg.*, I).

58. For the history of Brescia, see especially Pasero, "Il dominio veneto."

The city was divided by social conflicts of an economic and political nature. Brescia suffered an economic crisis that became particularly evident in the seventeenth century. Furthermore, in the sixteenth century the council came under the control of a narrowly based oligarchy. The wars of Italy, in addition, caused political tension and demographic crises. The middle strata of society, especially craftsmen, suffered most during these social upheavals.

Economy and Society

In the late Middle Ages Brescia was a wealthy city. The Brescian territory was rich in natural resources and the many city workshops testified to the economic importance of crafts.[59] The two main trades were wool (which employed the highest number of workers) and iron. In the early fifteenth century, with the Venetian annexation, the Brescian economy had experienced a new expansion, due especially to the commercial privileges granted by Venice and the end of the wars between Venice and Milan. By contrast, the late fifteenth and early sixteenth centuries were a period of economic instability caused by the increasing corporative interests, the Venetian taxation system, and warfare. For Brescian craftsmen it was a period of insecurity and transformation. Although manufacturing still kept production up to good standards, important changes occurred: some sectors in crisis (such as the wool and the shoemaking industries) converted to low-quality products, others declined (for example, the gun industry), and new ones emerged.[60] Furthermore, several guilds (such as that of the weavers) and independent masters of workshops were in conflict with merchants who tried to impose their monopoly over commerce by controlling the volume of

59. There is no comprehensive description of Brescian manufactures based on guild records. The only sources are the reports of the Venetian officials and the petitions for tax relief from the local ruling class.

60. The linen industry became more important and new workshops were opened. Other expanding sectors were the production of musical instruments, the paper industry and the printing of books, and the glass and ceramic industries. The production of building materials, and especially the wood and leather industries, were also important.

production of manufactured goods, of imports and exports, and of the supply of raw material.[61] Another cause of concern for Brescian craftsmen and commerce was the Venetian taxation system. From the end of the fifteenth century, and in particular from 1517, Venice introduced different types of indirect and personal taxes (*dazi*) on commercial activities, goods, and agriculture. These taxes provoked protests and led to the smuggling of both exports and imports, a practice that the Venetian authorities could never quell. This situation hurt Brescian competitiveness with foreign products, especially iron and wool. Workers and owners of workshops connected with these trades were particularly at a disadvantage.[62] Finally, the wars of Italy had a significant impact on Brescia, especially in the years 1509–16, when the city was the theater of the contest between the French, the Spanish, and the Venetians. The working population was severely reduced by the wars (in particular by the sack of Brescia carried out by Gaston de Foix) and by subsequent famine, epidemics, and emigrations.[63] Nevertheless, the Brescian economy survived thanks to resources from the surrounding territory, the protectionist policy of the mercanzia, and because Brescia was no longer affected by wars.

61. Especially the "carders" (*garzatori*), "shearers" (*cimatori*) and "lesser weavers" (*tessitori minori*). Though, in the fifteenth century, the Venetian government often supported the protesters, after the 1509–16 experience Venice became more cautious in supporting local corporative bodies, which were always a danger for the state. Venice dealt with the social tensions and conflicts of interest among different social classes in a pragmatic way, evaluating the particular circumstances and its own interests.

62. In 1560 the situation was worsening, as we learn from a *supplica* of the *podestà*, Paolo Correr: "Your most faithful city of Brescia used to have two kinds of merchandise with which it gave livelihood to its poverty and enriched that country with the money of strangers, iron work and the wool trade . . . now these two important trades have little by little become almost extinct in the Brescian territory. . . . One can see in this city innumerable poor families fall into ruin because there are no means for trading merchandise, and furthermore the idle sons are turning to crime, many poor who have nothing left, and cannot support themselves and their families with their work, go begging, and resort to crime" (*Lettere pubbliche*, 18 June 1561, in Pasero, "Il dominio veneto," 336).

63. Brescia faced the great famine in 1512–16. After that there were other periods of famine in 1523, 1527, 1531–33, 1540, 1546, 1548, 1559–60, 1569–70, and 1590.

Politics

At a political level there were significant changes that penalized the lower-middle classes. As with other Italian cities, the Brescian Council underwent a progressive aristocratization that eventually excluded the middle class from political office.[64] A concomitant shift in values discredited manual labor, industry, and commerce.

At the time of the Venetian annexation, the Brescian ruling class was composed of both nobles and nonnobles.[65] The composition of the council was not fixed, since families died out and new families entered. Between 1426 and 1473 the ruling class expanded to include families of industrial, artisan, and commercial origins. Between 1473 and 1488, however, the most important families, which still had the greatest control over the council, began to defend their position of power and limit entrance to their ranks. During the French occupation (1509–12), however, the council accepted into its ranks families connected with trade and industry and, in 1517, after Venetian dominion was reestablished, the classes excluded from the council in 1488 were readmitted because of their support during the liberation of Brescia. Within a few years, however, the few families who had previously held power in the council managed to reassert the old laws and reestablish their oligarchy. In 1528 and 1546 further provisions excluded people whose relatives were involved in commercial activities ("lowly trades") and made the seats in the council hereditary.

These changes were connected with a wider debate over the nature of nobility that found its greatest expression at the end of the sixteenth century.[66] The Brescian ruling class developed an aristocratic consciousness, stressing the importance of ancestry and proof of nobility. The notion of honor found expression, among other

---

64. The same phenomenon took place in other cities of the Brescian territory, where the local government became more oligarchic.

65. In Brescia there were influential families who did not participate in the civic government and families in the council with little authority.

66. See Donati, *L'idea di nobiltà in Italia*.

things, in separation from other social groups in public events and in the code of precedence in seats and in the streets. According to foreign observers, the Brescian aristocracy prized luxury and the display of wealth.[67]

Finally, another category of people who suffered social discrimination were the "foreigners," who were denied the same rights as Brescian citizens. They were a significant portion of the population, having moved to Brescia from other cities and the Brescian territory in the second half of the fifteenth century and the sixteenth in order to benefit from the 1440 privileges acquired by the city over the *territorio*. They included small landlords and merchants who became active in the Brescian economy through their many commercial activities and land investments. They were members of the guilds and merchant associations but were excluded from citizenship and from holding office in the council and in the mercanzia. As they became more aware of their status and importance within Brescian society, their discontent increased.[68]

Social Motivations for Entering or Rejecting the Company

What was the impact of Brescian social conflicts and economic crises on the social makeup of Merici's company? As we have seen,

67. An agent from the Medici in 1568–69 reported: "They are Brescians, and as rich persons they are very haughty and their ostentation is to have many servants and to flaunt themselves and their women in fine garments and liveries and have beautiful horses with magnificent coaches and carriages; and besides, to hold a splendid and most honoured table" (A. Segarizzi, "Le relazioni di Venezia dei rappresentanti esteri," *Atti Istituto Veneto* 81, no. 2 (1921–22): 148–50, in Pasero, "Il dominio veneto," 370). As a Venetian observer put it: "They are lax and full of idleness . . . most of the time they stay on the ground floors of their houses with open doors; they visit one another and gamble, in the morning they walk around, in the evening they ride a great deal around the city" (Relaz. C. Zen, 1553, 68, in Pasero, "Il dominio veneto," 370).

68. In 1572 the most active and wealthy "foreigners" (all merchants) started a protest, which failed because of the opposition of the Brescian Council, which presented the revolt to the Venetian government as politically dangerous. The status quo was maintained and the privileges of the Brescian oligarchy confirmed.

Angela founded her company in a period of general instability that especially penalized those very classes that proved more receptive to her ideas. To explain the reasons why the artisans participated in the company while the aristocracy rejected it, we should analyze the social and economic significance of Angela's way of life.

In the first place, it may be that the economic and demographic instability and exclusion from political power of the middling groups made them more vulnerable and more concerned about protecting the honor of their daughters. Given the ideological context that considered women who remained single disreputable, craftsmen may have worried that they would be unable to marry off their daughters. A failure in that regard would erode their social status. In the sixteenth century, convents had absorbed unmarried women. These, however, as they required substantial dowries, were mainly reserved for the aristocracy, and Brescia was no exception. From this point of view, Merici's company, not requiring a dowry, offered the lower classes a solution. The Company of St. Ursula protected the honor of women at both a material and an ideological level. The company defended the sexual honor of the artisans' daughters because by entering the company women were committed to maintaining their virginity and their secular behavior was supervised by the Colonnelle and the Matrone. The company also offered material assistance—economic, legal, and medical. An artisan's daughter could sustain herself through her work or through the help of the company. She could continue living at home with her family without scandal. These social considerations were persuasive not only for families but for the artisans' daughters themselves, who, by entering the company, gained financial and social security. For the poorer Ursulines the company represented a way to eschew poverty and social degradation, with its risks of crime and prostitution.[69]

69. Seduction and abandonment were other risks, when men could dangle empty promises of a marriage or a subsidy for an eventual dowry. See, for instance, Cohen and Cohen, *Words and Deeds in Renaissance Rome.*

In this context it is possible that the artisans' families saw the presence of the aristocracy in the government of the company not only as a guarantee of protection but also as an opportunity for social improvement. Angela depicted the company as a family, where the "mothers" were aristocrats and the "daughters" artisans. In a society where familial strategies were used to strengthen the power of lineage and individuals, craftsmen may have seen in their daughters a means of establishing useful social ties with the aristocracy. The company in this sense could have been seen as a sort of idealized and more harmonious version of society in which the powerful were committed to the protection of the weaker classes.

In addition, entering the company gave lower-middle-class women a higher status because they were considered Brides of Christ. As Merici explained in the prologue to her rule, regardless of their social condition, life in the company gave women a new dignity that was greater than that of powerful secular people. The life of the Ursulines was elevated: "You have to thank Him infinitely that, to you especially, He has granted such a singular gift. For *how many important persons* and others of every condition *do not have* nor will be able to have such grace! Therefore, my sisters, I exhort you, or rather I beg and entreat you all, that having been thus chosen to be the true and virginal spouses of the Son of God, you be willing to recognize what such thing this is, and what a new and *astonishing dignity* it is . . . we are called to so *glorious life* as to be spouses of the Son of God and *to become queens in heaven* . . . not only shall we easily overcome all dangers and adversities, but also, to our great *glory and jubilation,* we shall defeat them . . . and our every sorrow and sadness will be turned into joy and gladness, and we shall find thorny and stony paths *blossoming for us, and covered with paving of finest gold*" (*Reg.,* Prologue); "How many *lords, queens and other great persons* there are who, with the many riches and possessions they have, *will not be able to find true relief* in some extreme need" (*Ric.,* 5).

Furthermore, as recent historiography on confraternal activities has shown, religious devotion went hand in hand with corporate pride and social affirmation.[70] In a period of political exclusion and economic uncertainty, the lower-middle class and foreigners may have seen in Merici's company a means of reinforcing their social bonds and identity as a group. The company, like guilds and confraternities, gave them some public identity and visibility through the public role of their daughters, who were an example of virtue to the city. Moreover, since confraternities became more aristocratic in their composition in the late fifteenth and early sixteenth centuries, artisans may have been even more receptive toward the new forms of confraternal activities open to them.

Interestingly, there were many craftsmen among the people who backed Protestant ideas in both Italy and Europe. Recent scholarship has shown how artisans' participation can be explained in connection with their sensitivity to issues of social justice and to forms of religion that gave people more responsibility. The link between communal ideals, which belonged to the late medieval urban tradition, and the Protestant religion has been adopted to explain the artisans' involvement in the Reformation in the cities of southern Germany and Switzerland between 1519 and 1525 especially.[71] Another significant reason for the success of the Protestant Reformation in its initial phase was that common people were "flattered" by the reformers because they were invited to hear and judge doctrine and because the "common man" was placed at the center of the religious experience.[72] The success of the company among artisans may be seen through a similar perspective, especially in view of the progressive aristocratization of Brescian society. Even though the company was not Protestant, it presented some of the new religion's early features, such as democracy and communalism. For ex-

70. For this type of analysis see, for example, Weissman, *Ritual Brotherhood;* Henderson, *Piety and Charity;* Terpstra, *The Politics of Ritual Kinship.*

71. Moeller, *Imperial Cities,* 41–115. Blickle, *The Revolution of 1525* considers communal values in the Peasants' War.

72. Cameron, *The European Reformation,* 311–13.

ample, as we shall see, Angela placed the Ursulines at the center of the religious experience, giving them control of religious life. The Ursulines were given the right to appoint their common spiritual father and to elect the government of the company and were free to choose in which church to attend mass. Besides, their relationship with God was conceived as direct, and the company did not interfere with how they wished to live it (the rule does not indicate any particular activity they must follow in the world). Furthermore, the company's concern for material solidarity in the form of mutual help brings to mind the horizontal ties typical of the communal mentality of the lower-middle classes.[73]

A similar trait that may have appealed to the artisans was the fact that Angela's company was fundamentally "meritocratic" and "democratic": though no sources specifically concern relations among the Ursulines, Merici's and Cozzano's writings indicate that there were no class-based hierarchies or prescriptions. The Ursulines were considered equal among themselves and vis-à-vis the Colonelle and the Matrone. Any Ursuline, without class distinction, could become a spiritual guide (Colonella) and instruct others of higher social rank (in 1537, for example, two Colonelle were working or living in other people's houses). The Colonnelle could disobey the Matrone—who were members of the aristocracy—if these did not do their work properly. The Matrone were elected by the virgins, women from a lower social stratum. Another mark of the company's relative indifference to considerations of class was the absence of dowries. In sixteenth-century society and convents a woman's dowry was a measure of her worth and wealth: Angela thus removed an element of social discrimination among the Ursulines, especially against those who were poor.

The aristocracy, in contrast, largely refused to let their daughters become members of the company. As Cozzano testified, the main

---

73. Hughes, "Domestic Ideals and Social Behavior."

reason was that the members' virginity was not protected as in the convent (see above). The upper classes had stricter conditions for honor that the company, due to its secular nature, did not satisfy. Another explanation lies in the fact that the aristocracy did not want their daughters to mix with girls from the lower social classes. Cozzano says that the aristocracy despised the company because of the presence of members belonging to the classes involved in manual or "vile" work: "Neither gentlemen, nor gentle women or other persons of importance are pleased nor wish that their daughters should enter, for it is a company of a low sort of person, servants and poor creatures";[74] "They also try to disparage it, going around saying that noble girls do not enter it, but only artisans[75] and other girls without nobility."[76] The attitude of the aristocracy toward the company was thus a reflection, on a smaller scale, of the exclusivity that distinguished the mentality of the sixteenth-century Brescian elite.

Moreover, Merici's rule spurned the aristocratic codes of honor. The absence of social hierarchies within the company may have played a part in the aristocracy's refusal to let their daughters enter. The aristocracy had often been hostile to any attempt to limit or interfere with its power in the religious sphere. This was true, for example, of the nobles' resistance to the introduction of the observance and the decrees of the Council of Trent into monastic life, which promoted a religious life detached from family power.[77] From this point of view it is interesting that some changes occurred toward the end of the sixteenth century, after noblewomen en-

74. *Risposta,* f. 15r, in MTS, 569.

75. *Artiste* in the original text.

76. *Risposta,* f. 22v, in MTS, 572.

77. For the observance in Brescia, see Cistellini, "La vita religiosa." On the Tridentine decrees, see Lowe, "Secular Brides and Convent Brides"; Zarri, "Gender, Religious Institutions, and Social Discipline." One of the most interesting cases was Teresa of Avila's battle to introduce a strict version of the primitive Carmelite rule against the will of the local aristocracy; see Bilinkoff, *The Avila of Saint Teresa.*

tered the company. The company became much more hierarchical and directed from above. The distinction of identities between the classless virgin/Bride of Christ and the aristocratic widow/Matrona became blurred, as the Ursulines could become Matrone and even mothers general. The Ursulines, possibly according to their wealth and status, were having careers within the company, climbing the ladder of the new hierarchy. Some aristocratic families created dynasties of Ursulines and counted several Matrone and protectors in the company. This may suggest that the aristocracy brought strategies of prestige and family power into the company.

In conclusion, although Angela did not found her company for socioeconomic reasons, these were important to explain its reception. The characteristics of the Company of St. Ursula (in particular its democratic features, the material protection, the aristocratic supervision, and the dignity offered by the figure of the Bride of Christ) may have appealed to a sector of society that was economically insecure, was being marginalized from political and religious institutions and discriminated against at an ideological level. Angela's model of religious life, by contrast, did not meet the requirements of the aristocratic notion of honor, in particular because it did not protect virginity through the convent and challenged matters of rank. Although these social considerations are important, the main motivation for becoming a Bride of Christ, albeit a secular one, was religious. The Company of St. Ursula must have been very attractive to women who wished to pursue a spiritual life, since its religious ideal reflected many spiritual traits women expressed throughout the Middle Ages. Since we have already discussed how Angela conceived the material life of the Ursuline Bride of Christ, we must now analyze her spiritual life in greater depth. Before we do so, however, we must establish whether the texts that depict the core of the Ursuline's life—the rule and the advice for the Colonelle and the Matrone—were composed by Angela Merici.

THE AUTHORSHIP OF THE RULE OF
THE COMPANY OF ST. URSULA

The rule, the nucleus of the writings for the Company of St. Ursula, was written between 1532 and 1536. It consists of a prologue and eleven chapters addressed to the members of the company. The original rule of the company has not been found.[78] The oldest edition is a manuscript written between the end of 1545 and the beginning of 1546, the *Regula della Compagnia de Santa Orsola* (also known as *Codice Trivulziano*).[79] This edition of the rule is believed to be authentic, as its structure corresponds with the description of the original rule in the *Summarium additionale*.[80] The rule is preceded by a letter (*Al lettore,* which explains the utility of the company) that is not part of the rule and was written after Angela Merici's death. The dating of the manuscript is based on the inclusion of the prescription that the Ursulines wear a black leather cincture (established on 11 December 1545) and on the fact that the introductory letter states that the company did not yet have papal approbation (the bull was published on 14 April 1546).

Angela also composed the *Arricordi che vanno alli Colonelli* and the *Testamento della Madre suor Angela lassato alle Matrone* (also known as *Legati*). These are brief compositions comprising one

---

78. The original manuscript apparently disappeared during the canonization process, after 1770. One copy of the rule, together with the other writings of Angela Merici, was sent to the Sacra Congregazione dei Riti. During the canonization process, the priest Antonio Guelfi ("presidente della pubblica Biblioteca" di Brescia) stated that he had seen it (*Processus* 341, f. 710r). For these questions, see MTS, 17, 346–48.

79. It is published in MTS, 436–58.

80. The *Summarium* (compiled during the canonization process by the Congregation of Rites) describes the documents attributed to Angela Merici. In the *Summarium* the original manuscript is described as consisting of one prologue and eleven chapters as in the *Codice Trivulziano*. Both documents open and close with the same words. The only difference from Angela Merici's original rule is the introduction of the belt as a distinctive sign for the Ursulines. It is unlikely that other changes were introduced because Cozzano, who reported all the changes and the divisions within the company, makes no mention of them. See also MTS, 372–76.

prologue and nine chapters, written around 1539. They were directed respectively to the virgins' spiritual guides (the Colonelle) and
to the administrators of the company (the Matrone). The writings
suggest ways of dealing with these responsibilities and offer spiritual and pedagogical advice.[81] All texts were written in the vernacular.

Although the writings for the Company of St. Ursula (*Regula,
Arricordi, Testamento*) have always been considered a manifestation
of Angela's spirituality, attributing definitive authorship presents
some problems.[82] In the first place, Angela's name does not appear
in the *Regula*. Second, the *Regula, Arricordi,* and *Testamento* were
not written in Merici's hand but dictated by her to Gabriele Cozzano, the secretary-chancellor of the company. As historians of female
religiosity have frequently pointed out, the problem of the mediation and alteration of the men who wrote down women's words is
serious and must be considered.[83] Now I want to demonstrate that
Angela Merici should be viewed as the author of the writings for
the Company of St. Ursula.

The *Arricordi* and *Testamento* are less problematic since both are
in the form of a letter by Angela to the Colonelle and Matrone.[84]
They are written in an oral style, in the first person, and Angela men-

81. The original manuscripts are lost, but we have the transcriptions in the *Processus* 341, ff. 946v–58v (it is also published in MTS, 507–17).

82. The main biographers of Angela Merici, such as Mariani, Tarolli, and Seynaeve
and Ledòchowska, maintain Angela's authorship although they do not discuss system-
atically certain aspects involved in the problem. Less specific historiography and more
traditional accounts of her life do not tackle this issue directly, and two contradictory
tendencies sometimes coexist: on the one hand Angela's authorship is maintained for
apologetic reasons; on the other it is assumed that Cozzano is the author—possibly
because he was a man. More recently, Zarri has discussed this issue in "Orsola e Caterina."

83. See, for example, Mooney, "The Auctorial Role of Brother A." I will discuss
this historiographical issue in chapter 3.

84. The beginning of the *Arricordi* reads: "Sister Angela, unworthy servant of Jesus
Christ, to her beloved daughters and sisters." The same words are also used at the beginning of the *Testamento:* "Sister Angela, unworthy servant of Jesus Christ, to Count-
ess Madonna Lucrecia."

tions her own name throughout these writings. Neither the churchmen responsible for her canonization nor later historians have ever
questioned Merici's authorship. By contrast, there are some contradictions in the sources concerning the circumstances in which the
rule was written. Angela Merici's authorship of the rule is based on
a letter by Cozzano, where he affirms that the rule was dictated to
him by Angela alone: "It was written in my hand and the whole
composition was mine. But the sense was of the Holy Spirit, dictated through the Foundress . . . . She alone, divinely inspired, was the
foundress of all these works. She is the true and living mother, who
in the Word of truth and in the Blood of Jesus Christ has generated
and regenerated them . . . as she and I alone have made this Rule;
and even so no part of it is mine, except a small ministry of writing
as faithfully as I could her sacred meanings and documents."[85]

So far as Angela's literary skills and background are concerned,
we know that she could read[86] but apparently could not write. Angela had a solid theological background: she read religious books
daily and was asked by theologians and preachers to give her personal interpretation of the Old and New Testament.[87] So it seems
perfectly possible that Angela was able to develop the complex religious proposal expressed in the rule. In content and style there are
many similarities between the *Regula*, the *Arricordi*, and the *Testamento*. These writings appear complementary and form a whole
and complete spiritual system that shows no contradictions.[88] References to the Holy Scriptures with quotations, the use of certain
linguistic patterns (for example, the use of the verb *volere* instead
of *dovere*), and the warm—but at the same time determined—style

85. *Dichiarazione,* ff. 973v–74v, in MTS, 586–87.

86. As testified by Giacomo Chizzola and Agostino Gallo at the Processo Nazari
(*PN,* ff. 941r, 944r–v, in MTS, 536, 539).

87. Ibid.

88. We find, for example, that in the fifth *Ricordo* Angela asks the Colonelle to
make sure that the Ursulines do a number of things that correspond to what is prescribed in chapters 3 and 8 of the rule. The meaning of certain theological points (such
as "charity": *Reg.,* 8; *Ric.,* Prologue; *Tes.,* 1) is also consistent.

are also consistent. Given these shared traits, it would seem likely that the author was the same.

Another source, however, indicates that Cozzano was not the only person who may have been involved in the writing of the rule. The introductory letter to the oldest edition states that it was composed by a group of people, and especially by the wiser virgins of the company:[89] "Thus, the judgement of many wise and experienced persons contributing to it, and in particular that of the older and more expert virgins of the Company, with the help of God this brief institution has been composed, which we desire be called the Rule of the Company of Saint Ursula."[90]

In Cozzano's writings, however, we find another hint that can help explain why in the preliminary letter to the rule Angela does not appear as its author. Cozzano revealed that Angela had asked him to write an introductory letter *(epistola proemiale)* in which she did not want her name to appear, wishing to be considered among the other virgins: "But in an introductory letter she made me write, she wished to be placed among the common number, and her name not mentioned by me through humility, or maybe for other reasons and causes which are hidden in the divine secrets."[91] This letter he mentions may have been the introductory one to the rule, and its formulation concerning the origins of the company may have reflected Angela's request. It is likely that Cozzano was the author of the letter because its content and style recall his writings. There are a series of common themes in both the introduction to the rule and Cozzano's writings:[92] the comparison between the company and the original church;[93] the reference to certain criticisms of the com-

89. As noted by Zarri, "Orsola e Caterina," 541.

90. *Al lettore*, in MTS, 434.

91. *Dichiarazione*, f. 974r, in MTS, 586.

92. In particular with his *Risposta*. I will refer to the introduction to the rule as *Al lettore* and to Cozzano's letter as *Risposta*.

93. *Al lettore*: "This way of life has seemed to me . . . almost a spark of the life of the primitive Church" (MTS, 433); *Risposta*: "may this way of life be according to the apostolic life of the primitive Church" (f. 11r, MTS, 568).

pany and the style of the polemical reply;[94] the considerations regarding the decision of some Ursulines to leave the company;[95] the emphasis on the free choice of individuals in seeking the path toward salvation and the consequent absence of forms of command in the rule of the company.[96]

Angela's authorship of the rule does not exclude the possibility that other virgins contributed to the development of some of its features. As Cozzano tells us, it was common practice for Angela to discuss what she was proposing with the Ursulines, sharing the merit for decisions taken with them: "What she communicated to others she impetrated in these virgins, and gave them the ability to practice it. Then she consulted with them, and exhorted them to proceed, and said that she had done this not alone but with them."[97] It seems, therefore, that Angela was the author of the precepts and that she was open to the virgins' reactions and opinions. Since the rule most likely was written when she and the virgins were already sharing a religious life, it is probable that the virgins' contribution to the writing of the rule took place at a preliminary stage of its formulation and consisted especially in discussing some of its aspects.[98]

Finally, Angela used to discuss spiritual issues with theologians and friends. She probably spoke of her intentions for the compa-

---

94. *Al lettore:* "Who then is the invidious and malicious person who dares here to rashly open his mouth?" (MTS, 434) *Risposta:* "to turn up one's nose and speak badly over the Company" (f. 14v, MTS, 569); "this malicious voice is impious and wicked . . . a malicious doubt over the salvation of every saint" (f. 19r, MTS, 571).

95. *Al lettore:* "If she . . . climbs aloft to then come down; leaving what is better to take on what is worse" (MTS, 435); *Risposta:* "Becoming nuns, they leave this primitive and apostolic life, and fall from high to low" (, f 11v, MTS, 568).

96. *Al lettore:* "Here nobody lays down laws and obligations . . . . Each person is exhorted, each person is invited" (MTS, 435–36); *Risposta:* "God inspires, calls the creature, to where he can save her according to his will, if she wishes to follow his counsel" (ff. 29r–v, MTS, 574).

97. *Dichiarazione,* f. 974r, in MTS, 586.

98. As we have seen, they began to share this life in 1532. The rule was written between that date and 1535.

ny with other "experienced persons" (for example, her confessor, Serafino da Bologna), and it is possible that she received advice. The role of external contributions, however, should not be over-emphasized. As we have seen, the author of the introductory letter affirmed that the main contribution was given by the virgins ("in particular . . . expert virgins"). The *Processo Nazari* and the various hagiographies do not mention any spiritual figure close to the Brescian saint who could have had a significant impact on the writing of the rule.

Concerning the authorship of the *Regula, Arricordi,* and *Testamento,* the question of the nature and extent of Cozzano's involvement should be considered. Cozzano was certainly very close to the foundress, and his writings reveal similarities with those of the company. His impact on the composition of the writings of the company, however, was probably limited. Historians have often assumed that Cozzano was a priest, but it has been demonstrated that he was a layperson, a notary and teacher of grammar.[99] That he was a layperson associated with the legal profession is important because it gives more credibility to the statements he made concerning Merici's authorship of the rule. He was not Angela's confessor or a churchman interested in exalting the role of the saint as a means to gain personal fame or give luster to the religious order, as was the case with many religious women.[100] Cozzano's role consisted in ensuring the preservation of Angela's doctrine, defending the company, acting as legal representative and as the material executor

---

99. See MTS, 121. That Cozzano was a priest is affirmed by, for example, Guerrini, "La Compagnia di S. Orsola," 89, and Cistellini, *Figure della riforma pretridentina,* 198. In the epigraph on Angela's gravestone he appears as "Domini Gabrielis Cozzani litterarum professoris" (Nazari, *Libro della Vita,* in MTS, 547), in the will of Lucrezia Lodrone he is mentioned as "domino Gabrielo Cozalo infrascripto, qui se subscribet pro secundo notario ad laudem sapientis" (*Processus* 341, f. 926v), and in a legal act of the company in 1556 Cozzano is elected as legal representative and described as "gramaticum."

100. See Benvenuti Papi, "Frati mendicanti e pinzochere."

of the most important documents of the company.[101] He explained
that Angela herself gave him these roles: "[the] foundress made the
chancellor write the Rule and all things pertinent to it, and imposed on him to write many other things; and she made him the
protector of this Company, to defend the Company especially from
evil doctrines and opinions, and to manifest the truth of her own
doctrine. But these must not be changed, because the Mother left
them and made them . . . . But those orders made by the foundress . . . she wants them to remain intact and immutable."[102]

Throughout his letters Cozzano saw himself as the faithful follower and guardian of Angela's ideas. His commitment to fulfill his
duty emerges constantly: "another chancellor of this kind could not
be appointed, because he could not have the foundress' mind as I
have had it."[103] When, after Angela's death, the company became
the target of criticism and some Ursulines left, Cozzano wrote two
letters to support the Ursulines who remained in the company and
in reply to the argument that virgins should stay in convents. Then,
when the institute was finally approved by Paul III, he composed
another letter in which he translated the papal bull of approval.[104]
When the company was split by the decision to adopt an exterior
distinctive sign not prescribed by Angela, Cozzano belonged to the
faction that opposed this novelty.

A significant indication in favor of Merici's authorship is given
by stylistic considerations. A comparison between the writings of
the company and Cozzano's writings shows that the style is very
different. The *Regula*, *Arricordi*, and *Testamento* succeed in express-

101. Cozzano exercised this role through active involvement in the company from
its beginning as chancellor *(Cancegliere)* and from 1555 as "protettore." Cozzano is no
longer in the documents of the company from 1559.

102. *Dichiarazione*, f. 979v, in MTS, 591.

103. Ibid.

104. As we have seen, these letters are *Epistola confortatoria alle Vergini della Compagnia di Sant'Orsola composta per il suo cancegliere Gabriello Cozzano; Risposta contro
quelli persuadono la clausura alle Vergini di Sant'Orsola;* and *Dichiarazione della Bolla
del Papa Paolo III.*

ing very complex religious concepts in simple and clear language. Cozzano's writings lack these qualities. They are confused, repetitive, and difficult to follow, though they are addressed to the Ursulines and were thus intended to be clear.[105] The same conclusion was reached during Merici's canonization process. The calligraphic expert Vincenzo Bighelli compared the company's *Arricordi* and *Testamento* and Cozzano's *Epistola confortatoria* and affirmed that the handwriting belonged to the same person, but that the author was not the same: "Definitely . . . they are written by the same hand, however all three are not by the same author."[106]

Finally, it is unlikely that Cozzano influenced the content of the rule during the process of writing it down, in its passage from the spoken to the written language:[107] Angela's words were not translated from the Italian vernacular into Latin, and a religious rule is a type of text that leaves little space for interpretation and alteration. Compared to that of the *Arricordi* and the *Testamento,* the language of the rule is less colloquial and the words are carefully chosen and thought out. This also means, however, that it is unlikely that Angela's words were recorded exactly as they were said, and the text implies an elaboration of the language. Cozzano may have helped Angela in the process of writing the rule and discussing the words to be used.

In conclusion, Angela Merici should be regarded as the author of the rule, though she discussed some of its aspects (especially the organization of the company) with the other virgins and possibly with Cozzano or other spiritual people close to her. The synthesis of the ideas, the elaboration of the project, and the organization of the spiritual concepts, however, were distinctly Angela's.

---

105. Cozzano's letters have been recently translated into modern Italian: Tarolli, *Lettere del segretario.*

106. *Processus* 341, ff. 880v–81r (see MTS, 21).

107. Mooney argued that the *Memorial* by Angela of Foligno was modified by Brother A., who transcribed and translated into Latin the words spoken by Angela in the vernacular ("The Auctorial Role of Brother A").

CHAPTER 3

Female Spirituality

As we have seen, the form of life proposed by Angela's company reflected the kind of association practiced by the beguines, pinzochere, and tertiaries. This chapter will analyze in-depth the similarities between Angela Merici and late medieval spiritual women by examining their relationship with God and with the sacred in general. Angela's rule represents a very useful document for the study of the characteristics of female religiosity and its significance for women's relationship with society. In many respects Angela presented the Ursulines with a model of holy life that reflected the spiritual experience and active social roles of medieval mystic women. Her originality consists, above all, in her codification of women's spiritual experience into a religious rule.

My discussion also considers some traits of Angela Merici and of female spirituality within the context of medieval and Renaissance concepts of gender. I am not concerned here with what is biologically "female" about women's spirituality. I treat gender as a relative and historical cultural construct. Angela's spirituality appears to reflect some contemporary assumptions concerning the female, but at the same time she also rejects the negative consequences that possibly flow from these assumptions. Her case reveals a pattern that can also be valid for late medieval spiritual women. It will be useful to start with an overview of this late medieval experience before examining Angela's precise relationship to it.

THE BRIDE OF CHRIST IN HISTORICAL PERSPECTIVE, TWELFTH TO SIXTEENTH CENTURIES

Mysticism

Female religiosity has taken different forms over the centuries. And the status of devout women (nuns, tertiaries, or laywomen) implied certain differences between them in their spirituality.[1] But, generally speaking, the similarities override the differences. From the thirteenth century to the sixteenth, many women shared the same religious model whether rich or poor, married or unmarried, tertiaries or nuns—that is, mysticism. To be sure, not all spiritual women were mystics,[2] but this was a very important form through which women experienced the sacred and expressed their creativity within the religious sphere. It is also true, however, that mystic experience in women's lives was particularly emphasized by those men (confessors, hagiographers, and secretaries) who wrote women's biographies and mediated women's writings. Mysticism was not gender specific, as men, too, expressed themselves through this manner of communication with God. It was, however, more frequent among women and it was believed that they had a special relationship with the divine.

The origins of medieval mysticism lie in the diffusion of an affective spirituality from the twelfth century on. This diffusion is especially associated with authors such as the Cistercian Bernard of Clairvaux, who interpreted mystic marriage as a type of personal mysticism rather than as an allegory.[3] At the same time, veneration for the life of the human Christ became central to the spirituality promoted by the penitential movement led by Francis of

---

1. Bynum, "Women Mystics in the Thirteenth Century: The Case of the Nuns of Helfta," in *Jesus as Mother,* 170–265.

2. See, for example, Dor, Johnson, and Wogan-Brown, *New Trends in Feminine Spirituality* and Winston-Allen, *Convent Chronicles.*

3. Matter, "Mystical Marriage." For a recent compelling explanation of the growth of affective piety, see Fulton, *From Judgment to Passion.*

Assisi. Medieval men and women increasingly viewed Christ as an object of love and pity—as a man who had suffered. Furthermore, compared to the idea stemming from traditional monasticism, the emerging model of relationship with God was individual (rather than collective) and was conceived in terms of union (in traditional monasticism contemplation kept the individual and God more apart).[4]

Several studies on medieval female religiosity have noted that a privileged relationship existed between women and transcendency. As pioneering historian of sainthood André Vauchez has shown, women's claims to sanctity were more often based on charismatic authority, especially visions and supernatural signs.[5] Canonized men were, in some instances, represented as being in union with God, but an intimate rapport with the sacred characterized all reported women's religious experiences. As another quantitative study of sainthood confirms, male saints more often owed their power to ecclesiastical or even secular office.[6]

The sheer number of medieval visionaries about whom some information has come down to us seems to confirm that we are face-to-face with a society that privileged the connection between women and God.[7] Women visionaries outnumbered men in the

4. The main aspect of this new religiosity, however, rests on the type of relationship with God rather than the actual form of life in which this was lived. See Leonardi, "La santità delle donne," 48–50.

5. Vauchez, *La sainteté en Occident*, 410–48.

6. According to Weinstein and Bell, there were two types of "saints" in the period in question. One was a masculine type: "holder of temporal or ecclesiastical power, missionary to the heathen and fiery preacher of the word, champion of public morality, heroic defender of his virtue"; the other was common to both men and women, though some traits were particularly valid for women: "penitential asceticism, private prayer, mystical community with the Godhead, and charity" (*Saints and Society*, 237).

7. Dinzelbacher, *Vision und Visionliteratur im Mittelalter*. Dinzelbacher calculated that between the sixth century and the first half of the twelfth, visions were exclusively a male affair but that from the second half of the twelfth century to the thirteenth, women visionaries reached numerical equality with men, while in the following century they constituted the majority of visionaries. Dinzelbacher's data are partial as they refer only to visionaries approved by the church.

sixteenth century, too. During that period, the association between spiritual women and the supernatural was evident also in the privileged position women had in their access to divine secrets: the prophetic gift was often exercised by women. Churchmen encouraged female visionary activity because it was seen as an instrument for discovering God's will.

Studies of the hagiographical lives of male saints have shown that more emphasis was placed on conversion than on intimate relationship with God.[8] Men's conversion took place during adulthood, was public, and implied renunciation of wealth, social status, work, family, and sexuality. By contrast, where women's lives were concerned, it was their relationship with Christ that was emphasized rather than the moment of their conversion. Women's conversion came during childhood or adolescence; it was conceived of as a secret pact between the girl and Christ and was described in terms of a relationship of love. Although women, too, abandoned the values of secular life and their conversion was seen as an act of virtue, in the majority of cases their renunciation was far less emphasized than was their intimate relationship with God.

If we turn our attention from hagiographical sources to actual women's writings, we likewise find that these were dominated by a spirituality centered on ecstatic union through contemplation of the Passion. Women's religious writings were also more direct, affective, introspective, and colloquial than those of men. Women wrote more often about their personal mystical experiences of union with God. By contrast, in describing their search for union with God, men tended to deal in a more theoretical way with the steps needed to reach God. Moreover, when mystic men spoke of their ecstatic experiences, they did so either because they were influenced by women or they were using female images for themselves.[9]

---

8. Coakley, "Friars as Confidants of Holy Women."

9. These points have been made by several historians of spirituality. See, for example, Bynum, "The Female Body and Religious Practice in the Later Middle Ages," in *Fragmentation and Redemption*, 190–91.

Nuptial mysticism constituted the main ideological framework within which female relationship with God was conceived. Since the early centuries women's conversions to Christianity was viewed through nuptial images. In accounts of newly converted couples, the bride speaks of receiving marriage with the "true man," whereas the bridegroom interprets his conversion as receiving knowledge.[10] This view of female conversion was also endorsed by religious orders, in which women became *sponsa dei* and men soldiers of Christ.[11] Between the thirteenth and sixteenth centuries, bridal identity and mystic union characterized women's spiritual writings and correspondence with men.[12] Though women sometimes saw Christ as a judge, a father, or a baby to nurse, he was, above all, a man to love. Women enriched their spirituality with discourses of love.

To a certain extent, women's mysticism and affective spirituality can be explained by the fact that they were excluded from ecclesiastical roles and formal education. Since women were barred from ecclesiastical careers, preaching, and administration of sacraments, mysticism was considered the main type of religious experience available to them. Furthermore, women's visionary language was more direct, affective, introspective, and colloquial because they lacked formal education (normally women who could read or write did so in the vernacular), while they were influenced by popular literature and the tradition of courtly love.[13] In addition, the style of women's mystical writings can be explained with the fact that many of them dictated (or told) their experiences, rather than

10. See Kraemer, "The Conversion of Women to Ascetic Forms of Christianity." She affirms that all women's stories contain a motif of erotic substitution (either with the male divinity or his agent, the apostle).

11. Barone, "Society and Female Religiosity"; Zarri, "Gender, Religious Institutions, and Social Discipline."

12. For collections of women's writings, see Petroff, *Medieval Women's Visionary Literature;* Leonardi and Pozzi, *Scrittrici mistiche;* Spearing, *Medieval Writings on Female Spirituality.*

13. See Newman, *From Virile Woman to WomanChrist,* 137–67; Guarnieri, "Angela da Foligno."

wrote them. These factors explain some traits of women's spirituality, but do not help us to understand why women were considered apt to experience mysticism even more than men and why they shaped their relationship with the sacred with some specific traits (such as extreme penance).

As has been observed, saintly women are "portrayed constantly as living on the boundary as it were between this world and the other world. As conduits for God's word to this world, women function as bridges between these worlds." Men possess a sense of inadequacy and limitation concerning "their own office and learning, and their perception of women as 'other,' embodying in particular a connection with the divine that they do not find in themselves."[14] Some of the reasons that women were perceived to have a unique association with the divine and to be apt instruments to mediate God's power should be sought in the medieval ideology surrounding the female. Male writers portrayed women as possessing a dual nature: on the one hand weak, irrational, and lustful, on the other mysterious, numinous, and able to connect with the divine. Theologians stated, for example, that women's humid and soft nature made them more impressionable and therefore predisposed to visionary experience.[15] Aquinas affirmed that women were more suitable and receptive to this kind of contact with God be-

14. Coakley, "Introduction: Women's Creativity," 7–8. Man's sense of frustration at his incapacity for enlightenment by God clearly emerges, for example, in a letter written by the cofounder of the Theatines Gaetano da Thiene to the mystic nun Laura Mignani. A distressed Gaetano accords Laura a special relationship with God and the power of interceding with her celestial husband. Consequently, he asks for her help in various private matters: "I hope that God has truly enlightened your soul. . . . Oh beautiful gift! . . . the likeness of which I pray Your Reverence to impetrate in the same way in me. . . . I commend to Your Reverence and your sisters my niece and myself, a sinner, that you may love us all in Christ. . . . I certainly hope Jesus Christ will wish to do [this], if he is prayed to do so. The selling of my office, the marrying off of my niece, staying and going to Rome, God has put me in such a state that I neither know what to think or what to do" (Andreu, *Le lettere*, 30–31).

15. On beliefs regarding the power of female imagination and similar issues, see Elliott, *Proving Woman*, esp. 204–11.

cause of their "less rational nature." It should be noted that the association between the female and the realm of the supernatural also connected women with the demonic. Indeed, in the early modern period the speculations on "woman's nature" led men to persecute women as witches: the *Malleus Maleficarum* (1468) explained that women, being feeble in mind and body, were more inclined to credulity and therefore to temptation by the devil.[16]

Men's frustration and women's ability in relation to mystical experience can also be considered from a social perspective. As we have seen, men's sanctity was identified more with powerful renunciation of wealth than with intimate relationship with God. As we shall see in the next chapter, a similar model can be expounded in sixteenth-century male manuals of perfection, which stressed renunciation of codes of honor. If renunciation of worldly power was important to women, too, contact with the divine was more strongly emphasized. Women's renunciation was considered less significant because they lacked control of wealth, status, and family. Men, by contrast, who identified themselves with creation and management of these worldly values, considered this act of great worth. At the same time, however, men's concern with social renunciation tended to become the main aspect of religious life. Although renunciation was part of the male attempt to become "powerless" like Christ, it also represented a powerful act, which men viewed as sacred in itself. Thus, at least in part, men achieved holiness at the moment of renunciation—and union with God implied a further step. By contrast, because women did not sacralize the moment of renunciation, their holiness was more strongly tied to personal contact with the divine.

16. Many aspects of female sainthood (ecstasy, the ability to visit other places in spirit, and so on) were the positive image of the same traits of witchcraft (see Craveri, *Sante e streghe*). The possibility that female living saints were witches in disguise was considered: see Zarri, *Sante vive*, 114–18; Dinzelbacher, "Sante o streghe." By contrast, when men were accused of witchcraft they were portrayed as having a learned or scientific approach (i.e., based on the knowledge of books of black magic) that gave them control over evil forces.

Finally, women's religious experience and identity was shaped in continuity with women's symbolism within society. As we have seen in chapter 2, in the fifteenth and sixteenth centuries a variety of sources (secular and religious literature, contracts, wills, and other documents) all suggest that women's identity was mainly associated with the reproductive role, sexuality, and family. The identity of religious women, too, was shaped according to these aspects. In describing religious affiliation to the divine, female mysticism was depicted through bridal and maternal images, which reiterated women's main social identities, those of the wife and the mother. The symbolic significance of virginity for religious women—virginity was "the" sign of worldly detachment and another important source of religious identity[17]—also stems from this conceptual framework: the renunciation of sex and family transformed and sanctified a woman's "nature."[18]

Penance

Another expression of women's direct experience of God was through physical penance. Food deprivation, self-inflicted suffering, and the interpretation of illness as a religious experience were particularly common to women. Men, when they did express the same type of religiosity, were more moderate. Francis of Assisi tried unsuccessfully to have his spiritual sister Clare moderate her penance, and Catherine of Siena starved herself to death at thirty-three years of age. Traditionally, historians of religion tended to identify women's extreme asceticism as a form of punishment of self and the body, the latter being considered a source of lust. It was assumed that women internalized the misogynist tradition that saw woman as inferior to man by nature and unable to represent God on earth.

17. Newman, *From Virile Woman to WomanChrist.*

18. As also argued by St. Jerome in his notorious statement: "As long as a woman is for birth and children, she is different from man as body is from soul. But when she wishes to serve Christ more than the world, then she will cease to be a woman, and will be called man" (*Commentarius in Epistolam ad Ephesios* III.5, in PL 26: 567a).

Asceticism and virginity were considered the means to escape from the female condition.[19] Another theory viewed female ascetic practices as a psychological answer to a misogynist society that did not provide a forum of expression for women.[20] Making an analogy between modern female anorexia and women saints, Bell argued that through fasting, spiritual women were rejecting misogynist culture and moving their fight for control of situations and self-recognition from society to their bodies.

Caroline Bynum has analyzed religious phenomena of this kind through a cultural perspective.[21] Her work criticizes the theory that identifies spiritual women as victims of patriarchy. She argues that women did not internalize the misogynist tradition and did not see themselves as weak and incapable of relating to God. Whereas men, in order to approach God, adopted images of role reversal that expressed weakness and renunciation, spiritual women did not articulate their relationship with God through contrasts such as male/female, superior/inferior, spirit/flesh. Furthermore, medieval religion sacralized the body, and penitential practices were pursued in imitation of the suffering Christ on the Cross, as a means of attaining salvation and direct contact with the divine. Spiritual women manipulated their bodies in extreme ways in order to experience Christ. Penance should be seen in parallel with other physical phenomena (such as illness) that are interpreted as religious experiences. In addition, certain paramystical phenomena and miracles were connected with the sacrality of the body: trances, levitation, stigmata, miraculous lactation, mystical pregnancy, pictures etched on hearts, and the incorruptibility of the corpse. All these phenomena were centered on the body and were typical of women and of their relationship with the divine.[22]

19. For a historiographical review of this interpretation, see Bynum, *Holy Feast and Holy Fast*, 390.

20. Bell, *Holy Anorexia*.

21. See esp. *Holy Feast and Holy Fast*.

22. According to Bynum, Francis of Assisi was the only famous man to receive the

One explanation for the presence of bodily phenomena in women's religiosity is the association that late medieval society made between "woman" and "body."[23] Examples of this can be found in the theological assumption by which "man is to woman as soul is to body," in scientific ideas of conception and generation and in physiological theories, in which the woman provided the matter and nourishment (the blood) for the human body. Furthermore, there was a tendency to see female sin as bodily or sexual but male sin as mental, the result of external temptation. Women's social roles were also connected with the body: women gave birth and assisted births, nursed children and prepared food, took care of the sick, buried the dead. Bynum has used such association to explain extreme penitential practices in women's religiosity. Within a religious culture that sacralized the body and that saw Christ as body as much as spirit, both men and women agreed that female flesh was more "fleshly," and they identified Christ's humanity with the female body. This is why women's penance was more significant and more easily identified with Christ's suffering. This association between woman and the body also led medieval people to see some of Christ's bodily functions as female: he bled, nurtured (through the Eucharist), and gave birth (through redemption). His love for souls was identified with the love of a mother for her child.

A-institutional Religion

A further important characteristic of female religiosity during the late Middle Ages and early modern period lies in the fact that women did not seem to create and manage the sacred through institutional forms and exterior structures. Administration of sacra-

---

stigmata (and in more recent times, Padre Pio). One might add that Pope John Paul II could be seen as another example of a man who gave religious significance to the body. By making his sickness public, he identified the suffering of his body with both that of humanity and that of Christ.

23. Bynum, "The Female Body and Religious Practice in the Later Middle Ages," in *Fragmentation and Redemption*.

ments, sharing of ecclesiastical and monastic hierarchies, and the creation of rules of perfect behavior, with few exceptions, were the preserve of men. Though abbesses indeed were important figures in the high Middle Ages, they were still subject to male authority and, with a few exceptions, ruled only over women. Women's exclusion from positions of power can also be found in confraternities and even in heresies.[24] Furthermore, the creation and perfect interpretation of outward devotions was part of men's experience of the sacred. In late medieval hagiographical representations, male sainthood consisted mainly in exterior and imitable acts. As Kieckhefer put it: "If we want to write the story of male piety we must turn primarily to the pious acts, the devotional behavior of the saints: their veneration of statues and of relics, their daily regimens in the spiritual life, their pilgrimages and quest for indulgences."[25]

This aspect of female medieval religion reflected an important trait of women's condition within culture, that is, their exclusion from institutional forms of power.[26] Women were denied the "powerful" word (they could not sit as judges, preach or teach, write laws) and, with dynastic exceptions, lacked access to official politics. Ancient philosophers (like Aristotle), church fathers (for example, Tertullian), humanists (for example, Vives), and theologians (both Catholic and Protestant) all saw a natural incompatibility between women and positions of command.[27] Medieval women's piety was shaped in continuity with this cultural condition.

24. Casagrande, "Confraternities and Lay Female Religiosity." Similarly, with the hierarchization of the heretical sects women lost their condition of equality to men (initially a woman could be a *perfecta* and had the right to administer the sacraments): Anderson and Zinsser, *A History of Their Own*, 214–27.

25. Kieckhefer, "Holiness and the Culture of Devotion," 293.

26. Women, however, could have access to real informal power via patronage, counsel, spreading ideas, and complaint.

27. In 1558 John Knox affirmed: "To promote a woman to bear rule, superiority, dominion or empire above any realm, nation, or city is repugnant to nature, contumely to God, a thing most contrarious to his revealed will and approved ordinance, and finally it is the subversion of good order, and all equity and justice" (*The First Blast of the Trumpet against the Monstrous Regiment of Women*, in Aughterson, *Renaissance Woman*, 138).

Female religiosity, however, was not shaped merely by exclusion, because women showed a relationship with the sacred that did not seem to value the establishment and sharing of "powerful" institutional structures. As Bynum has pointed out, women's piety can be labeled as "a-institutional," "because [it] lacked rules, complex structures, permanent vows, hierarchical leadership roles, endowments and so on."[28] This does not mean that men could not follow a similar religious ideal: for example, Francis of Assisi emphasized spiritual values instead of hierarchy and structure. Spiritual women, however, more often experienced the sacred in this manner. For late medieval women who emphasized a mystical union with God, the convent, as a powerful space that articulated God's presence, seemed less important. As beguines, bizzoche, and often as tertiaries, women lived without vows. They also frequently changed their institutional affiliation, moving from one religious order—or religious status—to another and changing convent. Furthermore, hierarchies, positions of power, and perfect compliance to external norms seem not to have been central to female spirituality. Clare of Assisi's rule, for example, envisaged very little hierarchy and many exemptions from usual restrictions such as enclosure and perpetual silence. By contrast, these exceptions were absent in the version of the Poor Clares' rule drawn up by Cardinal Hugolino.[29] Though spiritual women who lived after the Council of Trent did often defend the strictness of their rules (for example, Teresa of Avila, Maria Maddalena de' Pazzi, and Maria Domitilla Galluzzi), by then women wanted to defend the convent, the main space for their creativity.[30]

28. Bynum, "The Mysticism and Asceticism of Medieval Women: Some Comments on the Typologies of Max Weber and Ernst Troeltsch," in *Fragmentation and Redemption*, 64.

29. See, for example, Bartoli, *Chiara d'Assisi*, 122–28; and Petroff, "A Medieval Woman's Utopian Vision: The Rule of St. Clare of Assisi," in *Body and Soul*, 66–79. Petroff notes: "Her vision of community is horizontal, not vertical, and collaboration, not hierarchy, is the key" (70).

30. Bilinkoff, *The Avila of Saint Teresa;* Matter, "The Commentary on the Rule of Clare of Assisi by Maria Domitilla Galluzzi."

Male Mediation

One main difficulty when discussing the features of female sanctity is that most of our information comes from men, especially from women's spiritual fathers, disciples, or later hagiographers.[31] In addition, most of these women did not write but dictated their thoughts to male writers. We thus run into the problem of men's mediation and distortion of women's deeds and words. Scholars have often dealt with the issue of the hagiographers' intentional or unintentional projection of personal ideas and expectations concerning female sanctity. Careful evaluation and comparison of existing sources of male representations of women with women's self-images have shown patterns. Hagiographers, for example, often stressed women's nuptial and corporeal mysticism at the expense of their active roles or public visibility. Female spirituality was more likely to be described as passive, caused by God's intervention and authority over a woman's life, and as marked by supernatural phenomena and by an intimate and secret relationship with God.[32] Studies of spiritual women must therefore seek to gauge the hagiographer's intervention in female writings and not assume that the woman's self-image coincided with the hagiographer's representation. One must bear in mind in particular the themes that recur in the male view of women's piety.

Active Roles

Women did not see themselves as passive vessels in their mystical experiences. We need to stress the active and public dimensions of mysticism. In many spiritual women, mystical practice was inextricably linked with active life in the community. Many of the social roles women filled should be considered in light of the role

---

31. For a thorough examination of the complex relationship between confessors and spiritual women, see Bilinkoff, *Related Lives.*

32. Men's perception and alteration of women's spirituality is the subject of the essays in Mooney, *Gendered Voices.*

of the medieval and early modern saint. The saint was an expression of a culture in which the relation with transcendency was still very important, and he or she was at the center of the veneration of the faithful by virtue of a life in imitation of Christ or of charismatic gifts. Having gained the consensus of large parts of society, she or he learned to operate in the social and political milieu.[33] Mysticism, therefore, in a society that recognized a religious value and space for social action in individual relationships with God, meant not retreat from the world but participation in its events. Some spiritual women were granted a public role as mediators of the voice of God or by virtue of an authority derived from their relationship with him.

A common active role of spiritual women in society was to reproduce God's power on earth in a variety of ways, as in prophetic, thaumaturgic (or healing), apotropaic (or protective), and salvific functions. Women could interpret God's will and exercise their prophetic gift in many milieux, public and private.[34] Supernatural healing was part of women's charitable works in convents, hospitals, and in their own neighborhoods.[35] Both spiritual women in the world and nuns in convents interceded for supernatural protection in everyday matters and for salvation. They corresponded with people asking for divine favors, received visitors, and prayed for the souls of the community. Intercession for supernatural protection was also a role given to the recluses who, in the thirteenth century, lived alone or in small communities near the gates of Ital-

33. Zarri, *Le sante vive,* 87–88.

34. For Italy, see, for example, Zarri, *Le sante vive;* Valerio, "L'altra rivelazione: L'esperienza profetica femminile nei secoli XIV–XVI," in *Donne, potere e profezia,* 139–62. Valerio discusses the relationship between prophecy, preaching, and theological knowledge in her *I sermoni di Domenica da Paradiso.*

35. Clare of Assisi performed several "miraculous healings" in her convent (Bartoli, *Chiara d'Assisi.* 144–45), while Gentile da Ravenna used to visit the sick and cure them through prayer: "she visited the sick and prayed over them, and they were miraculously healed" (Colosio, "Serafino da Fermo," 249). See also Pomata, "Practicing between Earth and Heaven."

ian cities.[36] Mystic women were often seen, and saw themselves, as saviors of humanity, taking responsibility for sinners and repeating the Savior's sacrificial suffering. Some mystic women, for example, affirmed that they abstained from food to alleviate the suffering of others or to relieve souls in purgatory.[37] These important active and public religious roles were probably accepted by society because women's authority came from God and thus did not challenge the hierarchy of genders. Furthermore, women were repeating the role of "mediator," championing the needs of the community with God and channeling divine will and power.[38]

Not all religious and public roles, however, were connected with the supernatural experience; some were the expression of rational capacities. Holy women could participate in civic life by giving political and moral advice and acting as peacemakers. They took part in the creation of religious culture by participating in religious debates, converting, teaching, preaching, promoting or resisting reform, and founding convents and even religious orders. Women promoted the cult of the Eucharist, devotion to the child Jesus, and the feast of Corpus Christi.[39] Furthermore, spiritual women wrote not only about personal mysticism, they wrote theological treatises that should be seen as part of a philosophical and intellectual tradition.[40] Hildegard of Bingen wrote theology, science, and poetry, Hadewijch religious poetry, Marguerite Porete mystical theology, Catherine of Bologna and Catherine of Genoa theoretical treatises on sin and love. The spiritual works of Angela of Foligno and Marguerite Porete are masterpieces of Western mysticism, and Catherine of Siena and Teresa of Avila became doctors of the church.[41]

36. Sensi, *Storie di Bizzoche.*

37. Bynum, *Holy Feast and Holy Fast,* 120–2; Newman, *From Virile Woman to WomanChrist,* 108–36.

38. On the reception of women as mediators, see Mooney, "*Imitatio Christi* or *Imitatio Mariae*? Clare of Assisi and Her Interpreters," in *Gendered Voices,* 69–70.

39. See, for example, Rubin, *Corpus Christi.*

40. Dinzelbacher, "Mistica e profezia femminile."

41. It has also been said that, parallel to the male tradition of discourse on God

Many nuns wrote histories of their convents, copied and translated devotional literature, edited and disseminated sermons.[42] Finally, spiritual women were active and became public through the production and diffusion of sacred objects.

A FEMALE APPROACH TO THE SACRED: ANGELA MERICI'S RULE

Angela Merici's rule for the Company of St. Ursula is a precious document, a rare instance of the codification of female spirituality. Medieval women seldom translated their spirituality into the form of a rule. Indeed, the first rule written for women was by a man, Caesarius of Arles in 534, and it remained a significant influence throughout the Middle Ages.[43] Instead of writing their own rules, female branches of third and monastic orders normally adopted the rule of their corresponding male order, or a modified version of it. Those pinzochere living in communities either persisted without a religious rule or adopted an existing one, generally Benedictine or Augustinian.[44] Or they might follow rules inspired by their charismatic leader but in fact composed by men after that leader's death.[45] Communities of beguines followed statutes that consisted chiefly of arrangements for their conduct of their devout life

---

(Patristics), we should speak of a female equivalent, Matristics, which is characterized by certain distinguishing features: see Børresen, "*Matristics.*"

42. Winston-Allen, *Convent Chronicles.* See also Gill, "Women and the Production of Religious Literature."

43. Furthermore, Jerome's letter to Eustochium (letter 22) provided women with an early model of life as Brides of Christ.

44. After 1298, with the bull *Periculoso* (which prescribed enclosure for all religious orders), the penitential women's communities adopted the rule of the third order (the only one that allowed them to avoid enclosure). See Makowski, *Canon Law and Cloistered Women.*

45. So, for example, the rules of the communities of penitents living in open monasteries led by Angelina of Montegiove (d. 1435), Francesca Romana (d. 1440), and Ludovica Torelli (d. 1569) were drawn up after their death and consisted mainly in instructions concerning conventual life.

and that did not include the mystical approach of their charismatic exponents.[46] It is true that in a few extremely important instances, women did write religious rules for the monastic orders they founded: no one would want to overlook Clare of Assisi (d. 1253), Bridget of Sweden (d. 1373), and Teresa of Avila (d. 1582). But these women often wrote under certain restrictions—Clare of Assisi, for example, had to adapt the penitents' spirituality to the limits of the cloister that was imposed on her, and Teresa of Avila worked within the limits reinforced by the Council of Trent.[47] To appreciate significant aspects of female spirituality in these rules, we must therefore read between the lines and think of the mystics doing so themselves, as they found inspiration in theological and devotional books, sermons, prayers, liturgical writings, spiritual directors, and art. Angela's rule is therefore of outstanding importance, as it both integrates that rich mystical world, depicting a relationship with God and with the sacred that medieval women would have understood, and codifies women's practice. For this reason it represents a key document for the study of female spirituality.

Angela's idea of relationship with God and of perfection further clarifies and reinforces what has been said about the characteristics of female spirituality. Her model of religious life presents many of the characteristics that we have seen associated with female spirituality in the Middle Ages: it consisted in a secular, individual, unmediated, and mystical relationship with God. The Ursulines lived in a transcendental dimension, while the institutional aspect of religion was marginal. Furthermore, she offered the Ursulines public visibility and an active social role and created a web of relations among the members, using female symbolism and manners of as-

---

46. Galloway, "Neither Miraculous nor Astonishing"; Ziegler, *Sculpture of Compassion,* esp. 80–84, 96–106.

47. Bridget of Sweden, who founded a "gynecocentric" monastic double order ruled by women in imitation of Mary's celestial hegemony, represents a very interesting case. Her *Regula* was never canonically approved in its original form. See Børresen, "*Matristics.*"

sociation. Though Angela was a mystic, she was very rational, and the spiritual peculiarities of the company are interwoven in an extremely logical way. Angela Merici provided precisely what women were lacking at an institutional level: she codified into a religious rule the "irregular" features of the female approach to the sacred.

Relationship with God

Obedience to God's Will

The most striking aspect of Angela's rule is that, like mystic women, the Ursulines were in direct contact with God without the mediation of the clergy. Angela outlined this radical position in the chapter on obedience. In her rule obedience was chiefly due to God and to the advice he sends continuously and directly to the Ursuline's heart: "above all: to obey the counsels and inspirations which the Holy Spirit unceasingly sends into our hearts" (*Reg.,* VIII). This interpretation of the precept of "obedience" is very unusual for a religious rule. The relationship with God was conceived in a direct form and without the mediation of the church. Angela allowed the individual Ursuline to take responsibility for the evaluation of God's advice. Note, too, that Angela viewed these inspirations as "continuous," stressing the existential condition of the divine relationship.

When Carlo Borromeo rewrote the rule in 1582, he inserted the confessor as mediator between God and the Ursuline's heart: "And also to obey the inner inspirations, which, with the *judgment and approbation of the confessor,* will be recognised to be coming from the Holy Spirit."[48] In Angela's rule, on the contrary, contact with God was unmediated and a confessor could have only limited influence on the Ursulines' spiritual life. Merici described the spiritual father's role as that of freeing the Ursulines from sin and watching over their fasting. Furthermore, she specified that the most important thing was obedience to God: "*above all:* to obey . . . the

48. *Regola della Compagnia di S. Orsola* (1582).

Holy Spirit." It is no accident that Carlo Borromeo changed this passage by writing: "and *also* to obey . . . the Holy Spirit," reflecting the greater importance he placed on obedience to the superiors of the company rather than to God.

We find confirmation of this controversial passage in Cozzano's writings where he states that the Ursulines were perceived as being in direct and continuous contact with God and that Angela established a hierarchy of obedience in which obedience to God was the most important thing: "*God gives and promises,* in the hearts of those who wish to live under this obedience, *the constant voice of the Holy Spirit* . . . [the Ursulines] live in uprightness and holiness, because of this *special assistance given them divinely.* Which gives them all the more strength *without mediation.* And insofar as *it touches their hearts directly.* And this is so true, that this *Holy Spirit, which now brings this about in hearts* . . . has pressed the foundress to give special importance to this in this Rule, saying: And *most specially we must obey the inspirations of the Holy Spirit.*"[49]

As with contemporary spiritual women, the Ursuline was alone responsible for her relationship with God, and it was precisely according to a relationship of this kind that she shaped her life. Merici's rule set no limits to the Ursuline's life; indeed, she had little to say about it. The significance of obedience to God in everyday life was reflected in the lives of Angela of Foligno, Catherine of Siena, and many late medieval women who decided their own lives according to their circumstances and their will. As Merici's own life indicates, on occasions she must have felt that earthly obedience was incompatible with God's voice or in disagreement with it. We find examples of this kind in her refusal to live in cities other than Brescia or to engage in a spiritual life that did not correspond with her aspirations. This is why, as we have seen, she declined Clement VII's invitation to remain in Rome, refused Duke Francesco Sforza's offer to stay in Milan, and rejected the proposal of some

49. *Risposta,* ff. 42r–v, in MTS, 578–79.

Venetian noblemen to remain in Venice. As Angela's close friend Romano affirmed, on two occasions (in Venice and Rome) Angela quickly left before she was ordered to remain:

She was begged by them [the Venetian noblemen] to remain in Venice for the common benefit of those pious places . . . . She, desiring to return to her beloved fatherland, and not wishing to wait for the following day (so that they might not possibly return with the Patriarch, whom out of obedience she would have had to obey) that same evening we came away from Venice, and returned to Brescia . . . the blessed Father begged her to remain in Rome in those pious places and She, excusing herself with very humble words, left, and the same evening, coming away from Rome, doubting that his Holiness would impose on her to stay out of holy obedience, she came to Brescia . . . she went to visit his Excellency the Duke, who receiving her with very sweet words insistently begged that she remain in Milan, but prudently excusing herself she left and came to Brescia.[50]

According to the rule, an Ursuline living in union with God was entitled, like Angela, to evaluate whether concrete situations accorded with the inner inspirations of God's voice. And so, as emerges from Angela's own case, divine contact gave the Bride of Christ control over her life.

Celestial References

According to Angela's rule—and similarly to many medieval mystical women—the Ursuline lived immersed in the divine relationship. A statistical linguistic analysis of the writings addressed to the virgins *(Regula* and *Arricordi)* shows that an Ursuline's religious reference consisted mainly in transcendental entities. By contrast, the institutional church did not have a central place. Whereas God, Christ, and other celestial beings are mentioned 110 times, the church and spiritual fathers appear only 14 times. Table 2 summarizes the roles covered by the divine in Angela's writings. According to the rule, God and Christ are responsible for the Ursu-

50. *PN*, ff. 939r–40r, in MTS, 535.

TABLE 2. DIVINE REFERENCES IN THE RULE OF THE
COMPANY OF ST. URSULA

Religious forms	Frequency	Features
Dio/Iddio, Altissimo, Signore	61	Bridegroom, father, master, judge, creator, providence
Gesù/Iesu/Christo/Figliol de Dio, Altissimo, Signore	26	Bridegroom, lover, master, example, savior
Spirito Santo	6	Source of inspiration; gives advice and strength

line's entire life: God is the creator, the architect, and judge of the world; both he and Christ inspire the rule of the company; they guide and protect the Ursulines in their spiritual and secular life. Angela describes the relationship between the Ursulines and the divine through the family imagery recurrent in the language of spiritual women. God is a father who takes care of the Ursuline's material needs and Christ, in particular, is her bridegroom.

The Ursulines lived their relationship with the divine as Brides of Christ. Throughout the rule Angela constantly referred to them in these terms, represented with vivid images. Celestial union was in contrast with worldly marriage and was its reverse positive image. Angela affirmed that her daughters were "spouses not of earthly, corruptible, and stinking husbands, but of the immortal Son of the eternal God" (*Tes.*, 4). Here the word "stinking" *(puzzolenti)* refers to the fact that secular men are sinners. According to sixteenth-century mentality, sin stinks.[51] By contrast, a good odor emanates from virtue: the incorruptibility of a saint's corpse and its good odor were seen as proofs of sanctity. We find equivalent descriptions of

51. Christ, in one of Osanna Andreasi letters, affirms that "the *stink [puza] of sin* rises up to heaven, such is the *stench [fetore]* that I can no longer bear it" (in Marcocchi, *La Riforma Cattolica,* I:136).

the divine relationship in several other spiritual women of the period.[52]

Like many other mystic women, the Ursuline's relationship with her divine referent consisted above all in a relationship of love. Christ, throughout the rule, is generally called "l'Amator" (the Lover): "Tell them . . . that I am continually among them with my Lover, or rather ours, the Lover of us all . . . let them have Jesus Christ for their only treasure, for there will be love" (*Ric.*, 5). If Christ is a truthful husband, God is mainly described as a caring father who will never abandon them: "your heavenly Father knows very well that you have need of all these things . . . do not trouble yourself about any of your temporal needs, because God, and he alone, knows, can and will provide for them; He who wants nothing for you but only your good and your joy" (*Reg.*, X); "they will never be abandoned in their needs. God will provide for them wonderfully" (*Ric.*, 5).

Interestingly, Mary has no family connotations for the company. As a matter of fact, Mary does not occupy a central role in Angela's writings: compared to God and Christ, Mary is rarely mentioned (only four times, against sixty-one and twenty-six respectively). Merici's spirituality seems thus to confirm that, despite what one might expect, Mary was far less central than Christ to female spirituality.[53]

The presence of the divine in the Ursuline's life was stressed in several contexts. In the rule's chapter on prayer Angela explained that an Ursuline should practice mental prayer continually in order to obtain God's help, which she always needs in her life: "One

52. One interesting example was the charismatic Angelic nun Paola Antonia Negri. She described detachment from the secular world and union with God through imagery familiar to secular women in their prematrimonial stage: "this miserable world, which constantly, with its deceptive and vain promises never fails to invite, entice, lead us to love it . . . while we have already come to *another lover, who offers us much finer ornaments, and gifts* than yours, and already *he has given us a pledge with the ring of his faith*" (Fontana, *Lettere spirituali*, f. 325; the italics are mine).

53. See, for example, Mooney, "*Imitatio Christi* or *Imitatio Mariae?*"

needs always to pray in spirit and mind given the continuous need one has of God's help"(*Reg.*, V). The Ursuline's secular life was lived in another dimension, replete with transcendental references. Heaven, the saints, and the angels were also mentioned in the rule and were perceived as concrete presences.[54] The dimension in which the Ursulines lived closed the gap between celestial life and worldly life. The life of the Bride of Christ was presented in a spiritual dimension, in complete immersion in the divine: "For the angels of eternal life will be with us, that is, in so far as we share in an angelic life" (*Reg.*, Prologue). Divine contact had a positive impact on the concrete life of the Ursuline. Together with the promise of eternal reward ("may return gloriously to our heavenly home" [*Reg.*, Prologue]); "in heaven a new crown of glory and joy is prepared for all of them, one by one" [*Ric.*, 5]), Christ's Bride could turn all the difficulties of her secular life into happiness: "Our every sorrow and sadness will be turned into joy and gladness, and we shall find the thorny and stony paths blossoming for us, and covered with paving of finest gold" (*Reg.*, Prologue); "Although at times they will have troubles or anxieties, nevertheless this will soon pass away and will be turned into gladness and joy" (*Ric.*, 5).

Finally, Christ's help was necessary for some of the company's tasks, such as those of guiding the virgins and changing the rule: "How much, therefore, must you pray God to enlighten you, and direct you, and teach you what you have to do" (*Ric.*, Prologue); "And if, according to times and circumstances, the need arises to make new rules or do something differently . . . always let your principal recourse be to gather at the feet of Jesus Christ, and there all of you, with all your daughters, to offer most fervent prayers. For in this way, without doubt, Jesus Christ will be in your midst, and as a true and good master, he will enlighten and teach you what you have to do" (*Tes.*, Last). This advice had an impact on the

---

54. Heaven (*Cielo* and *Paradiso*) is mentioned twelve times, saints (*Santi*) six times, and angels (*Angeli*) three times.

life of the company. As we know from Cozzano, the new precepts were introduced *(se fava legge)* "not without prayer, before, during and subsequently."[55]

Entry into the company offered the Ursuline both salvation in the next life and divine assistance in the present. She obtained a husband who loved her and established strong ties with eternal entities. Though she lived in the secular world, Angela's religious proposal allowed a radical change in the dimensions of her life.

Mystic Union

As with medieval and contemporary spiritual women, the highest moment of religious experience in Angela's rule consisted in mystical union. This was described in intensely mystical language, using the images of blood, death, love, and union current in female spirituality. In the chapter "On Prayer" (*Reg.,* V), she proposed a model of mental prayer involving elevation of the self toward God. Merici's prayer was divided into three moments: the Ursuline first contemplated her own sins, which led to identification with Christ/man; she then took responsibility for the sins of the world and pleaded for her own sacrifice in order to save it. At that moment she elevated her status and could reach mystical union with God. Several mystic women conceived their ascent toward God in similar terms: union with divine love was reached through the repetition of his suffering and identification with the Savior's role.[56] This kind of mysticism is particularly unusual in religious rules.

At the beginning there is the contemplation of one's own wretchedness, despair, and repentance, which are all reported in violent and imaginative language: "Alas! How grieved I am that, entering into the secret of my heart, for shame I dare not raise my eyes to heaven, for I deserve to be devoured alive in hell, seeing in myself so many errors, so much ugliness and vileness, so many monstrous and

55. Cozzano, *Dichiarazione,* f. 979r, in MTS, 591.
56. This mechanism, for example, emerges clearly in Catherine of Siena's *Dialogo della divina provvidenza,* 45–48.

frightful wild beasts and shapes. Therefore I am compelled, day and night, moving, staying still, acting, thinking, to call out and to cry to heaven, and to beg for mercy and time for penance" (*Reg.,* 5). The Ursuline was encouraged to extend her desperation from her own sins to those of the community and to sacrifice herself in repetition of the Christ's Passion. Angela's model of prayer was Christocentric in that it encouraged the Ursuline to identify with the role of the savior. The emphasis was on penance and self-inflicted suffering (in imitation of the Passion), offered for the sins of the world: "I implore this of you by your most sacred Passion and your precious Blood shed for love of us . . . . I deeply regret that I have been so slow to begin to serve your divine majesty. Alas! Until now I have never shed even the smallest drop of blood for love of you . . . Lord, in place of those poor creatures who do not know you, and do not care to be partakers in your most sacred Passion, my heart breaks, and willingly (if I could) I would shed my own blood to open the blind eyes of their minds" (*Reg.,* V).

The (desired) repetition of Christ's sacrifice allowed the Ursuline to raise her status before God. In Angela's rule this process culminated in the mystic fusion of the heart and passions with divine love: "My Lord, my only life and hope, I pray that you deign to receive this most vile and impure heart of mine, and to burn its affection and passion in the fiery furnace of your divine love" (*Reg.,* V). In successive editions of the rule (such as Borromeo's), there was a more negative view of love and passion, and the mystic fusion was no longer implied: Angela's "to burn its affection and passion" became "to burn *from the heart* its *evil* affection and passion."[57]

---

57. *Regola della Compagnia di S. Orsola* (1582), 5. In other women's writings we find similar words to Merici's. Paola Antonia Negri's vision of union with God very closely resembled the one envisaged in the rule of the Company of St. Ursula: "Oh what a beautiful thing it is to give oneself, speedily, and entirely to God, and not to go slowly . . . but with one's whole heart *to throw oneself at him, give oneself to him, be inflamed in this furnace of divine love,* consuming in it the branches, the leaves, and the things of the world" (Fontana, *Lettere spirituali,* f. 327; the italics are mine). A very similar image of union with God is also expressed by Osanna Andreasi: "*divine love which makes*

The Ursulines' Active Roles

Where the relationship between the Ursulines and the world
was concerned, although the rule did not explicitly prescribe activities, if we read between the lines we can find important indications
about the type of "apostolate" Merici envisaged. Angela proposed a
public and active role in society to be undertaken by virtue of their
privileged relationship with the divine and of the authority that derived from it. Angela indicated that the Ursulines should both mediate a supernatural power and use their rational faculties. Angela
was building on a well-established pattern that she herself and the
most famous spiritual women of the time experienced.

In the first place Merici granted the Ursulines a role in supernatural mediation for the salvation of sinners. Ursulines should, that
is, intercede with God through prayer to obtain forgiveness for the
sins of the people around them and beyond: "Deign to forgive the
sins, alas, of my father and mother, and of my relatives and friends,
and of the whole world" (*Reg.*, V). This was a function typical of
many holy women[58] and one that Angela herself exercised in the
Brescian community. Romano and Gallo asserted at the Processo
Nazari that Angela was regularly asked by various people in Brescia to intercede with the divine in order to obtain favors: "many
came to her from the city of Brescia [asking] for her most devout
prayers to impetrate a grace from the Lord";[59] "passing the entire

---

the soul blaze and burn without being consumed, being engaged in the sacred passion
for Christ" (in Marcocchi, *La Riforma Cattolica*, I:136; the italics are mine).

58. Women's supernatural intermediary role emerges, for example, in the correspondence between Gaetano da Thiene and the mystic nun Laura Mignani. Gaetano
asks Laura to intercede for the salvation of his mother, for his friend Bartolomeo Stella, and for corrupt Rome: "Pray to your Spouse that he may not disdain my prayers,
and, *for you, may he grant what I ask:* I commend to you she out of whose womb I
came; I commend to you your son and my brother; I commend to you once again the
holy city which now is Babylon, in which there are many relics" (in Cistellini, *Figure
della riforma pretridentina*, 243; the italics are mine).

59. Romano: *PN*, f. 937v, in MTS, 534.

day in various good offices, or in praying for herself and for sinners."[60] In addition, Romano affirmed that Angela asked for divine intercession to save them from the pirates who attacked their ship on their way back from Jerusalem: "through the constant prayers of the Mother Sister Angela . . . raised a most happy and prosperous wind."[61]

Together with intercession for others' salvation and protection, Angela proposed an affine and overlapping role, the actual repetition of Christ's salvific role. As we have seen from the chapter on prayer, the Ursulines were encouraged to identify with the Savior's role. This ideal is further developed in the chapter "On Fasting," where the Ursulines were asked to (symbolically) sacrifice themselves through fasting in repetition of Christ's Passion, in order to obtain forgiveness for the sins of the world: "They should fast . . . to subdue the senses and the appetites and sensual desires which then, especially, seem to lord over the world, and also to implore mercy before the throne of the Most High for the many dissolute actions committed by the Christians during that time, as is more than obvious to all . . . they should fast . . . to implore divine help for the Christian people . . . they should fast . . . and at the same time they should remain in prayer with as much strength of spirit as is possible . . . asking that great promise made by Jesus Christ to his chosen ones who are well disposed" (*Reg.*, IV).

The repetition of Christ's assumption of the sins of the world was characteristic of the female spirituality of this period.[62] Angela

---

60. Gallo: *PN*, f. 944v, in MTS, 539.

61. *PN*, f. 939r, in MTS, 535.

62. For example, we can find this attitude in a prayer written by Lucia Broccadelli da Narni, a "santa viva" and Angela's contemporary: "*Of the ruin of this world I am the cause . . . I commend to you all my enemies,* may you forgive them. I commend to you all my benefactors. I commend to you your immaculate bride. I commend to you all my sisters . . . . I pray that you do this to all the world because it needs it. This is my spouse, whom the entire world offends" (in Pozzi and Leonardi, *Scrittrici mistiche*, 293; the italics are mine). The same concepts are expounded in Osanna da Mantova's correspondence. Writing to her biographer, the friar Girolamo Scolari, Osanna takes responsibility for the sins of humanity and obtains the salvation of a number of peo-

herself had performed this salvific role. One early example was her intercession for the salvation of her deceased sister. According to several sources Angela took responsibility for her sister's sins by carrying out penitential practices. She was eventually rewarded with the vision of her sister in heaven.[63] It is also possible that Angela's illness in 1529 (which almost led to her death) stemmed from her penance for the salvation of Brescia when the city was threatened by Charles V's army.[64]

Clearly, then, the distinction between active and contemplative life is not very useful for understanding the religious practice Angela Merici's rule proposed. Praying and suffering (engaging in penitential practices) to obtain the remission of sins and supernatural protection were both contemplative (or mystical) and active practices. They were private activities with a public dimension (which the community often explicitly asked Angela to perform). Angela's case, thus, confirms that "ascetic suffering is both union—ecstatic, glorious, pleasurable union—with the suffering Christ and (because it can substitute for others' time in purgatory) service to one's fellow."[65]

Angela also proposed another type of intervention in society, made possible by the authority derived from the Ursulines' relationship with God and by their human and intellectual capacities.

---

ple. Osanna very vividly describes her vision of her union with Christ, who presents the people saved by her prayers to her: "my soul does not deserve grace from you, my Lord, for I have been wretched and *greatly the cause of all the evil that is done in the world.* Then [Christ], almost smiling in a way which it seemed to me united my soul with him . . . started to say: My soul my spouse and daughter, you have remained enough in humility and prayer for your creatures who themselves have the power of reason. At these words He presented to me all those I commended to him" (in Marcocchi, *La Riforma Cattolica,* I:136; the italics are mine).

63. On this episode, see MTS, 80–83.

64. Ibid., 190.

65. Bynum, "The Mysticism and Asceticism of Medieval Women: Some Comments on the Typologies of Max Weber and Ernst Troeltsch," in *Fragmentation and Redemption,* 69.

An important feature of her rule was their role of peacemaker. She pledged the Ursulines in this sense: "In speaking, that their words be wise . . . and leading to concord and charity. . . . And seek to spread peace and concord where they are" (*Ric.,* 5). Angela thus envisaged a "political" role for the Ursulines, one that society often asked of female saints and one that she herself filled. Angela helped people solve quarrels, and powerful noblemen agreed to her intercession and to her solutions. Sometimes Brescians visited her to "pacify discord which had arisen between citizens and other nobles of the city. Among which I remember the discord between Domino Filippo Sala and Domino Francesco Martinengo, which, with the intervention of the Duke of Urbino, the Rectors and Nobles of the city, were never appeased and pacified; and she, Mother Sister Angela, whom the wives of the above-mentioned begged to do so, with a very few words did so much that they made peace in such a way as to remain satisfied; her fame spread in the surrounding places, so much so that every Lord granted her whatever she asked."[66]

As we have seen, like many other contemporary religious women who were asked by the community to perform roles of public utility, Angela became a point of reference for the city. Within the Brescian community she provided help in various ways, such as counseling people. Angela's rule expressed an awareness of the public role the Ursulines played. They were advised to be virtuous and an example to others, helpful and available to assist people with their problems. This could include, as in Angela's case, help and advice concerning spiritual and civic matters: "tell them that, wherever they are, they should give good example. And be to all good odour of virtue" (*Ric.,* V); "let all words, actions and behaviour always be for the instruction and edification of those who have dealings with us" (*Reg.,* VIIII).[67]

66. Romano: *PN,* f. 938r, in MTS, 534. One other occasion is known in which Angela obtained from Alovigio da Castiglione the restitution of some land to one of her friends (or relatives).

67. The perception of the company's public dimension also emerges in Angela's

Finally, in the rule, Angela provided advice on how to deal with other people. As we have seen, her method contributed to her widespread popularity. Her advice was based on love and patience: "And let all behaviour, their actions and their words be with charity; and let them bear everything with patience, for with these two virtues especially, one crushes the head of the devil" (*Ric.*, 5).

These are the only activities that Angela proposes to her daughters. The reason she did not propose specific activities to carry out in the world is that Angela did not want to set limits on the Ursulines' actual life. As the experience of late medieval and early modern spiritual women's lives showed, the specific features of spiritual life depended on individual characteristics, time, place, and circumstances.

Institutional Dimension

A striking characteristic of Angela's rule was the lack of external institutional structures to manifest the sacred. Though at this time the external aspects of religion were often criticized by religious reformers and humanists (see chapter 4), this attitude was an important aspect of many spiritual women's experience of the sacred, and especially of those who lived in the world as tertiaries and beguines.

Angela represents a remarkable example of this characteristic of female religiosity because she proposed a form of consecration without convent, solemn vows, and habit. Other characteristics also qualify Angela's company as a-institutional: the absence of life in common and of hierarchies and the presence of a pedagogical model that does not deem perfect execution of precepts as important. The "sacred" was not projected onto exterior actions and institutional arrangements but emerged above all in the Ursuline's individual experience of the divine. The company can be seen as a

---

recommendation to the Matrone to avoid discord, as it would be a "bad example to the city" (*Tes.*, 10). Also, in the introduction to the rule, we read that with the Company of St. Ursula "the neighborhoods are consoled; the city is ennobled" (*Al lettore*, in MTS, 434).

sum of individuals who established vertical connections with the celestial dimension and lived in the world guided by, and united with, God. In this sense the rule can be defined as a nonrule and the company as an "invisible structure" that permitted the relationship between God and the Ursuline but did not mediate it.

The Ursulines' exterior life was not carefully prescribed, and the company had no common life. The only gatherings were the periodical meetings called by the Matrone to discuss spiritual matters and once a month to receive communion. As we have seen, Angela's rule did not impose a detailed set of limitations concerning the Ursulines' everyday life. Instead, Angela allowed them to take responsibility for their daily activities. Furthermore, when she prescribed something, she left a margin of decision to the people who were to carry out the prescription: "If they wish to pray longer . . . pray *as long as the Spirit and their conscience dictate*" (*Reg.,* VI); "Please go often, *as you have time and opportunity . . .* visit your dear daughters" (*Ric.,* 5); "If, according to times and circumstances, *the need arises to make new rules* or do something different, do it" (*Tes.,* Last); "Diminish these fasts *as they* [the Matrone and the spiritual fathers] *see that to be needed*" (*Reg.,* 4).

Moreover, the government of the company did not represent a form of "power," a structure sacred in itself, as this would have been alien and external to individual relationship with God. The government of Angela's company was conceived in a practical and simple way and was presented in one short chapter of the rule. This contrasts with other rules that devote several chapters to defining the organization of power. This does not mean, however, that the company was not properly organized, but rather that the organization was different and sustained by an alternative logic. Angela was conscious that she was proposing an alternative type of religious life and organization. She explicitly said so in the *Arricordi* when she warned the Colonelle of the difficulties their duties implied: "Do not be afraid of not knowing and not being able to do what is rightly required in such a singular government" (*Ric.,* Prologue).

The scope of the company was to establish the conditions for celestial union and, therefore, the role of the superior was to take responsibility for the success of this aim. Within this logic, Angela established not a hierarchy but roles functional to the material and spiritual needs of the virgins—those of the Matrone and of the Colonelle. Significantly, Angela resorted to a head of the company (the *madre principale*) only when necessary for practical reasons.[68] This shows that she attached no sacrality to the office.[69] Furthermore, the way she used the concept of "superior" indicates the absence of power positions within the company. The term *superiore*, used nine times in the rule, never referred to the Matrone: it referred six times to people in the secular world with whom the Ursulines had a relationship (parents, tutors, landlords), twice to the Colonelle, and once to Pope Gregory I (as a model of authority associated with charity and humility).[70] When she employed the term *superiors* in reference to the Colonelle, Angela used it only to reject it, propounding service in its place: "Do not consider yourselves worthy to be superiors and leaders. Rather regard yourselves as ministers and servants, reflecting that you have more need to serve them than they have to be served by you, or governed" (*Ric.*, 1).[71]

The foundress's main preoccupation was the spiritual health of the virgins rather than respect for hierarchy. As we have seen, the members of the government—who were elected by the vir-

68. In 1537, in order to inherit some money that Patengola had left to the company. It must be noted that Angela did not create specific duties for this position and did not leave any writings concerning this office (in the *Testamento* there is no distinction between the madre principale and the other Matrone). This could indicate that Angela intended this office mainly to comply with legal issues.

69. In this sense, also the fact that parts of the rule could be changed shows that Angela did not invest it with a sacred value.

70. As noted already in MTS, 241.

71. A similar precept can be found in Catherine Vigri's counsels, which she left to her sisters in the convent of Corpus Domini: "It is so grateful to God and useful to the subordinate when the superior helps before she is asked" (Caterina da Bologna, *Sette Armi spirituali*, 132).

gins—could be removed from office if they did not fulfill their duties properly. The Colonelle had the right to question the authority of the Matrone if they neglected the Ursulines' needs. In the *Arricordi* Angela warned the Colonelle to give priority to their responsibility toward the virgins rather than to the obedience and respect due to the Matrone. In the passages of the *Arricordi* where she explained this delicate matter, Angela began by asserting that the Colonelle should obey the Matrone, criticize them very mildly, and bear with their inappropriate and eccentric responses: "Remain obedient to the principal Mothers whom I leave in my place, since this is just . . . . Now, if it should happen that you have some just reason to contradict or reproach them, do it with discretion and respect. And if they do not want to pay you heed, have patience. And know that it is right to love the mothers if they are good, and bear with them if they are eccentric. And be very careful never to complain, or grumble, or speak ill of them, whether with others or with your daughters" (*Ric.,* 3). Angela added, however, that if the Colonelle were seriously upset or hurt, they should not hesitate to talk to someone they could trust: "Still, if you have something in your heart that disturbs you in them, you may rightly and without scruple talk about it in confidence with some person who is good and faithful in many respects and ways."

Angela drew the line where the virgins were in danger because of the Matrones' behavior. In this case the Colonelle must confront the Matrone directly without concern for the respect due to them: "Know, however, that where you see clearly that the salvation and honour of your daughters are in danger, you must on *no account consent to it, nor tolerate it, nor have any respect.* Yet all this with discernment and maturity of judgement."[72]

Angela stated clearly that if the Colonelle were unable to solve

---

72. It is significant that this passage was changed in Borromeo's rule, which gave the father of the company the authority to sort out the problem. It read: "You must with humility and maturity have recourse to the Father of the entire Company that he with his prudence may provide for everything" (*Ric.,* 3).

a virgin's problem, they must unhesitatingly seek help from the Matrone, with no reluctance because of their position. If they had no immediate response they must importune them: "You will be careful and vigilant to know and understand the behaviour of your daughters, and to be aware of their spiritual and temporal needs . . . . But if you cannot provide for them yourselves, go to the principal mothers, and quickly, and *without hesitation* explain to them the needs of your lambs. And if you see them slow to provide, *be insistent;* and in that case, in my name even be *importunate and troublesome*" (*Ric.,* 4). Considering the importance of hierarchical structures both in religious orders and in society, Angela's attitude toward authority was unusual.

Another testimony to the absence of institutional and powerful traits in Angela's ideal of religious life is her advice to the Colonelle (especially) and the Matrone on how to guide their daughters. In her pedagogical advice, perfect execution of external practices was not central. Her instructions for the government of the company also proposed an innovative pedagogical model based on exhortation and love. Furthermore, her pedagogical method respected the diversity of persons. All these characteristics form a distinctive model of government, alternative to one based on perfect obedience.

In advising the members of the government on how to deal with the Ursulines, Angela made it clear that each person is different and deserves specific treatment. Angela considered types of personalities and suggested actions to take according to their differences: "If you see one faint-hearted and timid and inclined to despondency, comfort her, encourage her . . . . And on the contrary, if you see another presumptuous, and who has a lax conscience and little fear of anything, into this one instill some fear" (*Ric.,* 2). She was very precise in her description of personalities and understanding toward the difficulties the Ursulines might experience. She never yielded to the temptation to simplify the complexity of human responses to a new form of life: "When you see that one of them finds great difficulty in deciding to give up fashionable trifles and other similar frills . . . do not have too high a hope about her that she will persevere under this Rule. For if she does not want to do what is lesser, much less will she do what is greater. But here, however, you must be prudent, because it can happen that a person has set almost all her desire on a bagatelle, so that, having conquered herself on this point, she will no longer find any other too difficult" (*Tes.*, 6). Her pedagogical model reflected the fact that the company did not propose a form of "power" in relation to which the members must mold themselves. Respect for the individual lay at the basis of Angela's pedagogy.

Angela recommended that the members of the government be humane and gentle rather than strict and harsh. However, she conceded that in certain situations and with certain people one might sometimes need to resort to corrective rebuke. To know which was the most appropriate behavior, Angela maintained that the Colonelle should love their daughters:

Be gentle and compassionate towards your dear daughters. And strive to act solely out of the sole love of God and out of the sole zeal for souls when you admonish and advise them, or exhort them to some good and dissuade them from some evil. For you will achieve more with kindness and gentleness than with harshness and sharp rebukes, which should be reserved only for cases of necessity, and even then, at the right place and time, and according to the persons. But charity, which directs everything to the honour of God and the good of souls, charity indeed teaches such discretion, and moves the heart to be, according to place and time, now gentle and now severe, and little or much as there is need. (*Ric.*, 2)[73]

Love played a very important part in the government of the virgins. Love allows the guides to get closer to their daughters and, consequently, enables them to judge what they really needed: "For the more you esteem them, the more you will love them; the more you love them, the more you will care for and watch over them. And

---

73. Angela gave the Matrone very similar advice (*Tes.*, 3).

it will be impossible for you not to cherish them day and night, and to have them all engraved in your heart, one by one, for this is how real love acts and works" (*Ric.*, Prologue); "I beg you that you willingly hold in consideration and have engraved on your mind and heart all your dear daughters, one by one; not only their names, but also their condition, and character, and their every situation and state. This will not be difficult for you if you embrace them with an ardent charity . . . because this is how real love works" (*Tes.*, 2).

In her writings concerning governance Angela did not prescribe detailed duties for the governors. Instead, she simply set a principle to follow: their decisions must be guided by love and charity, for the good of the virgins: "That you are moved to this care and government solely by the love of God and by the sole zeal for the salvation of the souls. Because all your works and actions as governors, being thus rooted in this twofold charity, can bear nothing but good and salutary fruits" (*Tes.*, 1). Angela's concept of love was in opposition to "power" in its antihuman and anti-individual sense. If one acts for the good of others, there is no need to establish perfect behavior. This was summarized in her interpretation of the Augustinian saying: "'Ama, et fac quod vis'; that is have love and charity and then do what you please . . . charity cannot sin" (*Tes.*, 1).

The characteristics of Angela's pedagogy reflect her personality and type of sanctity. Cozzano, albeit apologetically, described her attitude toward the daughters and the people who asked for her help: "amongst them all [the virgins of the company] . . . . She had such gratitude and gentleness that it seemed to her that she could not ever [sufficiently] reward with courteous acts those who did even a small but heartfelt service for her. She so thirsted and yearned for the health and well-being of her neighbour . . . . With motherly love she embraced every creature."[74]

Angela's pedagogical model fit into the spiritual logic discussed

74. *Dichiarazione,* f. 974v, in MTS, 587.

above. The imposition of perfect behavior and the expectation of perfect obedience do not fit into a proposal of religious life conceived as a personal relationship with God, the forms of which were in many respects left to the Ursulines themselves rather than established by the company. Angela's pedagogy, ideal of government, and worldly routine reflect the fact that women's relationship with the sacred during that period does not seem to prize exterior institutional and powerful structures. In the case of Angela Merici, this female approach led to an emphasis on humanity, love, and the individual.

Despite the absence of institutional aspects, the company did represent a solid structure ("mighty fortress, or tower impregnable" [*Ric.,* Last]) that enabled the Ursulines to carry out their spiritual life. Angela created a network of "informal" relationships among the virgins that provided material security, solidarity, affection, and new "family" bonds.

In the first place, as we have already seen, Angela's writings describe the relationships between the members of the company and with the divine through the family imagery recurrent in the language of spiritual women. As we have seen, Christ is a truthful husband and God mainly a caring father. The virgins are "sisters" among themselves, while the Matrone are the "mothers of so noble a family" and "mothers-in-law . . . of the Son of God" (*Tes.,* Prologue and 4).

Furthermore, love, trust, and friendship, presented in their human significance, were important assets gained through the life offered by the rule. The Ursulines were bound together, and both Angela and Christ could be trusted as true friends: "Live in harmony, united together, all of one heart and one will. Be bound to one another by the bond of charity, esteeming each other, helping each other, bearing with each other" (*Ric.,* Last); "immense and inestimable grace that my Lover, or rather ours, will grant you at the supreme moment of death, for *in times of great need, true friendship is recognized*. And believe firmly that then, especially, *you will recognize me to be your faithful friend*" (*Ric.,* Last); "And when you visit them, I give you this charge, to greet them, and *shake hands with them, also in my behalf*" (*Ric.,* 5).

If they followed this path, the company and heaven would form one single force: "For if you strive to be like this, without any doubt, the Lord God will be in your midst. You will have in your favour our Lady, the apostles, all the saints, the angels, and finally all heaven and all the universe" (*Ric.,* Last).

Finally, as we have seen in chapter 1, Angela created a network of female relations that protected women economically, legally, and medically. The affiliation among the Ursulines allowed women material detachment from society.

Conclusions

Angela Merici's rule thus represents an outstanding example of institutionalized female spirituality. By entering the company, women could follow a rule that featured several aspects of an approach to the sacred experienced for centuries by mystic women who lived in the world. Her rule illustrates clearly some fundamental characteristics of female spirituality and shows the importance of medieval religion from the perspective of women's life in society.

Furthermore, Angela Merici's rule lends itself to an investigation of the interaction between female spirituality and concepts of gender. Angela's ideal suggests that women approached the sacred in continuity with some of the roles, symbols, and ideals that were involved in the Renaissance notion of "woman." Angela's model, however, also indicates that women adapted some of these ideas and rejected others, turning certain gender assumptions in their favor and managing to overcome many of the constraints society placed on them. Angela's rule thus suggests that women's empowerment within religion took place through an adaptation of mainstream ideas about femininity.

Mystic Life

Angela's rule seems to confirm that spiritual women developed their religiosity in association with transcendency, in accord with the male perception of woman as naturally disposed to mystical experience and liminal to the realm of the supernatural. The Ursuline lived in "another," "transcendent" dimension where the most significant moment was mystic union. However, Angela's religious model presented significant differences from the male perception of women's spirituality and of the female. Angela did not view the Ursuline as a passive vessel filled with God's love and power. First, in their mystical relationship the Ursulines could express their will and become subjects who stood independently in front of God.[75] As we have seen, their relationship with God was unmediated and gave them the authority to decide their own lives independently. Thus women could overcome dependency on men. Second, the Ursulines' role in mediating and providing supernatural protection and reenacting Christ's salvific role empowered women, offering them social visibility and an opportunity to exercise a political and social role.[76] Third, Angela did not see women as irrational and weak and able only to channel divine power. As we have seen, not all the public roles of Ursulines were conceived of as a reflection of God's power or as the fruit of mystical experience. Angela also gave women the possibility of exercising their human, rational, and intellectual capacities in a variety of contexts such as theology (discussing religious issues with others), civic matters (advice, peacemaking, and so on), and friendship. In these roles their relationship with God granted the Ursulines the necessary authority but did not appear as the source of individual capacity.

Men, by contrast, seem invariably to see spiritual women's worth in terms of divine inspiration. For example, Angela's roles as "coun-

75. Women's subjectivity in mysticism is discussed in, for example, Slade, "Alterity in Union."

76. This role also shows that the traditional distinction between active and contemplative life does not serve to frame Angela's religious experience.

selor" and theologian were seen by her male friends as the result of God's intervention. Gallo affirmed that Angela was used to "counseling and consoling each person as much as she could, in such a manner that her works had more of the divine than the human" and stated that "to hear from her such an interpretation [of the sacred books, listeners] were struck with amazement, so that one could say that this woman had more of the divine than the human."[77] Cozzano sees Angela's ways of speaking to people in the same way: "These were her fiery, powerful, and gentle words, and spoken with such new vigor of grace that each person could be forced to say: 'Here is God.'"[78] And he reaches the same conclusion in relation to the rule of the company: "the reasoning was of the Holy Spirit, dictated through the Foundress . . . She alone, divinely inspired, was the foundress of such an institution."[79]

A-institutional Religion

Angela's company also reflected the a-institutional dimension of female spirituality and further clarifies the logic that sustained it. Merici created a structure without convent, habit, vows, common activities, obligations, and hierarchy. These characteristics seem in continuity with women's cultural incompatibility with the establishment and management of institutional forms of power. Angela's lack of institutional forms of power, however, did not throw the company into chaos and religious relaxation, as Angela's ideal of religious life was sustained by an alternative spiritual and organizational logic. Angela created a "nonpower," as the external features were not sacralized. In Merici's religious model "sacred reality" was given solely through interaction between the individual and God. Angela's rule granted greater freedom and responsibility to individuals in shaping their religious life. Angela substitutes order and the

---

77. Respectively in *PN*, f. 942v–43r, in MTS, 537; *PN*, ff. 944r–v., in MTS, 539.

78. *Dichiarazione*, ff. 974v–75r, in MTS, 587.

79. Ibid., ff. 973v–74v, in MTS, 586–87.

obedience to strict codes of behavior with a pedagogical model that was shaped around individual needs. Finally, Angela does not sacralize positions of power, but she establishes rational roles for the management of the company. And in relation to these she rejected the idea that the "female" was naturally incompatible with positions of responsibility and leadership.

Female Identities

Like medieval mystic women, the figure of the Ursuline is based on traditional female identities. As we have already seen in greater detail in chapter 2, in Angela's rule the Ursulines reiterated the social roles of wives, mothers, and sisters to describe their religious affiliation to the divine and among themselves. Angela structured her company according to women's sexual status—virginity and widowhood. It offered virgin women the identity of Bride of Christ, while widows were viewed as mothers-in-law of the celestial Lord. Furthermore, Angela prized the ideal of virginity, a concept originating in the identification of "womanhood" with sexuality. The Ursulines were also encouraged to cherish, toward Christ, love and tender feelings, frequently regarded as female. In this identity, however, Angela does not accept the limitations that we find associated to female roles, such as obedience, confinement to the private, incapacity to govern, and irrationality. As with the tertiaries, the beguines, and the bizzoche, Angela's ideal of the Bride of Christ outside the convent offered women the possibility of living as single women in the world and of shaping their own daily lives. As virgins the Ursulines shouldered heroic virtues and affirmed their symbolic and practical independence from male control; as brides of Christ they displayed a privileged union with the divine and gained public functions; as mothers and widows they held managerial and educational roles. Through the reiteration of mainstream identities and social roles, Angela could thus achieve a condition that surpassed dismissive notions of female identity.

Penance

Finally, another trait of medieval female piety by which to evaluate Angela's company is the stress women put on physical penance. This spiritual feature fit the medieval and early modern association between "woman" and "body." In Angela's rule, physical penance appears associated with certain aspects of the Ursuline's life, such as pleading for divine intercession and assuming the sins of others. Angela Merici, however, did not fit this model exactly. The cultural link between women and the body shaped female spirituality at a time when the body was an important model for expressing the sacred. As will appear in the next chapter, in Angela's times and milieu physical penance was no longer considered a sign of sanctity in itself. Indeed, Angela recommended caution and warned of the danger of excessive forms of penance: "reduce and diminish these fasts, as they see that to be needed, because to afflict one's body indiscreetly . . . would be to offer in sacrifice something stolen" (*Reg.*, IV). Angela made it clear that penitential practices were ascetic techniques or instruments that predisposed the individual to the life of the spirit rather than operating as direct signs of contact with God. Her model of sainthood suggests, therefore, that in the sixteenth century some spiritual women were less inclined to show their union with Christ through their bodies.[80] Furthermore, her case shows that even within a form of religiosity that did not sacralize the signs of the body, women could be perceived and might see themselves in association with transcendency. The absence of bodily miracles did not prevent supernatural intervention in Angela's life via sacred knowledge, mystical marriage, and divine intercession. To understand why Angela veered from the tradition of female mysticism with which she was clearly associated, we must turn to other religious influences. That is the subject of next chapter.

80. Saintly women like Elena Duglioli (1472–1520), Margherita da Russi (1442–1505), Gentile da Ravenna (1471–1530), and Paola Antonia Negri (1508–55) should be considered from this perspective.

CHAPTER 4

Spiritual Trends in Pre-Tridentine Italy

This chapter examines Merici's spirituality amid some significant spiritual themes that characterized the period before the Council of Trent (1545–63). The season of Angela's religious work knew a host of spiritual currents and manifestations. It saw new forms of religious perfection, millenarian expectations, campaigns for church reform, and the spread of Protestant ideas. As historians have pointed out, the 1520s and 1530s in particular were a time of religious "experiments," when new forms of individual perfection and projects for the reform of the church's institutions were discussed in many spiritual circles.[1] While reform of the existing religious orders, with the movement of the Observance, had started more than a century earlier, the first half of the sixteenth century witnessed the mushrooming of new congregations such as the Theatines (1524), the Capuchins (1528), the Somaschi (1528), the Barnabites (1533), the Angelics (1533), and the Jesuits (1540). The Theatines, the Barnabites, and the Jesuits—also known as Clerks Regular—followed a new religious life, mixing clerical and monastic practice. They persued stricter observance of the three vows of poverty, chastity, and obedience; an ascetic regime; and common life under a rule. They also pursued apostolic life, administering the sacraments, working in hospitals, promoting education, and performing other charitable works. During this period new confraternities developed, too, such as the Company of Divine Love, the Company of Buon Gesù, and the Company

1. See, for example, Prosperi, "Riforma cattolica."

of Christian Doctrine. These included both laymen and ecclesiastics who sought personal sanctification through the common exercise of religious practices and through various apostolic activities. Another significant religious manifestation of the time was represented by a new vernacular literature composed by members of reformed religious orders, such as the Dominican Battista da Crema and the Lateran Canon Serafino da Fermo, which promoted new devout models for individual perfection both to religious people and to the laity.

As recent scholarship has proven, these pious foundations can no longer be easily seen as a composite movement.[2] Research on the Jesuits, the Barnabites, and the Company of Divine Love has shown that at the outset each institution had its own distinctive character and that by the time of the Council of Trent they had altered their original physiognomy. Initially, they were influenced by a variety of mystical and ascetic traditions; they were quite fluid and often out of alignment with the expectations of the ecclesiastical hierarchy. The project of church reform—either considered as a genuine movement of reaction against the loosening of Christian morals, doctrines, disciplines, and codes of institutional conduct or as an opposition to the Protestant reformers—does not fully explain the proliferation of religious models endorsed by the new orders and spiritual writers.[3] As scholars have also pointed out, charitable solicitude for the needy—supposedly the chief trait of the piety of the time—cannot by itself account for the diverse ideals of Christian perfection the new foundations fostered.

The case of Angela Merici reinforces these arguments. Angela Merici and the Company of St. Ursula have long been linked to the new religious orders amid a church reforming itself *in capite*

2. O'Malley, "Was Ignatius Loyola a Church Reformer?"; Bonora, *I conflitti della Controriforma;* Solfaroli Camillocci, *I Devoti della Carità.*

3. For a critique of "counterreformation" and "Catholic Reform" as terms able to capture the spirit of the Catholicism of the period, see O'Malley, *Trent and All That* (esp. 130–34); Hudon, "Religion and Society."

et in membris and cultivating charity and teaching. But this conventional picture fails to capture Merici's spirituality. Although Angela supported the reform of the church, her company was no attempt to carry out this ideal. If she was aware of the problems faced by women in the world, support for the needy was peripheral to her spirituality. In order to find a common ground between Angela Merici and other contemporary institutes and writers, we should look toward a spiritual trend that stressed the inner and moral aspects of religious life. This attitude, already present a century earlier in the Flemish *devotio moderna* and in the Italian movement of the Observance, was central to the main sixteenth-century religious circles and foundations.

ANGELA AND THE DEBATE ON THE REFORM OF THE CHURCH

Since Jedin historians have used the category of "Catholic Reformation" to explain a series of phenomena that, during the fifteenth and the early sixteenth centuries, signaled an attempt to renew Christian society and reform the Catholic Church. Some of these phenomena include the Councils of the Church, such as that of Constance (1414–18) and the Fifth Lateran Council (1512–17)—where Giustiniani and Quirini advanced proposals for church reform—the accusations against the corruption of the clergy made by preachers such as Girolamo Savonarola, and attempts to correct the ecclesiastical institutions by bishops such as Jiménez de Cisneros. The campaigns to reform traditional religious orders and the foundation of new ones, together with the flourishing of confraternities, are often seen as regeneration of the ecclesiastical body.

Doubtless the reform of the church is a main theme of late-fifteenth- and early-sixteenth-century Italian religiosity. In the 1520s debate on the reform of the church was led by circles linked to the Savonarolan tradition, which fostered a millenarian hope for Christian *renovatio*. Harkening to the revelations of charismatic women, these groups looked forward to the arrival of the figure of the *papa angelico*.[4] By contrast, in the 1530s the project of church reform was pursued by evangelical circles, groups of nobles with a humanist background. Unlike the circles of the previous decade, they rejected prophecy and, unlike the Protestants, they proposed a reformation of the church without subversion of ecclesiastical institutions.[5] How does Angela Merici fit in with all these developments? Was she influenced by these debates? Can her company be seen as a product of the attempts to reform the church? And what was her position in relation to Protestant ideas?

In Merici's time, the situation in Brescia reflected the general problems of the church.[6] The bishops were often absent and the clergy corrupt and bereft of pastoral guidance.[7] Religious life re

4. A notable example of these circles was the Oratorio dell'Eterna Sapienza (1500–30). Important religious and lay personalities of the time (such as the bishop of Toulon, Denis Briçonnet) gathered around the revelations of Arcangela Panigarola (an Augustinian nun of the convent of St. Marta in Milan). These groups remained isolated, and the failure of political projects linked with prophetic visions brought their experience to an end. There is a discussion of these circles in Prosperi, "Dalle 'divine madri' ai 'padri spirituali.'" For an analysis of popular prophetism, see Niccoli, *Profeti e popolo.*

5. We find exponents of these circles (based in Venice and Viterbo) in Pietro Bembo, Gasparo Contarini, and the cardinals Iacopo Sadoleto, Reginald Pole, and Federico Fregoso. Some members of these circles wrote the *Consilium de emendanda Ecclesia* in 1537 which, although impressive in its proposals for reform, did not have an immediate impact on the organizational reform of the church. The milieu of Contarini and others was also connected with Valdés's circle in Naples, through Marcantonio Flaminio. The demise of this movement coincided with the last attempt to reconcile Protestant and Catholic doctrines Contarini conducted at Regensburg (1541). After that date the more repressive approach toward reformist ideas led by the future Paul IV, Pietro Carafa, became dominant. For a general overview of these themes, see Firpo, *Riforma protestante,* esp. 89–141.

6. See Cairns, *Domenico Bollani;* Caprioli, Rinoldi, and Vaccaro, *Diocesi di Brescia;* Montanari, *Disciplinamento in terra veneta;* Cistellini, "La vita religiosa."

7. Though in the second half of the fifteenth century religious reform occurred under the bishops Malipiero (1457–64) and De Dominici (d. 1478), the period between 1478 and 1558 (the election of Domenico Bollani) was characterized by the absenteeism of bishops and the lack of religious reform. There were abuses in the admin

volved around monasteries, which, however, were also centers where families paraded their prestige.[8] The upper classes installed their daughters in cloister, many doing so just to shed excess daughters, who often became reluctant nuns. The Brescian Council tried in vain to repair the situation.[9]

Furthermore, Protestant ideas were circulating in Brescia. Commercial contacts with German traders, the influence of Venice,[10] and the presence of several Protestant preachers made Brescia one of the Italian cities most receptive to the reformed ideas. Lutheran ideas existed at every social level (both in the city and countryside), and several monks and friars left their orders.[11] The Company of St. Ursula itself was not immune to Protestant conversions: Cozzano says that after Angela Merici's death some Ursulines left the company and supported "heretical" ideas.

The ideas promoted by the humanist reformist circles were widespread in Brescia in the 1530s, particularly because of the presence of adherents of Erasmus of Rotterdam.[12] It was in Brescia, in 1531, that Erasmus's *Enchiridion Militis Christiani* was published in Italian for the first time. Among Angela's friends, Gabriele Cozzano and Giacomo Chizzola showed an interest in Erasmus's ideas. Cozzano's letters often discussed the reformation of the church, advocating

---

istration of ecclesiastical benefices and the chapter of the cathedral was controlled by a small group of aristocratic families.

8. At the end of fifteenth century there were fifty monasteries (many of them empty) and ten female convents, which counted about eight hundred members. Public preaching took place in the Franciscan and Dominican monasteries or was conducted by wandering preachers.

9. The council, for example, invited famous preachers such as Bernardino da Siena, Giovanni da Capestrano, Jacopo della Marca, Bernardino da Feltre, and Girolamo Savonarola.

10. Venice was the leading publisher of reformist books. In Brescia Britannico was the main publisher.

11. About one hundred friars left their monasteries either in Brescia or in the surrounding territory (Cistellini, "La vita religiosa," 450). Many individuals belonging to important Brescian families converted to Lutheranism. See Caponetto, *La Riforma protestante*, 205–18.

12. On the Erasmian circles in Brescia, see Seidel Menchi, *Erasmo in Italia.*

the model of the church of the apostles. In 1548 Chizzola (less close to Merici but nevertheless a witness at the *Processo Nazari*) founded some "academies" for children (a type of boarding school) in and around Brescia in collaboration with Erasmus's Brescian friend, the humanist Vincenzo Maggi. Chizzola was also in contact with other people of humanist background active in church reform, in particular Reginald Pole and Bartolomeo Stella (Pole's collaborator and the founder of the Company of Divine Love in Brescia).[13]

The crisis of the church and the question of its reform certainly colored Angela Merici's spirituality. In the first place, passages in Angela's writings link her with the debates between Catholics and Protestants. In the controversy on divine grace and free will, Merici sided with the church. Angela affirmed that religious choice is based on free will: "God has given the free will to everyone." God grants the grace, the Ursuline is responsible for keeping it: "Then that you strive with all your might to remain as you are called by God, and to seek and desire all the ways and means necessary to persevere and make progress to the very end. For it is not enough to begin, if one does not also persevere . . . blessed are those into whose hearts God has breathed the light of truth, and to whom He has given the will to yearn ardently for their heavenly home; and who then seek to persevere within themselves this voice of truth, and this holy desire" (*Reg.,* Prologue).

Another significant doctrinal issue raised by Protestants and discussed by Angela is that of confession. Angela acknowledged confession as a necessary medicine for freeing the individual from sin. Angela granted the church this role: "no one will ever be justified from sin, if she does not first, with her own lips, confess her faults to the priest . . . whatever you bind on earth shall be bound in heaven . . . By which is clearly demonstrated that sin cannot be taken away except by a priest and through confession" (*Reg.,* VII).

---

13. Stella was also in contact with the Roman circle of Sadoleto, Vittoria Colonna, and Michelangelo. He was also very close to Gaetano da Thiene, a member of the Roman Divine Love and founder of the Theatines.

In chapter 7 of the *Arricordi* for the Colonelle, Angela condemned Protestant doctrine altogether, warning them that the heretics might preach things against the church or the rule of the company. The duty of the Colonelle was to protect the virgins from these dangers: "As for protecting them from the *pestilential opinions of heretics,* when you hear that some preacher, or other person, has a reputation for heresy, or preaches new things outside the common practice of the Church, and contrary to what you have received from us, then, tactfully, prevent your dear daughters from listening to such person."

Angela, however, also referred to the corruption of the church. If she warned the Colonelle that they must guard the daughters from heretics (the "robbers"), they must also defend them from the immoral clergy and from secular men (the "wolves"). Lax clergymen might convince the daughters to abandon some aspects of the religious life established by the rule, or even the rule in its entirety: "Know that you have to defend and protect your lambs from wolves and robbers, that is from two kinds of pestilential people: worldly persons or false religious with their deceits, and heretics. Firstly . . . take care especially that they not become familiar with young men, and other men too, even if they are spiritual . . . Be on your guard lest a confessor, or some other religious, turn them away from some good inspiration, or from fasting, or from the purpose of virginity, or from esteem for this holy Rule divinely ordained" (*Ric.,* 7). Nevertheless, Angela's loyalty to the church was beyond question. Rather than rejecting its institutions, Angela called for its reformation: "Keep to the ancient way and custom of the Church, established and confirmed by so many Saints the inspiration of the Holy Spirit . . . pray, and get others to pray, that God not abandon his Church, but reform it as he pleases, and as he sees best for us, and more to his honour and glory" (*Ric.,* 7).

Thus Angela was faithful to the church, while at the same time she was aware of its corruption and demanded its reform. As it has been noted, Merici's proposal for a religious life lived outside the cloister (as well as the absence of vows) recalls the antimonastic ideas expressed in Erasmus's *Enchiridion Militis Christiani* and the model of the primitive church, which was often at the center of the debates of the Catholic reformers.[14] Cozzano's writings treated monasteries as a symptom and cause of late antique decline and explicitly compared the Company of St. Ursula with the *chiesa primitiva:* "At first the Church was in its early and golden state of life, without cloistering. Then it declined and there were the monasteries. So that, preferring the cloistered life to every other life, they came to diminish the very perfection and the primitive and golden state of the holy Church: to which this one of ours resembles."[15] The symbolism used by the company, and in particular the reference to the myth of St. Ursula's ship, the ship everybody can join, would qualify the company as an *ecclesia*. And the introductory letter to the rule of the company states that everybody, not only virgin women, can follow the life proposed in it.[16]

It is difficult, however, to say whether this was the foundress's real intention. There is no doubt that Angela supported the idea of church reform. Furthermore, it is likely that the model of the primitive church, and especially the ideal of consecrated virgins in the world, provided an ideological point of reference for conceiving of religious life in the secular world. We must not forget,

14. Prodi, "Vita religiosa" and "Nel mondo o fuori dal mondo"; Zarri, "Orsola e Caterina." On Italian evangelism, see Simoncelli, *Evangelismo italiano.*

15. *Risposta,* f. 32v, in MTS, 575. Furthermore, the introductory letter to the rule of the company *(Al lettore)* presents the company through the same perspective: "This way of life seemed deign and right, and it appeared as an image and a spark of the way of life of the primitive Church" *(Al lettore,* in MTS, 433). As we have seen, it is likely that Cozzano was the author of this letter.

16. Zarri, "Orsola e Caterina." Zarri, however, discusses the introductory letter *Al lettore* as if it was the prologue of the rule and consequently gives this statement a greater importance than it should have. She has also argued that the connection with the primitive church emerges from the frescos of the chapel where Angela used to meet with the virgins. The images of the patron saints of the company, St. Ursula and St. Catherine of Alexandria, and those of the two Brescian martyrs Faustino and Giovita, show an association between virginity and martyrdom (ibid.).

however, that a choice of this kind had also been typical of many medieval spiritual women and of Angela herself (Angela became a tertiary well before she heard these debates). Secularity, therefore, was not adopted as a consequence of the debates on church reform, albeit these were present in the foundress's mind and may have influenced her. Moreover, it is important to stress that the company was not an ecclesia since it was open only to virgin women, who were considered Brides of Christ. The suggestion that the company could become a model for a future reform of the church was Cozzano's, not Angela's. Indeed, all the comparisons between the company and the primitive church were his. As a matter of fact, where these issues were concerned, Merici appeared cautious. Merici invited the Ursulines to remain outside the debates raised by Catholic and Protestants and not judge them: "Leave them alone. Consider each one as good, but be prudent for your own good" (*Ric.,* 7). Rather, Angela encouraged them to follow the *vita nova* proposed in her rule—in union with Christ, the only secure way to receive the light and find true spiritual life: "And live a new life . . . in these perilous and pestilential times, you will find no other recourse than to take refuge at the feet of Jesus Christ, because if he directs and teaches you, you will be taught" (*Ric.,* 7).

Finally, to interpret Angela Merici (as well as other religious individuals and associations) through the perspective of the return to the apostolic church is reductive because it does not account for her specific interpretation of the model. We cannot use the actual primitive church to expound its sixteenth-century evocations. As we have already seen, Angela Merici interpreted life in the world through the eyes of a female living saint of her times. In this sense her version of apostolic life was very distinct and significantly different from that of other promoters of the reformation of the church such as Erasmus. This said, as the final section of the chapter will show, Angela Merici and Erasmus of Rotterdam shared other spiritual ideals that have less to do with historical precedents and more with contemporary attitudes.

THE IDEAL OF "CHARITY"

Traditionally, historians viewed Merici's company as closely tied to works of charity. Catholic historians such as Guerrini and Cistellini reconstructed the network of religious activities in Brescia and the Brescian territory at this time, stressing charity.[17] In 1423 the council founded the Ospedale Grande, which provided assistance to the sick, medicines and food to beggars and prisoners, and instruction in trades to poor children. Later on, at the beginning of the sixteenth century, several charitable bodies were founded.[18] Some of these aimed to serve women in danger.[19] The figure of Bartolomeo Stella, who in 1521 founded the Hospital of the Incurables and in 1525, the Brescian Company of Divine Love, was important here. A rising population and the consequent plethora of the needy—exacerbated by the war and the sack of Brescia in 1512—led these charitable institutes to specialize. In 1548 the council unified and coordinated them.[20] As we have seen in chapter 1, although some of Angela's friends were involved in these initiatives, Angela, it seems, was not. Let us now go deeper into Angela's attitude to-

17. Guerrini, "Le condizioni religiose di Brescia"; Cistellini, "La vita religiosa" and *Figure della riforma pretridentina*.

18. These were: the hospice of Santo Spirito for the aged; the Luogo della Misericordia for orphans; the congregation of apostolic charity; the Monte di pietà; one Opera for the education of poor boys and another to provide assistance and funerals for the "shamefaced" poor. The council also supported young students and priests in their pastoral duties thanks to the income from legacies, oblations, and land possessions. In Salò another milieu (led by the Scaini brothers) was in contact with the founder of the Somaschi, Girolamo Emiliani (who founded an orphanage in Brescia), Thiene, Carafa, and the first Theatines. The Scainis founded another Company of Divine Love, which in 1541 developed into the Confraternity of Charity.

19. The noblewoman Laura Gambara founded the Casa delle Convertite della Carità in 1530, for assistance to women who were orphans or converted sinners. Other institutes were the Pio Luogo delle Zitelle di S. Agnese, for poor young girls, who were taught housewifery skills and placed in the houses of aristocratic families, and the Luogo della Carità, a house for orphan girls.

20. The Hospital of the Incurables became reserved for women, while men were treated in a section of the Ospedale Maggiore.

ward poverty and charity. For this we need to investigate the meaning the sixteenth century attached to these two important religious concepts.

Sixteenth-Century Attitudes
toward Charity and Poverty

As recent studies have suggested, in the early modern period the meaning and forms of charity were changing. Charity should not be identified simply as concern for the needy.[21] In the Middle Ages, for example, confraternities promoted a model of charity that consisted, above all, in encouraging support and love among neighbors.[22] Charity included preaching the end of conflicts, social harmony, love among men and for God. Concern for the poor and the sick was thus part of a larger solidaristic attitude aimed at establishing horizontal links of all kinds within the community. Furthermore, confraternal almsgiving was not universalist but particularist in spirit, aimed especially toward fellow members of the sodality. In the fifteenth century and especially in the sixteenth, this idea of *caritas* gradually evolved into a "new philanthropy" more organized and less personal, based on abstract benevolence as a duty of citizens.[23] The object of philanthropy became the outcast poor, to be redeemed from their condition and reinserted into a society that was becoming increasingly disciplined—or face expulsion.[24] So city councils founded new hospitals and charitable bodies, which taught the poor a trade for employment, introduced new methods of curing patients, distinguishing between diseases and types of

21. For example, Jütte, *Poverty and Deviance.* For Italy see Cavallo, *Charity and Power.*

22. Henderson, *Piety and Charity,* 411; Pullan, "Support and Redeem."

23. Bossy, *Christianity in the West,* 57–63, 140–49.

24. Organized charity "was now directed not only towards relieving the respectable, and ensuring that they continued to behave circumspectly and piously, but also at amending the character, morals and behaviour of the outcast poor in such a way as to integrate them with a highly disciplined Christian society, and to cause that society to prosper thereby" (Pullan, "Support and Redeem," 181).

poverty—and, at the same time, promulgated laws to expel the poor.

Among the motivations for the establishment of charitable institutions in the early modern period was the urge to banish the most unpleasant aspects of poverty, the fruit of migration, economic change, and war. Furthermore, the new attitude toward the poor reflected a new meaning of poverty. In the Middle Ages the reason for charity was the symbolic connection between Christ and the poor—and all outcasts. In the thirteenth century Francis and Clare of Assisi battled the ecclesiastical authorities to keep their foundations faithful to the ideal of absolute poverty, which to them best represented the *sequela Christi.* By contrast, in the sixteenth century, with the rise of capitalism, wealth shed its sinful stigma and poverty lost its halo, declining to a mere economic condition and sign of failure.[25] In the humanist treatises, like those of Erasmus and Vives, the poor were no longer viewed as figures functional to society, who gave the rich a chance to redeem themselves or recalled the Son of God, but were depicted as deviants, misfits in the new social order of early modern cities. The foundation of hospitals and institutions for the destitute promoted by the city councils and by the new confraternities (for example, by the Company of Divine Love, the Company of Charity, and the Jesuits) can be seen, at least in part, as symptoms of a new attitude of the urban elites toward poverty and diversity within a trend of social discipline.[26]

In Angela's times, another reason for pursuing charitable works was the attempt to achieve personal sanctification through renunciation of status. The religious and lay urban elites who developed the ideals of charity viewed their involvement in the service of the poor and the sick both as a deserving act and as a ritual of humili-

25. Magli, *Gli uomini della penitenza,* 55–62.

26. For example, the statutes of the Company of Charity, formed by noblemen and courtiers, reflect debates concerning deserving and undeserving poor (Solfaroli Camillocci, *I Devoti della Carità,* 180–87). The Compagnia della Grazia, established by Ignatius Loyola in the 1540s for women in peril or repentant prostitutes, reflects a preoccupation with those who did not fit accepted roles for women.

ation.[27] The Barnabites and the Divine Love are cases in point. Inspired by the doctrine of their spiritual leader, Battista da Crema, the Barnabites were a group of young noblemen who appeared to identify asceticism in particular with renunciation of codes of honor and status. For example, they rejected symbols of social distinction such as ornate clothing and long beards, and addressed each other without those gestures of submission that respected rank.[28] In addition, their constitutions reject haughtiness and prescribe accepting offense and criticism as central to a perfect spiritual life. The Barnabites sought to abandon pride and status via public humiliation: "There is no humility without *wishing at length for incivility* . . . through this humility man knows that he is God's enemy, unworthy of anything good, and *worthy of being scorned by all people.*"[29] As has been noted, renunciation of status was also the main value behind the Barnabites' acts of public penance, such as wandering about poorly dressed and preaching in the squares of Milan with a rope around their necks or bearing a cross.[30] Their service among the poor and the sick in the hospitals was part of their penitential exercise, and it belongs to this same ideological context. Thus, works of charity in hospitals or among the sick and the poor were not carried out merely to alleviate the sufferings of needy people but functioned as acts of penance, forms of public humiliation that enabled individuals to give up social honor and secular aspirations and thus come closer to God.

A similar motivation can be found at the root of the opposite behavior of the members of the Genoese Company of Divine Love, who wanted to hide their identity when carrying out charitable works. As has been observed, the reason behind this secrecy should

27. Prosperi, *Tribunali della coscienza*, 20.

28. As testified, for example, in the letters of Bonsignore Cacciaguerra, a nobleman and religious writer who spent a period with the Barnabites and who expressed his admiration for them. See Premoli, *Storia dei Barnabiti*, 473–79.

29. *Costituzioni*, XVIII, in Premoli, *Storia dei Barnabiti*, 450.

30. Bonora, *I conflitti della Controriforma*, 228.

be sought in their conviction that public recognition of good works could lead to pride and therefore undermine the progress achieved in the scale of virtue.[31] Charity was thus an ascetic activity conceived within a religious context that prized renunciation of status. It is possible that this spirituality became particularly important within a period of reaffirmation of codes of honor and redefinition of social identities—indeed, most of the men involved in these pious foundations were nobles.

Angela Merici's View of Charity

How did Angela Merici fit into this conceptual framework? Angela's attitude toward charity should be viewed in relation to her understanding of poverty. Merici, unlike Francis of Assisi—who inspired Angela's third order—invested material poverty with no profound religious significance. Angela's rule held no prohibition concerning property, and the Ursulines could keep their possessions. A number of Ursulines owned their own houses, some earned money, and others inherited from their families.[32] As will appear in more detail later, the type of poverty that interested Angela was the one identified with spiritual detachment from secular values.

Angela proposed a spiritual model in which the care of the needy was not central. As we have seen, there is no evidence of charitable works among the Ursulines' duties toward the outside world (as in the hospitals). In fact, in Angela's writings the word *charity* is used only twice in connection with helping the poor and the sick. However, there it refers to the Ursulines' duty to help fellow Ursulines in need. The only charitable works Angela envisaged, as in the medieval confraternities, consisted in the establishment of horizontal links among the Ursulines, ensuring material support to those members who needed it. But this in itself was not a central religious goal.

31. Solfaroli Camillocci, *I Devoti della Carità,* introduction.

32. The Ursulines' right of inheritance was officially recognized by the bull of approbation of the rule in 1544.

Another indication of Angela's attitude toward charitable works can be found in the concept of almsgiving that emerges from her writings for the company. Merici did not view almsgiving as a means of self-sanctification. She specified that it had a functional rather than spiritual or religious purpose. It was presented as a useful and practical means of forging cohesion within the company and motivating the Ursulines to carry on their life. Angela claimed that through occasional almsgiving and distribution of gifts (organized by the Matrone), the Ursulines would feel more bound to the company, much as a laywoman is indebted to a man who gives her a gift. Angela told the Matrone:

such income as you have, spend it for the good and development of the Company . . . as much *to urge and move those who are already in* [*the company*] *to greater love and obligation to do good,* as to attract still others to it. For this is the *real purpose,* agreeable to God, *of almsgiving and kindness* . . . Indeed, in this way people are so to speak *won over and compelled to do the very thing one wants.* Because just as for example, if a girl takes and accepts some present and gift from some worldly stranger, she remains obliged to gratify the wishes of that person, and it seems that she is no longer able to say no, so neither more nor less, *by gifts and alms people are drawn and somehow compelled to do good;* and thus they remain almost bound to do good. (*Tes.,* 9)[33]

In Angela's writings the concept of charity is used to describe in particular a general human—or inner—disposition toward others. For example, in explaining how the Ursulines should behave with those outside the company, Angela associated this term with "love" and "patience." Similarly, while advising the Colonelle and the Matrone on how to relate to their spiritual daughters, Angela identified "charity" with "love." Here these words indicate that one should not be defensive and attached to one's own good but open, acting only for the other person's good (see chapter 3). Angela viewed charity as a human quality as a tool for helping others.

33. In the *Polizza* of 1588 the company declared it had paid 40 lire for little gifts for the Ursulines at Christmas.

Why did Angela give less stress to charitable acts than other contemporary religious institutions (such as the Company of Divine Love, the Barnabites, and the Jesuits)? One of the reasons is that Angela shared with them neither the urge to restore social order nor the ideal of self-sanctification through renunciation of status.

In the first place, in Angela Merici's spirituality, the concept of charity was not associated with humility and renunciation of social honor. Unlike the Barnabites and the Company of Divine Love, she did not emphasize the importance of bearing with insults, accepting criticism, and humiliating oneself. Humility and self-abnegation are not viewed as renunciation of a social status. The reason Angela's rule did not propose renunciation of status as a form of personal sanctification must be sought in the fact that most of the Ursulines were not noble but came from artisan families. Furthermore, they were women, and women had less control over their social identity. That is also why Angela and the company were not involved in charity through motivations concerning social order. As women and as members of the lower middle class, the Ursulines were not part of the urban elite responsible for these matters. Note, too, that we cannot view the company itself as a means for restoring social order by offering a stable social identity to women in danger of losing their honor. As we have seen, the company was neither directed to nor composed of such women. Furthermore, Angela offered an original form of spiritual life and an alternative female identity that could easily switch from holy to scandalous. That said, some of the aristocratic Matrone may have perceived their role as charitable, in the sense that it offered a worthy form of life to Ursulines in need.

In conclusion, in the sixteenth century the concept of charity was multifaceted. While material poverty no longer seemed a sign of sanctity, the reasons for carrying out charitable works included personal renunciation of social status and an attempt to eliminate diversity in order to establish good social order. In Angela Merici's case, the desacralization of poverty led to other religious options.

Angela and the Ursulines did not give special attention to charitable works because they were middle-class women neither interested in restoring social order nor prone to see renunciation of status as a powerful act that could lead to personal sanctification.

INDIVIDUALITY, INTERIORITY, AND MORALITY IN RENAISSANCE CATHOLICISM

One of the key themes in the spirituality of Renaissance Catholicism consisted in the stress on individuality, interiority, and morality. Ascetic writers and the rules of new religious orders and associations contemporaneous with Angela Merici depict models of religious perfection with these characteristics. Angela Merici's spirituality can also be viewed in these terms. Indeed, her company represents a radical and institutional synthesis of this spiritual trend. Angela's religious model, however, shows significant differences from those of her contemporaries concerning the relationship with the divine.

Italian Religious Circles

Although examples of a concern for individuality, interiority, and morality in spirituality can already be found in the high Middle Ages, spirituality was increasingly characterized by these traits from about the fourteenth century onward, especially in the urban elite. The movement of devotio moderna was probably one of the most articulated and early systematizations of this spiritual trend. Its spirituality has often been described as individual, inner, and affective as well as ascetic and practical, Christocentric and distant from theological reasoning.[34] In the fifteenth century Italian men and women of different religious traditions, whether influenced by the devotio moderna or not, favored a religious approach of this

---

34. Vandenbroucke, *La spiritualité au Moyen Age,* 341–62. See also Trolese, *Riforma della Chiesa.*

kind. This was especially true of the Observant congregations.[35] Confraternities such as the Battuti of S. Domenico of Bologna also showed a similar type of devotion.[36]

In the early sixteenth century, this spirituality was promoted by many religiously inspired groups and individuals, particularly in northern Italy. We find this "devout" spirituality in several exponents of the Observant movement, such as the Dominican Battista da Crema and the Lateran Canons, Serafino da Fermo.[37] These men composed very influential ascetic writings in the vernacular for the laity, in which they proposed a devout life that fostered worldly perfection and eternal salvation.[38] This spiritual orientation also surfaced in the rules of several late-fifteenth- and early-sixteenth-century confraternities, such as the Company of Divine Love and

35. Some examples are the Franciscans Bernardino da Siena (d. 1444), Giovanni da Capestrano (d. 1456), and Bernardino da Feltre (d. 1494); the Dominicans Giovanni Dominici (d. 1419) and Girolamo Savonarola (d. 1498). Possible links between the Flemish and Italian devotio were Ludovico Barbo (1382–1443), promoter of the Observant Benedictine Congregation of Santa Giustina of Padua, and Lorenzo Giustiniani (1381–1455), member of the congregation of the secular canons of S. Giorgio in Alga. For a discussion of the origins of Italian Observant spirituality and of its differences from the Flemish devotio, see Picasso, "L'imitazione di Cristo." See also Petrocchi, "Una 'Devotio' moderna nel Quattrocento italiano," in *Storia della spiritualità italiana*, 55–67.

36. The confraternity of the Battuti was a lay confraternity of medieval origin that was reestablished in 1427 under the influence of the preacher Manfredo da Vercelli (the rule of the confraternity was composed in 1443). The members continued to live their secular life while observing several devotional practices and pursuing charitable activities.

37. Battista Carioni da Crema (ca. 1460–1534) was a preacher of the Dominican congregation of the Observance in Lombardy. He composed ascetic writings such as *Via de aperta verità* (1523), *Della cognitione et vittoria di se stesso* (1531), *Philosophia divina* (1531), and *Lo specchio interiore* (1540). Serafino Aceti de' Porti da Fermo (1496–1540) was influenced by the spirituality of Battista da Crema. Serafino's first work, *Del discernimento degli spiriti,* was published in 1535; his other works were published from 1541 and reprinted many times. A collection of his writings is contained in *Opere spirituali.*

38. Vernacular religious texts, together with preaching, were the main vehicle for the diffusion of religious ideas and precepts of moral behavior. See Zarri, "La vita religiosa femminile tra devozione e chiostro," in *Le sante vive*, 21–50.

the Company of Buon Gesù.[39] Moreover, we find the main traits of this type of devotion in the rules of the Clerks Regular and in other writings composed by their major exponents. Ignatius Loyola encouraged his brothers to read Thomas à Kempis's popular book *The Imitation of Christ*,[40] and his *Spiritual Exercises* represents a peak of this spiritual trend. At the same time, the foundation of the Barnabites and the Theatines was connected with the circles that promoted this spirituality. It was through the direct influence of Battista da Crema in particular that Antonio Zaccaria established the Barnabites. Gaetano da Thiene, the cofounder of the Theatines and a member of the Company of the Divine Love, was also a disciple of Battista da Crema, and the latter probably played a role in the foundation of the Theatines.[41] The female religious order of the Angelics, founded by Ludovica Torelli, was the product of cooperation between Battista da Crema and Antonio Zaccaria.[42] Within this spiritual movement we should also consider humanists such as Erasmus of Rotterdam, who had been religiously formed in the schools of the Brothers of the Common Life and whose *Enchiridion Militis Christiani* promoted a similar ideal of Christian life. Finally, the spiritual ideas promoted by the circles

39. The Company of Divine Love was founded in Genoa in 1497 by the layman Ettore Vernazza (ca. 1470–1524) and through the influence of Catherine of Genoa (1446–1510). The confraternity, composed of both laypeople and ecclesiastics, expanded in other cities. The brothers led a devout life and performed charitable work in hospitals and prisons. The Company of Buon Gesù (founded in the same year as the Divine Love) was a congregation of laypeople and clerics (including virgins, married people, and priests), whose rule is said to have been drawn up by Margherita Molli da Russi (1442–1505). However, the rule was reported by Serafino da Fermo, who probably codified what Margherita's disciples inherited from her: *Alcune regole cavate da gli ammaestramenti della divina vergine Margherita per la sua unione.*

40. O'Malley, "The Society of Jesus."

41. The rule of the Theatines, however, was mainly written by Carafa who, as is well documented, was opposed to Battista da Crema. It should also be noted that another very significant text belonging to this spiritual tradition (*Il combattimento spirituale*, published anonymously in Venice in 1589) was composed by a later member of the Theatines, Lorenzo Scupoli.

42. On the Angelics, see Baernstein, *A Convent's Tale.*

of the *spirituali* connected with Reginald Pole and Juan de Valdés were also rooted in the devout approach.[43] Most of these authors and founders—at least for a period—were viewed with suspicion by the church.[44]

Angela Merici, too, can be seen within this spiritual context, and she may have been influenced by some of these circles. As has been recently suggested, there is a connection between Merici and the Brescian Lateran Canons of the Observant Congregation of Fregionaia (Bologna).[45] In the last years of her life Angela moved into an apartment annexed to the church of St. Afra, which the canons had recently bought, and chose to be buried in that church.[46] Furthermore, her confessor, Serafino Torresini da Bologna, was a Lateran Canon and the author of spiritual treatises that show a clear affiliation with Battista da Crema and Serafino da Fermo.[47] Though Angela, who read "many holy books," could not have read Torresini's writings (composed after her death), she may have read the works of his spiritual masters. It is also likely that she read the *Imitation of Christ,* one of the most important books of the late Middle Ages.[48] Furthermore, it is not impossible that Angela read Eras-

43. The movement of the "spirituali" pursued an ideal of religion as interior enlightenment, gradually achieved through personal contact with God. On Valdés's spirituality, see Juan de Valdés, *Alfabeto cristiano.*

44. Battista da Crema, and possibly Serafino da Fermo, were accused of Pelagianism (Battista's writings were condemned by Julius III in 1552 and listed in the Tridentine index of prohibited books in 1564); Antonio Zaccaria's piety aroused suspicions for his close association with the Angelics and for his excessively penitential behavior; the charismatic Angelic Paola Antonia Negri was accused of presumption, discredited, and eventually imprisoned; Erasmus's books were also listed in the Index (after his death); and Valdés and his followers were persecuted as heretics.

45. Zarri, "Ambiente."

46. "Indultum pro moniali," in *Diversa Sacrae Penitentieriae Clementis P.P. VII. Anno IX. 1532,* reg. 79, Archivio Segreto Vaticano, in MTS, 520–21.

47. Serafino Torresini da Bologna (ca. 1498–1568) wrote several spiritual books in the vernacular. He was a follower of Battista da Crema and Serafino da Fermo. He advocated Battista da Crema's ideas in *Pharetra divini amoris.* This text is a free translation (as explicitly stated by Serafino himself) of the book attributed to the Carthusian Johann von Landsberg (1489–1539).

48. In Italy the work existed in multiple printed editions, both in Latin and in the

mus's *Enchiridion* (published in Brescia in 1531).[49] By contrast, it is very doubtful that Angela had contacts with Loyola, Zaccaria, and Thiene or was able to read any of their texts (since they were composed after or in the same period as her rule). Finally, it is unlikely that Angela was familiar with Valdés's writings and with the circle of the spirituali, since they were active between the end of the 1530s and the beginning of the 1540s, and Angela's writings were composed before that time.[50]

The remainder of this chapter compares Merici's ideal of religious perfection with the one emerging from the spiritual literature produced by this milieu.[51] The relationship proposed here is not, however, one of direct influence. My aim is to reconstruct a spiritual climate into which Angela fit. I want to expose a spiritual

---

vernacular. It was published for the first time in Venice in 1483; in Brescia, it was published in 1485 with the title *b. Bernardi opus saluberrimum de imitatione Christi et contemptu mundi, quod J. Gerson can. Parisiensi tribuitur* (Angelo e Iacono Britannici).

49. As we have seen, Cozzano explicitly supported the renovation of the church based on the model of the primitive church. This, however, occurred in 1544, that is, four years after Angela's death.

50. Besides, Valdés's writings were mainly discussed within an aristocratic elite with the aim of reconciling Protestant and Catholic doctrines.

51. Here I will consider several examples taken from the above-mentioned spiritual literature: the ascetic writings of Battista da Crema, Serafino da Fermo (see note 44) and Serafino da Bologna (see note 47), the letters of Gaetano da Thiene (written in the 1520s), the rules of several confraternities such as the Confraternity of the Battuti of S. Domenico of Bologna (composed in 1443), the Company of Divine Love of Genoa (laid down in 1497), and the Company of Buon Gesù (composed before 1540), as well as those of the Barnabites (conceived by Battista da Crema around 1533) and the Jesuits (composed between 1544 and 1550). I will also consider Ignatius Loyola's *Spiritual Exercises* (first drafted in 1523, later revised, and then published in 1548) and Erasmus of Rotterdam's *Enchiridion Militis Christiani* (1503). I will not consider the rule of the Theatines, as this was written by Carafa in the 1550s. Needless to say, I do not intend to present exhaustive discussions of the spiritual traits of each individual author or religious order. I also must mention that I will not specifically compare the Company of St. Ursula with the Angelics because unfortunately there are no written constitutions for them (except in a later edition, composed after Borromeo's reform of the order). We do not know exactly what spiritual life they followed and whether they were inspired more by the rule of the Barnabites or by the charisma of their spiritual leader, Paola Antonia Negri.

logic that can account for many spiritual traits and religious practices promoted by ascetic writers and religious associations between the mid-fifteenth and the early sixteenth century. Both Angela and her contemporaries proposed a religious model that stressed the inner experience of the individual. By contrast, they deemed exterior, ritual, and institutional aspects of devotion far less important. This attitude pervaded a vast array of religious experiences, such as penance, prayer, vows, monastic life, conversion, and relationship with the divine. Let us first turn to Angela's contemporaries and then to Angela herself.

Ideals of Perfection and Relationship with God

Penance and Prayer

The preeminence of inner involvement at the expense of more exterior religious practice arises with physical penance. Physical discipline (such as flagellation, fasting, and so on) ceased to serve as a means for achieving religious perfection. Battista da Crema, for example, believed self-punishment was not something everyone should do; on the contrary, it could even be dangerous since it could become a source of pride and a reason for judging those who did not practice it:

But because you tell me that penance appears to you necessary: because it is a restraint on sin: it seems that you wish to say that one must practice great austerity: fasting: vigils: the discipline and other similar things: because in truth with these means one curbs the flesh . . . . And speaking of such penance one must use mature discretion: because not everybody has equal need of great penance: because many are weak and cannot practice it. And yet being molested by sins one must find the medicine . . . . Where if someone, to punish the body, practices penance but, from this, impatience or pride were to grow in him, despising others or placing great confidence in his austerities.[52]

52. Battista da Crema, *Via de aperta verità*, ff. 135r–36r.

The position of the Dominican friar emerges in the writings of Serafino da Fermo, too, who maintained that "true" penance consists
in the acceptance of other people's criticism and in the mortification of one's own will: "There are many who harshly afflict their
bodies with fasting, and vigils, but they do not accept that *they
may be wrong,* and thus they nourish *spiritual pride,* the root of every passion. . . . Fruitful penance *mortifies our entire will,* and, with
a joyful heart, *bears will every sorrow.*"[53] Similarly, the rule of the
Buon Gesù confraternity states that self-discipline and fasting are
less important than the effort to suppress feelings for secular matters: "make an effort to overcome the passions of the heart, because
it is better to resist a passion either of anger or of cupidity than to
discipline oneself forty times and fast for an entire year."[54] Though
physical penance was still prescribed in rules and manuals of perfection, its practice was aimed at disposing the mind to spiritual
values. The statutes of the confraternity of the Battuti of Bologna
say: "May each person fast on the fasting days ordered by the holy
church . . . . Because fasting is enjoined to *dispose our minds* to the
feasts which follow."[55] Ignatius Loyola's *Spiritual Exercises* also states
that one of the chief purposes of external penance is "to ensure that
all our lower appetites are under the control of our higher powers";
one must "overcome oneself," thus disposing the individual toward
higher things.[56]

Another example of the preference accorded to inner spiritual
life in religious practice emerges in the opposition between mental
and vocal prayer. According to the Barnabites' constitutions, mental prayer is the food of those who pursue a spiritual life, whereas
vocal prayer provides only exterior satisfaction and does not alter

53. Serafino da Fermo, *Trattato brevissimo della conversione,* in *Opere spirituali,* 20,
in Marcocchi, *La Riforma Cattolica,* I:178–79.

54. *Alcune regole,* 17

55. *Statuti,* 22, in Marcocchi, *La Riforma Cattolica,* I:206.

56. Ignacio de Loyola, *Spiritual Exercises,* week 1, 87.

or improve the worshipper: "*The food and nourishment of those who are proficient lies in mental prayer.* But if you do not nourish yourselves of it, you will necessarily feel your strength fail. But mere *exterior prayer* (above all without mental involvement, or in other words not participating in it) *is merely exterior satisfaction, and hypocrisy of true prayer* and of the true spiritual food. And this you can understand since *starting from this you remain the same as before,* as, *verbi gratia,* light in conversing, negligent in your actions and in all things imperfect."[57] Serafino da Fermo shared the same attitude.[58]

If mental prayer is the true means for the inner ascent of the soul to God, vocal prayer without inner involvement is condemned: "They however do not have their heart intent on what they are saying, but only move their dry lips. When you pray do not wish to say many words . . . . Spirit is God, and he wishes to be adored in spirit and truth . . . . But this does not mean that we blame the custom of the church."[59] The rule of the Company of the Buon Gesù preferred mental prayer to vocal prayer: "strive to pray more with the mind than with the voice."[60] Vocal prayer, left to the end of the document, occupied a less central place in the rule.

This spiritual context turned against exterior manifestations of piety. The confraternity of the Battuti, for example, explicitly condemned exteriority as caused by the devil, in contrast to God's inspiration, which is interior. While praying, it suggested, members should not perform solemn gestures (unless divinely obliged to do so): "He who prays must not practice any innovation or singularity, for which he is observed by others, either sighing and crying out, beating his breast, stretching out his hands and arms, unless he is

57. *Costituzioni,* X, in Premoli, *Storia dei Barnabiti,* 434.

58. The Lateran Canons were the main promoters of mental prayer. Fifteenth-century Italian asceticism, on the contrary, was still based on vocal prayer (Petrocchi, "Una 'Devotio' moderna nel Quattrocento italiano," in *Storia della spiritualità italiana,* 55–62).

59. Serafino de Fermo, *Trattato utilissimo,* in *Opere spirituali,* 21–23, in Marcocchi, *La Riforma Cattolica,* I:180–81.

60. *Alcune regole,* 5.

forced to do this out of true devotion and not out of bad habit or flightiness of mind. There are in our times certain dangerous devotions, which are more smoke than fire . . . . The visitations of the Spirit are all occult, inner and hidden, and those of the Devil are exposed."[61]

Inner Conversion and Institutional Religion

A spiritual model focusing on individual and inner devotion also spurred criticism of more institutional aspects of religion, such as monasteries, vows, and rituals in general. Separation from the world and contact with God were sought through conversion of the heart rather than represented in exterior structures. For example, despite its diffusion within the movement of the Observance (a monastic movement), the devotio moderna could easily imply the abandonment of monastic life, as it is demonstrated in the experience of the Brothers and Sisters of the Common Life. Similarly, according to Erasmus of Rotterdam, separation from the world consisted in a spiritual attitude rather than in a physical condition. He held up as ideal the antique church, in which monasteries did not exist. This attitude also emerged in ascetic treatises that advised the laity to live a devout life in the secular world. The Clerks Regular also deemed traditional monastic life less important, as they sought perfection above all in the midst of society.

The new spirituality also questioned the significance of vows in religious choice. Humanists debated whether one could be saved and become perfect through an exterior ritual.[62] In Valla's words, a spiritual life could be pursued without vows: "I have wished to confute . . . that you have a prerogative and a privilege because you have promised obedience, poverty and chastity."[63] Valla affirmed the importance of inner commitment and saw vows as a mere ob-

---

61. *Statuti*, 22, in Marcocchi, *La Riforma Cattolica*, I:214.

62. Prodi, "Nel mondo o fuori dal mondo."

63. Lorenzo Valla, *De professione religiosorum*, in *Scritti filosofici e religiosi* (Florence, 1953), cited in Prodi, "Nel mondo o fuori dal mondo," 25.

ligation as opposed to free, inner choice: "you acted righteously for necessity, I did it voluntarily."[64] Similarly, according to Erasmus, man is called on to seek salvation, to be achieved through inner commitment rather than via a formal oath. In addition, as Battista da Crema asserted, religious status is not valid in itself since for success it depends on the acquisition of virtue: "You must however note that though it may happen that Religion has a status of perfection, this does not necessarily mean that he who has made it his profession is instantly perfect but he must well need to take pleasure in acquiring it."[65]

In place of rituals, the center of the "true" religious conversion of a devout person lay in an individual and inner detachment from secular values. A religious attitude of this kind was expressed in the struggle against vices (such as haughtiness, vainglory, and anger), which keep man chained to secular preoccupations and distant from God. This approach to religious life was particularly evident in the Dominican friar Battista da Crema, who explained how perfection should be attained through a long, tough battle against one's weaknesses. Man can cast off vice and acquire virtue without asking the Creator to carry out the job:

And note however that many pray that God may remove from them some temptation from which they themselves (though with the grace of God) could free themselves: as when someone feels tempted by anger: because others speak evilly of him: or cause him some other displeasure: and this person prays to God that he remove the temptation, appeasing those who are displeasing him: this prayer is certainly in vain: because one must neither expect nor believe that our patience lies in not having tribulations. But having them may we magnanimously bear with them: and overcome them . . . and not tempt God in waiting for him to bring down here a bag of patience . . . and remove the cause of the impatience [accusing him then if he does not do this] . . . If ever you need to have patience:

64. Ibid., 24.
65. Battista da Crema, *Via de aperta verità*, f. 24v.

there will need be someone who makes you acquire it with his behaviour which is contrary to your desire. And that you begin by overcoming yourself.[66]

This attitude was also reflected in the Barnabite rule, where religious perfection consists in the repression of self-love: "to extirpate their [vices'] roots, which are *love of self,* and other passions."[67]

This spiritual doctrine proposed an ideal of perfection consisting mainly in virtuous behavior and purity of heart. The rule of the Company of Buon Gesù prescribed that members should not be proud when carrying out good deeds ("to flee from vainglory . . . being born of good works it consumes and ruins them all");[68] that they must not judge ("never to judge others in our hearts and in our speech"), have bad thoughts ("to place every effort in fleeing from bad thoughts, because through these we are drawn away from God") or listen to evil conversations ("to flee from evil conversation"). Instead, they must have a good opinion of and pray for everybody, including persecutors and slanderers ("to have a good opinion of all people, and pray for all people, and most particularly for those who slander us and our persecutors"). In this spiritual current, tolerance and humility were central virtues. In the rule of the Barnabites the truly humble must bear with other people's weaknesses: "The humble person is accompanied by compassion, and tolerance for the defects of others."[69] Similarly, in the Battuti's rule the members must not disparage people but always be "gracious, pleasing and courteous."[70] Note that God's goodness lay in his willingness to bear offense. Man, on the contrary, is intolerant and prickly: "with what patience [God] bears with offences and

---

66. Ibid., ff. 32v–33r.

67. *Costituzioni,* XVII, in Premoli, *Storia dei Barnabiti,* 449; the italics are mine.

68. *Alcune regole.* The quotations in this paragraph are respectively from chapters 9, 8, 10, 18, and 23.

69. *Costituzioni,* XVII, in Premoli, *Storia dei Barnabiti,* 451.

70. *Statuti,* 10, in Marcocchi, *La Riforma Cattolica,* I:211.

awaits the repentance of sinners, and we cannot have a little patience for one small word."[71]

One's battle against vice and one's detachment from secular values were motivated by the desire to reach union with God and to follow his will in the world. In the ascent toward God freedom from secular values was the precondition to progress. Arrogance, anger, pride, and curiosity were all signs of attachment to secular values, which keep man distant from God. To be humble, pleasant, and patient, was, by contrast, a sign of detachment from the world. If Battista da Crema stated that "he who has not purged well his eye and has not become cleansed and pure of heart cannot contemplate God,"[72] Serafino da Fermo echoed him, saying that the aim of ascetic life was to remove the obstacles that separate man from the operation of grace: "to purge the soul from vice, and scorn every taste and sentiment because every time this is obtained . . . we will not be able to contain the impetus of divine grace which descends copiously in us."[73] The close relationship between inner purification and divine encounter found its most systematic expression in the *Spiritual Exercises* of Ignatius Loyola: "By the term 'Spiritual Exercises' is meant every method of examination of conscience, of meditation, of contemplation, of vocal and mental prayer, and of other spiritual activities that will be mentioned later . . . every way of preparing and disposing the soul to rid itself of all inordinate attachments, and, after their removal, of seeking and finding the will of God in the disposition of our life for the salvation of our soul."[74]

This philosophy also informed the meaning of other religious concepts such as religious "poverty" and "obedience." Battista da Crema intended the concept of "poverty" precisely to mean of spir-

71. *Statuti,* 23, in ibid., 215.

72. Battista da Crema, *Specchio interiore,* f. 95v, in Gentili and Regazzoni, *La spiritualità,* 106.

73. Cited in Marcocchi, *La Riforma Cattolica,* I:177.

74. Ignacio de Loyola, *Exercicios spirituales, Annotaciones,* 3.

itual detachment rather than paucity of goods: "And note that this virtue [poverty] is the summum of perfection. But this does not consist in having nothing . . . it consists (as the Gospel says) in poverty of spirit in order to have a free mind to think only of the crucified Christ and conform to the other virtues."[75] The rule of the Company of the Buon Gesù states that spiritual detachment (or spiritual "poverty") also consists in placing one's affections not in friends and worldly things but only in God: "place all one's trust in God, not in relatives, not in friends, nor in things of this world."[76] The concept of "obedience" in the rule of the Barnabites had precisely this meaning: obedience was necessary in order to suppress self-will toward secular attachments.[77] And, as Angela's confessor, Serafino da Bologna explains self-will as an obstacle to spiritual life: "But if you wish to follow and hold your own will, everything will be against you and will resist you and negate you. But certainly if you leave and mortify perfectly your own will for love of me, you will enjoy true inner peace, and will feel great contentment and consolation and serenity."[78]

The Importance of the "Will"

Within a religious model in which the road to perfection is individual and interiorized and is conceived outside institutional structures and rituals, personal commitment is essential. The concept of "will" as the effort to pursue a life of perfection was thus a common feature of these spiritual writers and in particular of Battista da Crema who, for this reason, was accused of Pelagianism: "Be sure, my Lord, that in my soul you will be safe; don't you know that human will is almost omnipotent, and that it can only be surpassed by itself?"[79] In his *Della cognitione et vittoria di se stesso*, Battista

---

75. Battista da Crema, *Via de aperta verità*, f. 9r.

76. *Alcune regole*, 12.

77. Bonora, *I conflitti della Controriforma*, 233–34.

78. Serafino da Bologna, *Pharetra divini amoris*, f. 331r.

79. Battista da Crema, *Philosophia divina*, f. 127r, in Petrocchi, *Storia della spiritualità*.

urged the fight against *tiepidezza* and *accidia* (laziness in spiritual life), the most dangerous of all sins: "I answer tepidity, her mother being sloth, who, for having been idle, was made pregnant by the devil."[80] The Barnabites' rule made the same claim: one must avoid worldly distractions since the devil conquers the *distratti,* the "absentminded." The members of the order must have their spiritual goal constantly in mind: "In travel as elsewhere avoid, my Brothers, *distraction and curiosity,* knowing that the Devil does not commonly win, unless it is over the heedless."[81] Serafino da Fermo, too, in his *Quarantadue problemi circa l'oratione* (1518), asserted that those who are not committed in their spiritual life are worse than those who never had one: "those who one time engaged in prayer, and then grew cold, become worse than those who never started . . . the tepid person gives God greater displeasure than the cold one."[82]

For this reason inner commitment to the search for God must always be pursued: "if we want to fulfill this undertaking, we must first make a strong and obstinate resolution that we wish to be unmovable in this inner exercise."[83] The emphasis on the will in the pursuit of a truly religious life is also present in a letter Gaetano da Thiene wrote to Laura Mignani. He advised the Brescian mystic not to rest, though already enlightened by God: "But you must not be content with this . . . and as one who is relentless always seek it in order not to fall into the abominable sin of sluggishness."[84]

Contact with God

Finally, in this spiritual current contact with God, too, was described in its inner dimension. According to the Battuti, God lives

---

80. Battista da Crema, *Della cognitione et vittoria di se stesso,* f. 141v, in Marcocchi, *La Riforma Cattolica,* I:256.

81. The only condition for entering the Barnabites' company was the commitment of the soul, while exterior, physical weakness ("li debili, o infermi, o vecchi") was not a limiting condition (*Costituzioni,* XI, in Premoli, *Storia dei Barnabiti,* 436).

82. *Problema trigesimoprimo,* in *Quarantadue problemi circa l'oratione,* 261.

83. *Trattato utilissimo,* in *Opere spirituali,* in Marcocchi, *La Riforma Cattolica,* I:181.

84. In Andreu, *Le lettere di San Gaetano da Thiene,* 30.

in man's heart and mind and guides human action: "You are God's temple and the holy spirit dwells in you. *May the altar be our heart and mind,* where every good action is offered to God. On this altar the fire of divine love must always burn, in other words the mind must be disposed to every request and wish of his Lord."[85] In the rule of the Company of Divine Love, union with God is reached by inner conversion—in particular, affection and mental prayer: "And since prayer and devotion are what unite us with God and render us impetrated with every grace . . . *let us turn our heart* to God and *offer it to him mentally* with great affection of heart, and pray to him that he make it walk all day according to his approval."[86] Serafino da Fermo refused a religious life based on exterior ceremonies and located true spiritual life in an inner attitude: "because you seek in exterior ceremonies what you can possess inwardly . . . looking with great diligence at the heart, that it be always united with God."[87]

In conclusion, the spiritual writers of the early sixteenth century promoted a notion of a perfect life founded more on individual and inner attitudes and less on exterior rituals. Conversion was realized through purification of the heart, not through institutional means; penance was conceived of as mortification of self-will, not flesh; and contact with God was mental and intimate, not vocal and collective.

Angela Merici's Inner Spirituality

Merici's religious ideal mirrors many traits of the spiritual logic. Angela's rule privileges the devout principles that promote an inner and individual experience of the sacred and reject exterior structures and ceremonies and interweaves them in an extremely logical and original way.

85. *Statuti,* I, in Marcocchi, *La Riforma Cattolica,* I:204.
86. *Capitoli,* VIIII, in ibid., 223.
87. Serafino da Fermo, *Trattato utilissimo,* in *Opere spirituali,* 20, in ibid., 179.

Penance and Prayer

As with the devotio moderna and sixteenth-century spiritual writers, in Angela's spirituality the importance of the inner conversion of the individual emerges in the pursuit of penance and prayer. Here the ritual and exterior is considered marginal and accessory to the predisposition to a life of the spirit. Although Merici engaged in penitential practices, they did not occupy a central place in her spirituality. In fact, as we have seen, she recommended caution and warned of the danger of excessive fasting (*Reg.,* IV). Angela distinguished between corporal and spiritual fasting and made it clear that the function of abstinence from food is to attain spiritual abstinence, that is, independence from the things of the world. If corporal fasting is a means, spiritual fasting is an existential condition: "Embrace bodily fasting as something necessary, and as a means and way to true spiritual fasting through which all the vices and errors are cut away from the mind . . . fasting and abstinence be the source and means of all our spiritual good and profit" (*Reg.,* IV).

As we have already seen in the texts of Angela's contemporaries, another issue for those who prized inner devotion, not outward rituals, is the contrast between "vocal" and "mental" prayer. Angela Merici made a clear distinction between the two and stressed how union with God takes place through mental prayer. Vocal prayer is also important but is a means to prepare the Ursuline for spiritual life: "Just as by fasting one mortifies the appetites of one's flesh and one's own feelings, so by prayer one obtains from God the grace of a spiritual life. And although one needs always to pray in spirit and mind, given the continuous need one has of God's help . . . nevertheless we also advise frequent vocal prayer, through which the bodily senses are awakened and one disposes oneself for mental prayer" (*Reg.,* V).

Evangelical Counsels as Virtuous Behavior

As Angela explained at the beginning of her rule, the life in union with God the company proposed implied separation from secular life. However, the company had no convent and the Ursulines followed the rule in the secular world: because separation from the world was invested with a spiritual significance rather than a material one. Angela proposed a worldly detachment and celestial union that must stem from the conversion of the Ursuline's inner self. In her rule the pursuit of the evangelical counsels of poverty, obedience, and virginity have precisely this meaning.

As we have seen with Battista da Crema, in Angela's rule the precept of poverty refers to spiritual or inner detachment from worldly things—from the possibilities offered by secular life, from worldly affections, and from self: "Finally, we exhort each one to embrace poverty, not only effective poverty of temporal things, but above all the true poverty of spirit by which man strips his heart of all affection and loving for created things, and of his very self" (*Reg.,* X). Angela enlarged on this concept by explaining its meaning, which referred to the Ursuline's real everyday life. The Ursuline should depend neither on her own needs nor on human relationships with relatives and friends. Instead, Angela asked the Ursuline to place all her expectations and affection in God alone: "And so, let each one strive to strip herself of everything, and to place all her wealth, and love, and delight, not in goods, not in food and gluttony, not in relatives and friends, not in herself and in her own resources and knowledge, but in God alone and in his gentle and ineffable Providence alone" (*Reg.,* X).

The Ursuline must abandon herself to this celestial relationship in every aspect of her life. She must not impose her will in an attempt to satisfy her secular needs (such as hunger, thirst, and sleep), since God would provide for her sustenance: "Seek first the kingdom of God, and all these other things of yours will be set before you . . . do not be anxious in seeking what you will have to eat or what you will have to drink, because your heavenly Father knows very well that you have need of all these things . . . do not trouble yourself about any of your temporal needs, because God, and he alone, knows, can and will provide for them; He who wants nothing for you but only your good and your joy" (*Reg.,* X).

After all, the concept of poverty depicts an existential conversion. It portrays the religious dimension in which the Ursuline lives: detached from the world and in union with God. Outside this union the Ursuline is *totalmente un niente,* "a total nothing," "does not exist": "And in God she has all her wealth; and apart from God sees herself to be completely poor, and a total nothing, and with God to have everything." Therefore, poverty is not an external perfect condition existing in itself (for example, as renunciation of a specific aspect of life, such as wealth). Detachment from material possessions follows from spiritual freedom from the secular world as an inevitable consequence of an inner attitude.

Spiritual detachment from the world was also at the center of the concept of obedience. Obedience was seen as a means to free the Ursuline's will from the material world. Angela considered the will toward secular ends as deleterious and asked the Ursuline to renounce it through obedience: "We also exhort each one to keep *holy obedience, the only true abnegation of self-will,* which is in us like a dark hell" (*Reg.,* VIII). Consequently, the Ursuline must obey everybody and, in particular, all her associates and superiors: the church, the bishop, her spiritual father, the governors of the company, her parents and superiors in the house, and civic law and God's commandments (*Reg.,* VIII).

The ideal of detachment from the world as transformation of the "inner self" was fully expressed in the ideal of virginity, not limited to just sexual abstinence (as in the rules of most other orders) but embracing a wider range of the soul's inclinations. Virginity entailed inner purity, involving behavior, thoughts, and feelings that expressed having placed one's love in God: "And so, above all, keep the heart pure and the conscience clear of any evil thought, of any shadow of envy and ill will, of any discord and evil suspicion, and of any other wicked desire and purpose . . . . Not answering haughtily. Not doing anything grudgingly. Not staying angry. Not grumbling. Not repeating any malicious gossip" (*Reg.,* VIIII); "Above all let them be humble and gentle" (*Ric.,* 5). Love for God implies virtuous behavior: the absence of envy, discord, suspicion, haughtiness, anger, ill will, gossip. As in the spiritual literature discussed above, here detachment from the world is achieved through the refusal of those feelings that attach us to the material world. As in the writings of Battista da Crema and Serafino da Fermo, in Angela's rule freedom from worldly preoccupations allows the Ursuline to hear God's voice more clearly: "He [God] whose voice we shall hear all the more clearly as we have our conscience more purified and clean" (*Reg.,* VIII).

The Will, Vows, and Obligation

As we have seen so far, the absence of the convent, the evangelical counsels, fasting, and prayer shows how in Angela's rule the Ursuline fulfills her religious conversion through inner detachment from the world and the projection of self in God, rather than through participation in institutional structures or exterior behavior. The centrality of inner conversion and the marginality of the exterior religious life emerge also in connection with the importance of will. Angela's concept of will resembles that of Battista da Crema.

In Angela Merici's writings the "will" *(volere/volontà)* was key for the religious life. First, the will was a condition for entry into the company: "she must enter joyfully and *of her own will*" (*Reg.,* I). Though this condition shows Angela's preoccupation with the coercion of girls into monasteries, indubitably the volontà had a specific place within her theology, and it is significant that we find it at the beginning of the Ursuline's life.

Moreover, the will is at the center of one of the most radical traits of Merici's spirituality. The Ursuline's conversion was sanctioned not by the profession of vows but by her will, a human element that depends only on inner commitment: "Each one should also preserve sacred virginity, *not making a vow on account of any human persuasion, but voluntarily* making to God the sacrifice of her own heart" (*Reg.,* VIII). The absence of vows fit Angela's vision of a human and individual relationship with God created by inner conversion and not mediated by the sacralization of exterior structures.

Angela's rule reflected her theological principles very consistently. Note, for instance, how the will of the Ursuline replaces the obligation to carry out the precepts of the rule. A statistical linguistic analysis of the rule shows that she used the word *volere* (want, wish, desire) sixty-two times and the word *dovere* (must, ought) three times. The extensive use of the verb *sforzarsi* (to make an effort, to strive) and *esortare* (to exhort) also testify to the involvement of the Ursuline's will. Thus, the Ursuline managed her religious life without the mediation of an "obligation." Angela considered the will of the Ursuline in every possible circumstance involving the life of the Bride of Christ. It was not sufficient for Ursulines to "carry out" what was prescribed in the rule, for they should "want" to do so. This applied, for example, to the practice of spiritual poverty ("Let each one *strive* to strip herself of everything, and place all her wealth . . . in God alone" [*Reg.,* X]), physical fasting ("Each one should be *willing* to embrace bodily fasting" [*Reg.,* IV]), vocal prayer ("Each one *will* say[88] everyday at least the office of Our Lady" [*Reg.,* V]), confession ("*Willingly* present herself before the priest . . . confess her sin" [*Reg.,* V]), and obedience ("We *exhort* each one to keep holy obedience" [*Reg.,* VIII]). Angela required of the Ursulines an active attitude toward spiritual life. The same applied to every other aspect of their existence—life in the world ("wherever they are *may they wish* to give a good example" [*Ric.,* 5]), the organization of the company ("*May* the Company [decide] to congregate" [*Reg.,* XI]) and the duties of the Colonelle ("*May* you frequently decide . . . to go and visit your daughters" [*Ric.,* 5]). Finally, the Ursuline's will replaced the external structures of the company and undergirded its unity: "And tell them that they should want to be united and in concord together" (*Ric.,* 5); "See then how

88. *Voglia dire,* in the Italian original.

important is this union and concord. So, long for it, pursue it, embrace it, hold on to it with all your strength; for I tell you, living all together thus united in heart, you will be like a mighty fortress and tower impregnable against all adversities, and prosecutions, and deceits of the devil" (*Ric.,* Last.).

Since Angela required the individual's will in accepting the religious life, she tries to convince her sisters of the utility of the rule rather than impose it: "Therefore, my sisters, I exhort you, or rather I beg and entreat you all, that having been thus chosen to be the true and virginal spouses of the Son of God, you be willing first of all to recognize" (*Reg.,* Prologue). The rule did not dictate strict rules but exemplified, inspired, exhorted, warned, and directed. It was written to be read often: Angela prescribed that the Ursulines occasionally meet and discuss the rule and compare their own behavior with it. Her pedagogy, too, was based on the encounter between God's grace and the Ursuline's will. She explained to the Matrone: "And above all, be on your guard not to want to get anything done by force; because God has given the free will to everyone, and wants to force no one, but only proposes, invites and counsels" (*Tes.,* 3).

Differences between Angela Merici and Contemporary Spiritual Writers

In Angela's rule this spiritual logic results in an institutional outcome possibly more radical than anything found in the other institutions discussed above. Angela did not contemplate the convent, vows, and habit; she codified the practice of virtue in the evangelical counsels; and, in prescribing religious life, she substituted obedience with the individual's will. By contrast, the religious models emerging from the rules of the Clerks Regular included some exterior aspects of cult such as vows, the habit, and some life in common. Furthermore, the evangelical counsels were considered in their traditional sense (renunciation of possessions, sexual abstinence, and obedience to superiors), and the inner dimension was covered by the requirement that members participate inwardly (that is, not think about sexual acts or desire possessions and obey both outwardly and inwardly). Finally, the rules of the Company of Divine Love and of the Jesuits lay more stress on externality in respect to the hierarchy and obedience.[89]

The most significant difference between Merici and her contemporaries, however, consisted in Angela's greater emphasis on the relationship with God. The spirituality of the Clerks Regular and ascetic writers stressed more the battle against the self that purified the devout individual.

The tendency to focus on human behavior rather than on supernatural contact was already present in the spirituality of the devotio moderna. The devotio moderna was less based on magic power and much more critical of the miraculous aspects of religion (such as visions, prophecies, healing, and the like) than was medieval spirituality—for instance, Francis of Assisi or Catherine of Siena. Furthermore, as several studies have pointed out, although colloquy with God and pursuit of his will in the world were the goal of the purification of self in the spiritual model of the devotio moderna, great stress still fell on the fight against the will, against vanity, haughtiness, and man's vicious nature.[90] The devotio moderna proposed a human perfection that amounted to a set of moral values.[91]

89. The same could be said about the rule of the Theatines. By contrast, hierarchy and obedience were not emphasized by the Barnabites. Lack of exterior structures also characterized the Company of the Buon Gesù. This, however, did not offer a life of consecration but a series of spiritual principles to be followed.

90. Picasso, "L'imitazione di Cristo," 270–71. A language analysis of the main text of the devotio moderna, the *Imitation of Christ,* has suggested that the emphasis is more on repression of self rather than on union with God. In this book 419 words refer to the spiritual fight; 256 to humility; 138 to spiritual consolation; 108 to inner peace; and 64 to the imitation of Christ (Debongnie, "Les thèmes de l'Imitation"). Also, Brezzi affirmed that the most appropriate title for the Imitation of Christ would have been "Il combattimento spirituale" (the spiritual fight): "La spiritualità della 'devotio moderna.'"

91. Tolomio, "Il primato dell'etica nella spiritualità della 'devotio moderna.'" As

The same position was taken by the authors of the new religious rules and ascetic writings, who viewed supernatural phenomena with increasing suspicion and tended to read spiritual life as a battle against vice. Although contact with God is their aim in self-repression, Battista da Crema and Serafino da Fermo concentrate on the effort to quell vices. This model was chiefly expressed in Battista da Crema's ideal of will, which hastens man through spiritual combat toward perfection. The Barnabites, who incarnated the ideals of this Dominican friar, were devoted mainly to the refinement of the individual through fight against vice.[92] The same attitude can be traced in the writings of Gaetano da Thiene. Though Gaetano declared that purification of the heart is necessary in order to follow Christ's will, the repression of self is clearly central: "I wish that Jesus would swiftly purify my heart so as to no longer rebel against his will, for certainly I now only desire to always be where and how it pleases him; because *in this obedience and death of myself lies the glory of my creator,* and souls are purified not in affective fervour but only in effective fervour."[93]

With the Jesuits' *Spiritual Exercises,* control of self and purification from weaknesses became a scientific method. Here the search for perfection was a way both for preparing man for contact with God and for praising and pleasing him. The centrality of virtue also appears in Erasmus's religiosity. Erasmus's *Enchiridion* consisted mainly in a thorough analysis of the weaknesses of human nature: by following the rules for dealing with them, the individual could achieve true Christian life. Here the aim was no longer a

---

Weiler has noted, the emphasis on self-control appealed to the middle classes (merchants, doctors, etc.) in their attempt to progress in virtue and improve their position in the secular world ("Il significato della devotio moderna").

92. The Barnabites were engaged in a process of "discussion and action" that consisted of several phases: analysis of individual weaknesses, establishment of the necessary remedies during the discussions in common *(collatione),* and extirpation of faults (especially through self-humiliation and renunciation of honor). See Bonora, *I conflitti della Controriforma,* esp. 170–83, 212–24.

93. Andreu, *Le lettere di San Gaetano da Thiene,* 30–31.

mystical status, as perfection (being a "good Christian") coincided with virtue.

Finally, within this spirituality the relationship with God was mediated by a spiritual father, a figure who, in the course of this period, became central to the devout life. Following Battista da Crema, Serafino da Fermo affirmed that to avoid pride one should submit to a spiritual father: "because it is the custom of the truly humble person, in order to flee from every danger of his own reputation, to wish to be governed by the *counsel of others* rather than through his own revelation."[94] Similarly, the rule of Buon Gesù recommended revealing one's thoughts to one's spiritual father for support in the fight against sin: "reveal all his thoughts to his spiritual father, because in this way the devil loses all his strength."[95] And the spiritual father was an essential in Loyola's *Spiritual Exercises,* as these were not supposed to be practiced without an experienced guide.

Angela does not share this view of religious perfection and relationship with God. Angela's writings stressed not the improvement of self but union with God. As we have seen, Merici's spirituality was highly mystical, emphasizing fusion with the divine and constant contact with the transcendent. Obedience to God's will focused not on the annihilation of self-will but on the actual contact between the Holy Spirit's counsel and the Ursuline's heart. And the relationship with God was not mediated by the spiritual father. Furthermore, Angela's idea of the relationship with the supernatural foresaw the presence of God in human actions and granted a role to the Ursulines in the mediation of God's power. Spiritual poverty, obedience, and virginity were hardly ascetic techniques that detached the believer from secular values before contact with

94. Serafino da Fermo, *Vita di due beatissime donne Margherita e Gentile,* in *Opere,* ff. 403v–4r, in Colosio, "Serafino da Fermo," 249.

95. However, if they did not find one who suited them, they could only confess (*Alcune regole,* ch. 11).

God. Rather, they described the existential dimension in which the Ursuline lived: detached from the world and in union with God. Angela described the Bride of Christ as an existential condition. The suppression of secular will or the practice of virtuous behavior reflected a status vitae; it was not its precondition.

Angela Merici emphasized the relationship with God at the expense of spiritual combat and jettisoned exterior aspects more radically than did her contemporaries because mysticism and indifference to the institutional side of religion marked the female approach to the sacred. The next chapter will conclude this analysis of the spirituality of Angela Merici and her contemporary spiritual milieu by examining the cultural context in which they developed.

CHAPTER 5

Holy Women, Modern Individuals

SPIRITUALITY, SELF, AND GENDER

This chapter seeks to establish a connection between spiritual models and the cultural context of Renaissance Italy. The stress that Angela Merici and contemporaneous writers of rules and ascetic manuals placed on inner spirituality can be discussed in relation to Renaissance notions of the individual. The perception that societies have of the "self" changes over time, and it has been made the subject of fruitful historical inquiries. The concept of the self in Angela's times was inherited from the Middle Ages. Increasingly, the self was perceived as unique, with a complex interiority, and as the agent of its own deeds. These traits have been associated with the development of a "modern" view of the individual.[1]

Historiography has discussed the growth of these views mainly with an eye to medieval theology, humanist literature and philosophy, Renaissance art and society, and the Protestant Reformation, but has said very little about late-fifteenth- and early-sixteenth-century Catholic spirituality. This neglect can be partly explained by the legacy of a historiographical tradition that labeled it with an "antimodern" character (in opposition to a "modern" Protestant

---

1. The "modernity" of the medieval or Renaissance self does not consist in the fact that it is like our own, but that some of its fundamental aspects developed in the early modern and modern times and contributed to the emergence of new worldviews.

Reformation). This ideological pattern, however, has recently been questioned by a historiography that has viewed Tridentine institutions and their impact on society as an expression of a process of modernization paralleling that of the Protestant churches.[2] I argue that a similar parallelism can be established from the perspective of spirituality. The trend toward individualization, interiorization, and moralization emerging within Catholic spirituality—as in the case of Protestant piety—should be framed within a cultural process in which a new understanding of the human being and its position in the universe was developing.

In her writings, Angela Merici allowed the Ursulines to live a profound experience of their personhood. Merici's case suggests, therefore, that women in the religious domain could experience a concept of the self that in many respects was "modern." To answer Joan Kelly's famous question, "Did women have a Renaissance?" it could be said that women had a Renaissance "self" in the religious domain.[3] Such experience of the self within religion, however, was not exclusive to Renaissance women, as individual and inner perceptions of this concept began to emerge from the twelfth century. Around the mid-sixteenth century, at least in Italy, women's chances for subjectivity within religion began to decline, because the conditions that fostered female sanctity waned. Such a development was reflected in the evolution of the Company of St. Ursula after Merici's death. In the first part of this chapter, I will briefly outline the development of some aspects of the concept of the self in the Middle Ages and in the Renaissance in order to subsequently evaluate them in relation to the writings of the new religious orders, confraternities, ascetic writers, and, finally, of Angela Merici. In the second part I provide an epilogue to the book that deals with the evolution of Angela's company.

2. Reinhard, "Reformation, Counter-Reformation, and the Early Modern State"; Prodi, *Disciplina dell'anima*; Hsia, *The World of Catholic Renewal.*

3. Kelly, "Did Women Have a Renaissance?"

Perceptions of the Self in the Middle Ages
and in the Renaissance

Recent studies have modified Jacob Burckhardt's groundbreaking hypothesis that placed the beginning of individuality and inner introspection in Renaissance Italy.[4] Scholars have pointed out that from the eleventh century on, one finds examples of psychological introspection and of the conceptualization of man as an individual rather than a member of a group.[5] As Benton stated, "In the century and a half which included the lives of Gregory VII and Francis of Assisi there did occur . . . a renewed commitment to the examination of the inner life and a development of modes of thought about the self and others which have profoundly affected our civilization."[6]

Thus, if we examine a variety of medieval sources expressing re-

4. Burckhardt, in *The Civilization of the Renaissance in Italy*, maintained that in Renaissance Italy man freed himself from medieval ecclesiastical and knightly schemes and asserted himself in the world with his individual capacities, creating a new society in his image and likeness. While in the Middle Ages man defined himself in respect to collective identities such as race, state, family, and guilds, in the Renaissance man became an "individual" with autonomous will, complex psychology, and self-awareness. According to Burckhardt, Renaissance man signaled the emergence of modernity and in particular of the modern individual. Burckhardt's theory, extremely influential in the first half of the twentieth century, in the last thirty years has been criticized very seriously from a variety of perspectives. Here, it is not my intention to review the criticism of Burckhardt's theory of the individual, but to discuss some of the new developments concerning the concept of the self in relation to Renaissance Catholicism.

5. These include Southern, *The Making of the Middle Ages*; Bynum, "Did the Twelfth Century Discover the Individual?" in *Jesus as Mother*, 82–109; Benton, *Culture, Power, and Personality*; Magli, *Gli uomini della penitenza*. Recently, Barbara H. Rosenwein has maintained that an awareness of self and of an "emotional" self existed already in the early Middle Ages ("Y avait-il un 'moi' au haut Moyen Âge?"). A very influential contribution was Greenblatt's *Renaissance Self-Fashioning*, which proposed an image of the Renaissance self as "fragmented and divided" and as a product of socioeconomic and political power. This view was also followed by Hale *(Civilization of Europe in the Renaissance)*. Martin *(Myths of Renaissance Individualism)* illustrates the variety of Renaissance identities and how the refashioning of certain religious and civic ideals helped to shape a more individual self.

6. Benton, "Consciousness of Self and Perceptions of Individuality," in *Culture, Power, and Personality*, 328.

ligious sentiment and doctrine (manuals, iconography, rituals, and devotions), we find that they attest to the growing importance of individualism, interiority, and human life in general. For example, from the eleventh century on, the artistic representations of Christ increasingly emphasized his humanity: unlike Byzantines, who depicted Christ as judge or king, artists began to represent him in significant events of his life, such as birth, childhood, suffering, and death.[7] Feelings (affection, love, sorrow) were central to the religious experience of men such as Bernard of Clairvaux and Francis of Assisi and of women such as Mary of Oignes.[8] Hagiographical accounts began to feature the individual life and virtues of the saints rather than exclusively their magical powers.[9] Furthermore, from the twelfth century on, monks were encouraged to live mystic marriage as a personal experience of the divine, and theologians developed complex psychological portraits of the human soul in its mystical ascent toward God.[10] Within monasticism the communal dimension declined, while more individual forms of life were brought in: the monastic vow (seen more as an individual pact between the monk and God) substituted for the *promissio* (addressed to the religious community);[11] private property and individual rooms were introduced in the Benedectine order; and new hermitic congregations, such as the Celestines, emerged.[12] Lay piety displayed an individual and inner relationship with God, too: though the collective and ritualistic experience of the sacred was still important, as in confraternities, a direct and personal relation-

7. Cousins, "The Humanity and the Passion of Christ." Fulton *(From Judgment to Passion)* argues that praying to the crucified Christ and Mary "forced medieval Christians to forge new tools with which to *feel*" (197).

8. For example, Leclercq, *La spiritualité au Moyen Age*, 283–29.

9. I.e., Vauchez, *La sainteté in Occident*.

10. Benton, "Consciousness of Self and Perceptions of Individuality." Other frequently quoted examples testifying to the importance of interiority in the Middle Ages include Peter Abelard's ethics, which emphasized the intention rather than the deed, and Aelred of Rievaulx's concept of friendship, viewed as an inner experience.

11. Prodi, *Il sacramento del potere*, 134–36.

12. Lawrence, *Medieval Monasticism*, 351–59.

ship between man and Christ, consisting in personal and intimate dialogues, came to the forefront. In addition, through hermitism and penance, the individual (either religious or lay) could reach salvation without the mediation of the church.[13] Finally, throughout the Middle Ages, the church promoted an individual and inner experience of the sacraments, especially communion and confession, at the expense of their collective and social dimension.[14]

If medieval piety shows increasing attention to individuality and interiority, externality and collectivity were also important. For example, in religious life and theory we find concepts emphasizing exteriority, such as "model," "example," "imitation," gestures, and rituals. The *Imitatio Christi* was based mainly on exterior and visible elements such as poverty, fasting, flagellation, stigmata, and preaching.[15] Interiority and exteriority were not clearly distinguished, since people tended to believe that through exterior acts (such as penance) the inner side of an individual followed his external conversion. Theologians promoted a concept of the person as a "psychosomatic unity," as body and soul together.[16] Furthermore, individualism and human agency were subordinated to an ideal of universal harmony that linked men among themselves and with the divine will.[17]

Scholars have shown that concerns with interiority further devel-

13. Magli, *Gli uomini della penitenza*, 101–5.

14. Bossy, "The Social History of Confession." In the Middle Ages confession was a social institution aimed at recomposing social conflicts. Gradually, however, it became a central religious practice used for controlling and inspiring individuals. The minute examination of conscience, the interiorization of sins, and the intimacy of self-revelation changed the focus of confession from satisfaction to contrition, from social sin to hidden guilt, from family, kinship, and the community to individual soul. However, this model had a limited impact in the rural areas.

15. Bynum, "Did the Twelfth Century Discover the Individual?"

16. Bynum, *Fragmentation and Redemption*, 222–23. See also Magli, *Gli uomini della penitenza*, 36–38. The association of objectivity and subjectivity in the ritual act is a mechanism that has been studied by anthropologists in connection with "primitive" cultures (for example, Lévy-Bruhl, *Le surnaturel et la nature dans la mèntalité primitive*).

17. Martin, *Myths of Renaissance Individualism*, 103–22.

oped in the Renaissance. This can be observed, for example, in the deep psychological analyses conveyed in Renaissance writings (from Petrarch's *Secretum* to Shakespeare's *Hamlet*), in the diffusion of portraits and self-portraits, and in early modern "good manners," which focused on the soul of the individual rather than on his body.[18] The novelty of the Renaissance concept of self, however, was above all the perception of the relationship between the inner and outer aspects of individuals: the two poles were increasingly viewed as separate, and the inner (thoughts and feelings) took central stage since it was seen as responsible for the exterior (words and deeds). For example, the theme of "dissimulation" emerged in treatises on the life of courtiers,[19] and the term *sincere* became very popular in French and Italian literature. As Burke puts it: "Like the literature on simulation and dissimulation, the rise of the new term suggests that people were becoming more aware of the difference between an inner and an outer self, a difference which was given its classic formulation by Descartes at the end of the period in his famous contrast between mind and body."[20] Furthermore, Renaissance medical practice began to conceive the body as separated from the soul and to understand it not through a spiritual and theological significance, but as operating according to the laws of mechanics.[21] In addition, the Protestant Reformation, which denied the role of the church in mediating salvation, placed greater responsibility on the personal commitment of the individual: "One no longer belonged to the saved, to the people of God, by one's connection to a wider order sustaining a sacramental life, but by one's wholehearted personal adhesion."[22] Finally, Martin argued that first nominalism (from Ockham on) and then Luther criticized the medieval idea of *concordia,* the idea of likeness

18. Knox, «Disciplina.»

19. Villari, *Elogio della dissimulazione.*

20. Burke, "Representation of the Self," 20. On "sincerity," see also Martin, *Myths of Renaissance Individualism,* 103–22.

21. Sawday, *The Body Emblazoned.*

22. Taylor, *Sources of the Self,* 217.

between man and God, between the inner and the outer self, and among men. This intellectual shift promoted a new way of understanding human beings, "one that placed greater stress on the internal self as agent or subject, as director of one's words and deeds."[23] Individuals were thus increasingly perceived as unique beings, characterized by a distinctive humanity, detached from a universal community of souls, responsible for their own deeds and guided by their internal selves.

Renaissance Catholic Spirituality and the Notion of the Self

The spirituality of Renaissance Catholicism reflected these developing views of the self. As we have seen in chapter 4, at the beginning of sixteenth century the new religious orders and confraternities, as well as ascetic writers and humanists, promoted a religious model that increasingly focused on individuality, interiority, and morality in an extremely articulated manner. First, inner life was central to the religious experience, while exterior, ceremonial, and bodily aspects were marginal. Relationship with God was described as an inner event, as it was lived in mind and heart. Real conversion was identified with purity of heart; indifference toward the shocks of secular life, such as insults and injustice; and a charitable disposition of soul. Exterior bodily discipline was subordinated to the fight against human weaknesses; mental prayer was preferred to collective and vocal prayer, and without inner involvement the latter lost meaning. Detachment from the world was above all interior; it needed no physical separation but demanded the abandonment of personal self-will. Such religiosity opened up a range of new obstacles on the road to perfection, due to inner resistance to the transformation of self. For this reason, Erasmus of Rotterdam, Battista da Crema, and Serafino da Fermo laid out particularly accurate maps of human vices and of the psychological battle to

23. Martin, *Myths of Renaissance Individualism*, 113.

keep one's mind aloft on spiritual things. According to Serafino da Fermo, the inner mechanisms of the human mind are responsible for the weaknesses of human nature: "The reason for this is, I believe, principally in corrupt and downward inclined nature, much aggravated by many passions . . . this difficulty because of the natural mobility of our imagination, which constantly follows now one thing, now another, and never rests, even while sleeping, as is shown in our confused dreams, and therefore without virtuous exercise it cannot be tied to the consideration of one object alone."[24] Religious writers' careful psychological analyses and portraits of character types testify to the stress on individuals and on inner life. The spirituality of the devotio moderna (through the Imitation of Christ) and of the Jesuits (with the Spiritual Exercises) played an important role in the development of modern introspection.[25]

Second, the individual was given much more responsibility in attaining righteous status. The quest for perfection was pursued individually—rather than collectively—as it emerges in several religious practices, such as in the Barnabites' Collatione and in the Jesuits' practice of the Spiritual Exercises, which enabled the individual to examine personal faults and to device ad hoc strategies to overcome them. Institutional forms of religion, such as monastic life, and communal activities, such as Divine Office in choir, were less central in or even absent from the life of the new religious orders. According to humanists and the writers of ascetic manuals, a life of religious perfection could flourish in the secular world without vows and ceremonies. Salvation was no longer a given fact attainable in a certain and definite way—it must include the acquisition of virtue, an aim to be pursued at an individual level. Conversion was an existential status to be sought in every moment of one's life. This is why *tiepidezza* and laziness were so frequently discussed as sins. To

24. Serafino da Fermo, *Trattato utilissimo,* in *Opere spirituali,* ff. 27–28, in Marcocchi, *La Riforma Cattolica,* 181.

25. For the devotio moderna, see Weiler, "Il significato della devotio moderna per la cultura europea."

be sure, the majority of these Catholic writers did not reject sacramental life, rituals, and monastic life, but they placed personal commitment at the center of religious life. Similarly to the Protestant believer, the Catholic follower of this spirituality is given more responsibilities and is—de facto—on his or her own in front of God striving for perfection. The idea of self endorsed here, thus, is one emphasising individuality, agency, and interiority.

Finally, in this spirituality, the new notion of the individual yielded an outlook that often stressed human behavior rather than contact with God. The idea of the self endorsed by male ascetic writers ultimately affirmed an idea of the human "per se." As we have seen in chapter 4, in the spiritual ascent described by ascetic writers and religious rules contemporaneous with Angela, contact with God was the final step on a path of self-purification, attained through mental prayer and marked by the perfect repression of self. It was a process, however, that focused on the path, on the search for perfection. The experience of the supernatural, through visions and mystic encounter, was less stressed and even viewed with suspicion. Within this spiritual logic God tended to become more distant, the authority that justified the spiritual battle against vice and the pursuit of proper behavior. Consequently, religious perfection was represented mainly by a set of moral virtues.

Behind this religious model lay a concept of "human" that shared much with the humanist philosophical tradition. Some humanists asserted that God created man in his image and likeness in his ability to rule over the things of the world. In the exercise of will, intellect, and actions, man plays a divine role and ultimately becomes like God.[26] This concept appears in the work of Battista da Crema, who claimed that man has within himself "the perfection of the entire world, of every creature, and also of God."[27] According to Battista da Crema, "through grace and industry" man can be-

26. Trinkaus, *In Our Image and Likeness.*
27. Battista da Crema, *Via di aperta verità,* in Grendler, "Man Is Almost a God," 237.

come more perfect than the angels and similar to God. Man stands between higher and lower things, between divine and animal nature. If man overcomes his most vile nature, repressing it by intellect and constant effort, he becomes similar to God and even comes to know things beyond human understanding: "To God by nature all things are present and manifest, occult things are manifested to man through his industry. Just as God operates with ease and does not feel difficulty because of his omnipotent power, so man because of his magnanimity does great things. Because he is almost omnipotent, in overcoming himself, which is almost every thing. And in this way he vanquishes himself and operates, for arduous things and which appeared impossible have become pleasing and easy."[28] Battista seemed thus to affirm that by repressing weakness man can become like God. Man can become a "Perfect" and rise above the rest of humankind (an ideal that Battista promoted in the Barnabite order). The underlying implication was that man's perfection could be obtained independently from God. Here this spirituality endorsed a concept of "individual" that existed in itself, even if within a sacral dimension of life.

This concept of the individual should be viewed as the religious equivalent of a concept of person per se, existing without a transcendental aim and belonging to the realm of nature, that was emerging in the philosophical and scientific ideas of the time—and that became part of the intellectual and material development of Western history in the following centuries. Pre-Tridentine Catholic spirituality shared with the Protestant Reformation a concept of the self that became fundamental in the formation of European identity. This notion of self developed in connection with a cultural process that separated the sacred from the profane, the spiritual from the material. The "sacralization" of virtuous behavior, the enhanced status of secular life, the suspicion of supernatural signs such as visions and access to divine secrets were all part of this his-

28. Ibid., 238–39.

torical development. Similarly, the criticism of rituals and ceremonies expressed in this milieu ran parallel to the Protestants' new theory of ritual, which denied the presence of the supernatural in worldly artifacts.[29] In pre-Tridentine Catholic spirituality, therefore, one of the main emerging historical-religious forms was the "devout" person striving for perfection, and not the "living saint" in its medieval connotations. This religious form should be considered as part (as well as an example) of a trend in which new attitudes toward the self emerged, increasingly emphasising individualism, interiority, and human agency.

Angela Merici's Views of the Self

How does Angela Merici's spirituality and her Company of St. Ursula fit within this history? On the one hand, Angela's spirituality reflected some traits of the Renaissance notion of the self (inwardly complex, individual, unique), which she interprets perhaps even more radically than the religious literature discussed above. On the other, Angela did not embrace the perception of a concept of the individual that exists in itself, as her proposed experience of personhood existed in close contact with the transcendent. Let's develop these points.

In Angela's writings the Ursulines are considered unique beings who relate to the sacred in an individual manner. In the first place, the Ursuline is considered an individual in her relationship with the divine, as emerges from her unmediated encounter with God. Second, the Ursulines did not live in common or carry out collective activities in the world, and they hearkened to their personal inspiration. Third, the Ursulines lived the experience of the sacred by converting their individual humanity rather than by adhering to institutions and ceremonies that transmit the sacred in an insti-

29. The term *ritual* itself was invented in the sixteenth century and was used in the pejorative sense ("mere ritual") in opposition to true religion. See Muir, *Ritual in Early Modern Europe*, 155–84.

tutional and supraindividual manner—for example, the convent, vows, rituals, and specific devotions. The Ursulines' individuality was also respected in the democratic nature of the company, which allowed them to choose their protectors, guides, and confessors and proposed neither a sacred hierarchy nor perfect obedience. Furthermore, Angela's pedagogical model acknowledged the diversity of single individuals and refused to impose common codes of behavior. Finally, as a Bride of Christ, the Ursuline did not lose her identity and was respected as an individual: unlike nuns and secular wives, the Ursulines did not change their name, did not bring a dowry, did not submit to secular men, were not segregated or controlled and protected by institutions established by men.[30]

In Angela's writings the specificity of the Ursuline's identity is located in the individual's interiority, in her heart and innermost secret thoughts. This idea emerges clearly, for example, when Angela warns the Colonelle that they must not judge or interfere with the Ursulines' choices for their lives: "who can judge the heart and the innermost secret thoughts of any creature? . . . [I]t is not up to you to judge the handmaids of God; he well knows what he wants to make of them" (*Ric.,* 8). The importance of will, in every aspect of the Ursuline's religious life, also demonstrates that the inner dimension (together with the will of God) figured as the agent of individual actions. According to Merici, the interiority of the individual was central to religious practice. The Ursuline received God's counsels in her heart. She separated from the world through inner detachment from secular values. Furthermore, as with her contemporaries, Angela's approach to fasting and vocal prayer shows that the she no longer assumes the correspondence between exteriority and interiority and that she does not invest the body with sacral value.

Finally, as in the writings of Erasmus, Battista da Crema, and

---

30. These were the common traits between secular and religious marriage: Lowe, "Secular Brides and Convent Brides."

Serafino da Fermo, portraits of character types and psychological analysis also emerge in Angela's writings (especially in the *Arricordi*). She described a wide range of personalities, citing positive and negative inclinations of character: being "humble," "pleasing," "human," "good," and "sober" were positive; while being "strange" (difficult), "pusillanimous," "cowardly," "presumptuous," and having a "wide conscience" were seen as negative. Other more ambiguous qualities were "disconsolate," "timid," "inclined to despair," "doubtful," "fragile." Angela also considered the Colonelle's preoccupations in response to their responsibility towards the Ursulines: "to be disheartened," "to worry," "to desire," "to regret." She also explored the attitudes the Colonelle should adopt in response to the various Ursulines: they were encouraged "to console," "open their hearts," "appreciate," "bear with," "help," "advise," "comfort," "vivify," "exhort," "love," "be nice to" and "give pleasure," "cheer," "correct lovingly," "not judge," "promptly provide," "be an example," "instill respect," "admonish."[31] Finally, she described the attitudes expected of the Colonelle toward the Matrone: they should be "solicitous," "vigilant," "pleasant," "sharp," "humble," "irksome and vexing," and "not be negligent"; they should use "dexterity," "reverence," "disapproval," "discretion," "earnest solicitation"; they should also "annihilate themselves," "skillfully and reverently contradict," and act "without scruple or any respect for authority."

Thus, Angela's rule respected the Ursuline as an individual in both her spiritual and material life. It considered her a complex human being with inner feelings, a will, and an intellect. The rule treated the Ursuline as an independent subject since it accorded her great freedom and responsibility in her relationship with God and everyday life (respectively unmediated and nonprescribed). From this perspective, therefore, one could say that the Ursuline was a

---

31. One notices that the terms used are all positive, with the exception of "admonish" and "instill respect," whose use is justified in a limited number of situations described in Angela's pedagogical principles.

"Renaissance" individual. It would even be possible to argue that the Ursulines lived such experience more thoroughly than the followers of the contemporary male rules and manuals. As a woman, Angela Merici tended to express her spirituality without projecting the sacred onto institutional structures and exterior codes of behavior. In her company, Angela pushed a religious model based on interiority and individuality to the extreme, abolishing all communal, intermediary, and exterior aspects more radically, thus allowing individuals to develop their personal and inner side more.[32]

In Angela's rule, however, the individual does not exist in itself. This represented the main difference between Angela's concept of the self and that emerging from contemporary spiritual writers. In Angela's spirituality the individual finds full affirmation of her own personhood and subjectivity in mystical union. Angela depicted the Ursuline's union with God as a projection of the individual self into the divine. The experience of thoughts, feelings, will, words, deeds, and any other inner and outer aspect of the self was best fulfilled in the relationship with God: "And strengthen my *affections* and *senses* . . . . I pray you that you deign to receive this most vile and impure *heart* of mine . . . receive my *free will,* every act of my own *will* . . . . Receive my every *thought, word* and *deed,* everything that is mine finally, both *interior* and *exterior*" (*Reg.,* 5).

In Angela's rule, thus, the self, through mystical experience, becomes sacred. Battista da Crema, by contrast, sacralizes moral virtues, a human experience that leads to divine contact but that is lived outside it. Angela does not share the idea that individuals could become perfect outside experience of the divine. In Angela's writings virtuous behavior takes place after the sacralization of the self; it is considered as a manifestation of the Bride of Christ's ce-

---

32. As we have seen, most new confraternities and religious orders, by contrast, kept exterior and institutional aspects such as hierarchy, order, obedience, and perfect execution of exterior practices even in connection with a religious trend that emphasized inner piety.

lestial status. Futhermore, God is viewed as the main agent of the
Bride of Christ's life. The Ursuline must obey the counsels of the
Holy Spirit and the Colonelle must respect the Ursuline's choices,
because "you do not know what God wants to make of them" (*Ric.*,
8). In Angela's writings there is no concept of self per se. Finally, Angela places the individual in connection with a transcendent dimension in granting the Ursuline a role of supernatural mediation. The
religious figure emerging from Angela's rule was a "living saint."

Therefore, Angela's rule promoted a concept of the self that presented some traits—such as its unique identity, inner orientation,
and self-determination—that were "modern" (because they further
developed in the following centuries), and others—such as a self
open to the influence of the supernatural—that can be called "medieval" (since they had already reached their zenith during the late
Middle Ages and were destined to decline).

Angela's rule shows how union with God was still essential to
women even when more secular views of the individual and reality were emerging. Women participated in the history of the emergence of a "modern" self and experienced subjecthood in the religious domain in close connection with the transcendent.[33] Angela
did not adopt a spiritual model that endorsed the ideal of the self
per se because in a society where things existed on their own (that
is, without a transcendental end), women's expression of their individuality was problematic. Without their divine counterpart they
were rarely given the right to exercise their will, intellect, and feelings because they were not considered equal to men. Given the
mainstream view of female nature (weak and sexual), in order to
become virtuous women had to adopt, above all, a submissive
model based on chastity, modesty, and obedience. Furthermore,

33. It is possible that other women who were in contact with men promoting "devout" spiritual ideas show a similar pattern to Merici. For example, Paola Antonia Negri—as spiritual leader of the Barnabites and of the Angelics—combined Battista da
Crema's ideals on annihilation of the will and supernatural charisma (see Baernstein,
A Convent's Tale, 58–61).

women's authority, signs of virtue, and creative possibilities were far more modest.[34]

Conclusions

In conclusion, Angela's case suggests that women's opportunity for the experience of self and creativity within religion was the product of the meeting between a spirituality that featured an emerging notion of the individual and patterns of gender norms. This opportunity lasted more or less from the twelfth century to the sixteenth, when a main model of relationship with God and of perfection, promoted by the penitential movement, was individual, unmediated, a-institutional, liminal, bodily, affective, and Christocentric. In this model the individual was expected to mediate supernatural power within society. Women became associated with sanctity because this religious model fit in well with cultural assumptions about them. Women became saints because they were seen as "bride," "body," "other," "mediator" and excluded from official power. Misogynist ideas and female religiosity were not in contradiction but were complementary expressions of the same cultural concepts. Religious women succeeded in manipulating, adapting, or rejecting some of the symbols and meanings in their actual lives. Thereby, more than their secular counterparts, they created new roles for themselves and overcame some of the limitations imposed by culture. Women used a set of values that associated them with the supernatural but rejected the idea that they were weak and irrational. They viewed their bodies as symbolically meaningful but used them to achieve a more profound union with the suffering Christ on the Cross. They employed familial and sexual symbolism, but used them as instruments of empowerment and independence and rejected the notion that they were lustful and unsuited for public life. Women interiorized exclusion from normative and

---

34. To a certain extent, this can be seen in the impact that the Protestant Reformation had on women. See Roper, *The Holy Household.*

institutional power but promoted forms of life that allowed them freedom and individuality.

Within the medieval religious context, the ideological construction of the "female" offered women an outlet for religious and cultural creativity. Besides, this was a time of "crisis," when the church's power was weak (Avignon and schism) and the forms of communication with the supernatural were redefined "from below" (laypeople became protagonists in religious life); and during crises of institutional power women have always gained influence—as also emerges in the popularity of spiritual women during the wars of Italy and the French wars of religion. Women were included within the emerging religiosity, and many became its highest expression. Women enriched religious symbolism and the forms of relationship with God (that is, affection, maternity, mysticism, penance, and interiority). Female saints filled public roles at various levels: intellectual (as theologians), political (as advisors), spiritual (as preachers, examples of life and piety, and objects of cults), and social (as points of reference for the secular community in which they lived). Within a society that recognized religious value and space for social action in individual relationships with God, women won their own role in mediating and repeating God's power (prophesying, healing, and providing daily protection and the salvation of souls). Spiritual women, however, did not always fulfill their roles in close association with divine power. Through religion women could also express intellectual and organizational skills (as writers and religious founders) as well as human and moral qualities (affection, altruism, patience, courage, integrity). Furthermore, women created a new religious figure in the form of an independent subject capable of expressing thoughts and feelings and aware of her own identity and agency. They could to do this because the history of the modern individual developed in close association with the sacred dimension of life. For all these reasons the female living saint was probably the most outstanding figure that women produced in premodern history.

Angela Merici's company represented a peak and an institutional outcome of this history. Angela used some ideas that were part of the cultural notion of "woman": modesty, obedience, virginity, otherness, and powerlessness. And through these ideas she proposed to women a religious model that could lead to individuality, independence, agency, self-esteem, self-awareness, public visibility, supernatural charisma, and to the exercise of rational and human qualities in a variety of contexts.

From the perspective of women's history, however, despite its great achievements, female religiosity had limitations. Female sainthood was constructed on the same ideals that led women to more restrictive roles elsewhere. Men accepted women's spiritual leadership largely because they believed that it reproduced a power that came from God. In this way, spiritual women did not challenge the traditional gender roles that cast women as subordinate to men. Female spirituality could not change the symbolic associations connected with "woman" because female saints owed their power precisely to that specific cultural construction, and when the demand for transcendental contact waned, women lost their religious leadership and social power while the misogynist ideology remained. Without their divine counterpart within culture, women were merely "other," "body," "bride," "mediator," and they remained excluded from power.

In connection with the progressive secularization of society and the decline of the medieval religious model based on supernatural union between the individual and God—which was taking place especially among the secular and ecclesiastical elite—the Tridentine church redefined the means of mediating the sacred and looked askance at God's revelations outside its institution, through individuals and especially women.[35] Signs of personal contact with the supernatural were believed to come more easily from the devil. In

---

35. Examples of this kind are provided in Brown, *Immodest Acts;* Sallmann, "La sainteté mystique femmine."

the sixteenth and seventeenth centuries female saints were greatly outnumbered by the new horde of witches. Constructed as negative mirror images of saints, witches, too, were believed to express contact with the supernatural through their bodies, by virtue of their weakness and "otherness," and to be instruments of a supernatural power. Although female mysticism continued—both in the world and, especially, in the convent (even achieving significant results, as in the case of Teresa of Avila and Maria Maddalena de Pazzi)—within an increasingly secular society, it was gradually losing outlets for expression and historical significance.[36] Convents, however, remained centers for women's religious creativity (producing spiritual writings, poetry, art, music, and theater).[37] Furthermore, the post-Tridentine church, with the development of new religious associations devoted to charity and teaching, offered spiritual women an option outside the convent. However, at least in Italy, these often fell under the thumb of the ecclesiastical hierarchy and had to promote an ideological program of the church's devising.

In the secular realm the experience of female spirituality had slight impact on the misogynist ideas that barred women from full participation in early modern opportunities. One lasting effect of female religiosity, however, was that women began to break down the identification of "female" with sexuality and reproduction. The tertiary-*bizzoca*-beguine-Ursuline—a Bride of Christ in the world—was the ancestress of the lay single woman. From the

36. There are obviously many cases of spiritual women who expressed a religious model similar to that of the "living saints" even in the seventeenth and eighteenth centuries. Especially in France, where the wars of religion made civic and religious life unstable, there occurred a revival of female mysticism that was involved in the events of society (see Diefendorf, *From Penitence to Charity*). However, here I am discussing a historical trend, which developed throughout the centuries. Individual examples of active female mystics also survive in twenty-first-century Italy (see "La restaurazione della visione: Il caso di Natuzza Evolo," in Lombardi Satriani and Meligrana, *Il ponte di San Giacomo*, 275–87).

37. Examples of women's creativity within convents are discussed in Monson, *The Crannied Wall*.

mid-sixteenth century it was no longer inconceivable that women could live in the secular world without marriage.[38]

The history of the Brescian Company of St. Ursula reflected this historical transition. On the one hand the post-Tridentine transformation of the Company of St. Ursula helped forge the status of the lay single woman. The Ursuline became the woman-schoolteacher and prototype of the spinster responsible for the religious education of the children of her family. On the other hand, however, the company largely lost its freedom, individuality, mysticism, and social action and became an instrument for the diffusion of an established doctrine under the direction and surveillance of a male hierarchy.

EPILOGUE: THE COMPANY OF ST. URSULA AFTER ANGELA MERICI

Evolution of the Company in the Sixteenth and Seventeenth Centuries

The history of the evolution of the Company of St. Ursula is complex and diverse. In the second half of the sixteenth century, the survival of the company was due mainly to support from the bishops of the Tridentine church, and in particular that of the Archbishop of Milan, Carlo Borromeo, who reformed the Brescian company and promoted its foundation in the Milanese territory. Subsequently, the company expanded in other Italian cities and in

---

38. Some female artists and writers rejected an identity based purely on traditional female roles and the concomitant restrictions—which seemed to characterize women's intellectual expressions in the earlier period (see Gottlieb, "The Problem of Feminism in the Fifteenth Century"). Two laywomen writers, Moderata Fonte and Lucrezia Marinelli, advocated with new energy and awareness women's right to participate in the sharing of offices and rejected (at least in their books) the role of wife (Cox, "The Single Self"). However, a wife's identity remained a point of reference that women always had to confront and that was influential in many respects, as emerges from the works of many of the female authors of the sixteenth and seventeenth centuries: see, for example, Aughterson, *Renaissance Woman.*

France. By then, however, the structure and aims of Angela's institute had been altered. It supported the Catholic Reformation as the Ursulines participated in the catechization of society. In this way the company became a pioneer in the education of laywomen and a prototype of the lay single woman. In Italy, however, the company was placed under a male hierarchy, and the Ursulines lost their freedom to shape their spiritual and material lives. In France, by contrast, they had greater power to mold their religiosity and enjoyed a good deal of public visibility during the Wars of Religion and up to the mid-seventeenth century.

The Brescian Company

In Brescia the history of the Company of St. Ursula is one of division and change. Angela Merici's religious proposal was ambiguous and its heritage difficult. After Merici's death, a period of conflict within the company began, caused by both internal divisions and external pressure. The unusual religious status of the company, in particular the idea of virginity in the secular world, became a target of criticism. As we know from Cozzano, this period saw several virgins abandon the company in the face of public disapproval. Some Ursulines became nuns and some married, while others turned to "heretical" ideas.[39] Furthermore, after 1545, the company split in two factions following the decision to introduce a black leather cincture as the exterior distinctive sign of the Ursulines. The initiative was taken by a group of Matrone led by Lucrezia Lodrone, the mother general of the company,[40] possibly in order to make the institute more acceptable to external eyes.[41] Another group of Matrone and virgins, led by Ginevra Luzzago and Cozzano, opposed the cincture to remain faithful to Angela's original ideal. Eventually, the dispute was won by the "cincture party," which, in 1546, man-

39. Cozzano, *Risposta*, ff. 6r–7r, in MTS, 566.
40. Lodrone had been chosen by Angela Merici herself as her successor.
41. The cincture was adopted on 11 December 1545.

aged to obtain papal approbation of the company,[42] the legitimization of Lodrone's leadership, and a decree threatening the Ursulines that they must accept the cincture or face expulsion.[43] Cozzano and Luzzago's party refused to sign, and the company remained divided.[44] The struggle continued after Lodrone's death in 1554, when the company elected two mothers general, each representing one faction (Ginevra Luzzago and Veronica Buzzi).[45] Though the group opposing the cincture was the smaller, it counted more Ursulines who had been in the company during Angela's lifetime.[46] The company was reunited in 1559, with the election of Bianca Porcellaga as mother general of both factions (after Luzzago's death and Buzzi's resignation).[47] During this period, probably from 1560, the Fathers of Peace became involved in the spiritual administration of the Company of St. Ursula and its founder, Francesco Cabrini d'Alfianello, became the spiritual father of Angela's institute (possibly up to his death in 1569).

---

42. The bull of approval was issued by Pope Paul III on 9 June 1544 and published on 14 April 1546: Bull *Regimini Universalis Ecclesiae*, Archivio Segreto Vaticano, Reg. Vat. 1696, ff. 223r–25r, in MTS, 547–49. It is possible that, already at the time of Paul III, the ecclesiastical hierarchy saw in the company a means for educating women. Furthermore, in those years there were discussions about the creation of the female branch of the Jesuits, and the Ursulines may have been seen as possible candidates (Elisabeth Wetter, "Gesuitesse," in *Dizionario degli Istituti di Perfezione*, vol. 4 (1977),1146–48.

43. The decree was issued by the archdeacon of Brescia, Aurelio Duranti (published in MTS, 490).

44. There is very little information concerning this phase of the history of the company (see MTS, 296–303).

45. Both acts of elections are published in MTS, 595–97, 600–601.

46. Buzzi's group comprised three Matrone and fifty-seven voters, of whom only five were among the virgins who elected Angela as mother general in 1537; whereas Luzzago's included a smaller number of voters (thirty-six) and no Matrone, but twelve virgins who belonged to the original company. A few months later the group led by Luzzago elected male agents and protectors for the first time, possibly in order to give more stability to their faction.

47. It is unclear how the company reached reunification. Besides Luzzago's death, one should note that Cozzano is no longer present in the documents of the company. Another reason frequently mentioned is the choice of Francesco Cabrini as spiritual father of the company (see below).

With the reunification under the direction of the Fathers of Peace began a new phase of change and consolidation. As we know from the letter written in 1566 by the confessor of the company, Francesco Landini, during this period the Ursulines became involved in teaching catechism in the schools of Christian Doctrine.[48] This duty was probably an initiative by Cabrini and by Brescia's new bishop, Domenico Bollani (1559–79). Bollani, the first resident bishop of Brescia for a long time, was committed to implementing Tridentine reform and placing lay religious activities under ecclesiastical control.[49] Cabrini was Bollani's confessor and both men were active in reviving the catechism in Brescia's schools of Christian Doctrine.[50] It seems therefore likely that they enfolded the company within their project and gave the Ursulines a new role. With the Fathers of Peace it is likely that a male figure (either as spiritual father or head of the company) took a central position in the life of the company.[51]

In 1569 the first printed edition of the rule was published[52] and the promotion of the cause for beatification of Angela Merici was set in motion with the Processo Nazari.[53] The printed rule featured some changes in language and revised the age and stages of admission in the company.[54] In 1572 the company introduced a ritual of

48. *Estratto d'una lettera del P.Francesco Landini,* in MTS, 531 (see chapter 1). The schools that gave Christian education (both moral and doctrinal) were first founded by Castellino da Castello in Milan in 1536. In Brescia they were established in 1554.

49. On Bollani, see Cairns, *Domenico Bollani.*

50. Roberto Lombardi, "La catechesi dal concilio di Trento al Vaticano II," in Caprioli, Rinoldi, and Vaccaro, *Diocesi di Brescia,* 222–25.

51. Landini states: "At a sign of his, the Father of the Company gathers all [the Ursulines] wherever he wishes"; "the Company elected a *head,* with the authority of our Bishop, Father Don Francesco [Cabrini]" (*Estratto d'una lettera del P.Francesco Landini,* in MTS, 532).

52. *Regola della nova Compagnia di Santa Orsola.* In Brescia per Damiano Turlino.

53. The Brescian notary Giovan Battista Nazari was also asked by the Matrone of the company to compose a biography of Angela on the basis of the testimonies given (*Libro della Vita della Reverenda et quasi beata Madre suor Angela,* in MTS, 541–46).

54. At age twelve the Ursuline was presented; at fifteen she was accepted; at eighteen she became a full member and signed the register.

admission similar to that of the consecration of the virgins, and the Ursulines took the vow of chastity.[55] While Elisabetta Prato was mother general (1572–80), the organization of the government of the company added new roles and a complicated hierarchy. The company was divided into seven districts (each including a group of virgins, a Colonella, and the new figure of the Maestra), individually ruled by a Matrona, who was subject to the mother general and the father general. These changes enhanced the authority of the Matrone and of the mother general at the expense of the Colonelle. Churchmen also became more influential; we find them at the top of the hierarchy and present at the institutional events of the company's life, such as ceremonies of acceptance and elections.[56] There also were eight men, four agents and four protectors, more external but influential. In 1582, when Carlo Borromeo reformed the company, he codified the new organization in a new rule and put the institute under the authority of the bishop (of which more below).

Beyond Brescia

Meanwhile, Borromeo had founded the company in Milan in 1567, with a new rule and a different organization.[57] In 1585 a branch of congregated Ursulines was founded, parallel to the secular Ursulines. Although they did not officially adopt clausura, they were in effect cloistered. In the meantime, the Company of St. Ursula was also established in other Italian cities, with different rules that often shared little with the original institute.[58] The founders were usually bishops who maintained the secular form but gave rules modeled on those of Borromeo (either that of Milan or, more rarely, that

---

55. *Ordine et Ceremonie* (ca. 1572).

56. See MTS, 317–29.

57. For the Ursulines in the diocese of Milan, see Di Filippo Bareggi, "Una riforma al femminile"; Turchini, *Sotto l'occhio del padre*, 288–97.

58. Some of these foundations were: Ferrara, 1587; Verona, 1590; Parma, 1590; Foligno, 1600; Bologna, 1603; Reggio, 1611; Modena, 1620. It seems that in 1565 Cremona was the first city to have a company dedicated to St. Ursula. However, there are no sources that clarify whether there was a link with Angela's original.

of Brescia). The Ursulines' communities were not unified under an overarching authority.

The Company of St. Ursula escaped enclosure by the bull *Circa Pastoralis* of 1563 because the spirit of catechization that animated the new breed of clergymen emerging from the Council of Trent prevailed over the anxiety to control women's honor through the convent. The Company of St. Ursula represented a valuable tool for spreading Christian values and doctrine. This idea emerges in many introductions to the rules, where it is stated that the Ursulines' duty is to teach Christian Doctrine to their relatives and friends at home and to pupils in schools. As we have seen, the Brescian company had started this activity in the early 1560s, under the direction of Cabrini and Bollani. Furthermore, this project emerges in a document sent to Carlo Borromeo in 1565 by the bishop of Bologna, Gabriele Paleotti, with reference to devout women who lived outside the convent in Bologna.[59] This document suggests creating a congregation of women for teaching Christian Doctrine and for other pious works. While in Bologna this project was postponed until 1603, in Milan Borromeo acted immediately, possibly in an attempt to regularize the informal groups of devout women present in the city. In 1566 Borromeo made inquiries concerning the Brescian Company of St. Ursula and was sent a copy of the rule.[60]

The Company of St. Ursula expanded in France, too. It was first founded in Avignon in 1592 by Françoise de Bermond, and by 1610 there were twenty-nine congregations in southern France.[61] Initially the French Ursulines kept the secular form and pursued teaching

59. Zarri, "Il terzo Stato," in *Recinti*, 461–63; Di Filippo Bareggi, "Una riforma al femminile," 63–66.

60. The rule was sent to Franceschino Visdomini by Landini (with his letter quoted above).

61. Some of these foundations were in Aix (1600), Arles (1602), Toulouse (1604), and Bordeaux (1606). There is now a rich bibliography on the Ursulines in France: Rapley, *The Dévotes;* Lierheimer, "Preaching or Teaching?"; idem., "Redefining Convent Space"; idem., *The Life of Antoinette Micolon;* Diefendorf, *From Penitence to Charity.*

Christian Doctrine to girls. In Paris in 1612, following the initiative of Madame de Sainte-Beuve, the company assumed a cloistered form (under Augustinian rule), and most Ursuline congregations followed suit.[62] In 1620 there were already sixty-five convents. On the eve of the French Revolution the Ursuline order existed in three hundred cities. From 1639 the Ursulines also became the first female missionary institute. Thanks to the initiative of Marie Guyart (known as Marie de l'Incarnation), French Ursulines went to the colonies of New France (Quebec) pursuing their educational mission.[63]

As has been recently demonstrated, throughout the first half of the seventeenth century, the French Ursulines were able to exercise an active role in their communities, as both a secular and an enclosed institute. In some cases they claimed the role of preachers, since they taught catechism in churches and barns to crowds whom they wished to convert.[64] Though enclosure limited the impact of their preaching, they found other ways to participate in public life.[65] Finally, at least in France during that period, conventual life ought not to be considered a restriction imposed by a male hierarchy, because it was often sought by women themselves and, within the historical context of the wars of religion, it still offered them an opportunity to exercise their mystical and prophetic gifts at a public level.[66] In Italy, on the other hand, we find a much quieter political context and a stricter, more officious church, which left less space for individual initiative. Although we lack documents attest-

62. In some cases, the duty of teaching became their fourth vow, in addition to obedience, chastity, and poverty.

63. On the life of Marie de l'Incarnation, see Zemon Davis, "New Worlds: Marie de l'Incarnation," in *Women on the Margins*.

64. Lierheimer, "Preaching or Teaching?"

65. Some continued to teach Christian Doctrine publicly in the convent church or at the choir grill. Furthermore, they saw their teaching in the convent classrooms as a way of participating in public life since their pupils would then raise their children in the outside world according to what they had learned (idem., "Redefining Convent Space").

66. Diefendorf, *From Penitence to Charity.*

ing to the Ursulines' teaching activity and their perception of their role as teachers, their restrictions in the Italian dioceses were tighter. The Ursulines' educational role was limited to the schools of Christian Doctrine, where teachers followed manuals for catechism and where women's teaching was closely supervised by men.[67] This, however, did not completely trammel women from finding some autonomous spaces and gaining public visibility or fulfilling their aspiration for an apostolic life.[68]

The Social Outlook of the New Brescian Company

As we can see from table 3, the number of Ursulines in the Brescian company increased in particular during the early years and between the last two decades of the sixteenth century and the beginning of the seventeenth. It almost doubled in 1582, that is, when Carlo Borromeo placed the company under his rule and the jurisdiction of the church. It seems that by that time the company had regained the respect of Brescian society.

In the second half of the sixteenth century and in the seventeenth we also find a change in the social profile of the Company of St. Ursula in Brescia. Many more Ursulines were wealthy or belonged to important families. Many names of prominent families after 1550 are listed in the company records. Some of the Ursulines were daughters and granddaughters of women who figured among the Matrone of the original company and belonged to the Brescian aristocracy: these included the Avogadro, the Buzzi, and the Mei.[69] We also find Ursulines belonging to other noble families: Alfianello, Asti, Capriolo, Fisogni, Iseppini, Manerba, and Ugoni.

---

67. See Di Filippo Bareggi, "Una riforma al femminile," 78–82.

68. See, for example, the case of the Ursulines in Parma: Culpepper, "'Our Particolar Cloister.'"

69. Costanza Avogadro (she entered the company in 1561) probably was the granddaughter of Maria Avogadro, Matrona in the company since 1537 (MTS, 250). In 1583 we also find the name of Hippolita Avogadro. Marta, daughter of Veronica Buzzi, was admitted in 1545. Maddalena di Mey entered the company in 1560; Domicilla Mey entered in 1583 (Caterina di Mey was Matrona in 1537 until at least 1546).

TABLE 3. NUMBER OF URSULINES IN THE
BRESCIAN COMPANY

Year	Number	Year	Number
1535	28	1572	114
1537	75	1580	100
1540	150	1582	180
1545	73–100	1592	229
1555	93	1602	229
1566	130	1616	297

The Capriolo, Fisogni, Manerba, and Ugoni were all represented in the city council.[70] If we look at the Ursulines' patrimonial declarations for 1617 and 1627 we find that, out of twenty-two, only three declared poverty.[71]

It is also interesting that from the second half of the sixteenth century, important families created real dynasties of Ursulines who, over the years, occupied many positions in the company.[72] In some

70. Ferraro, *Family and Public Life,* 70–71.

71. Camilla di Corti, aged sixty, stated that she had to work to earn her living: "I have nothing else, unless I earn a living, and that is little . . . from home I have nothing and no valuables." She also said that the company gave her a room that she did not pay for: "I pay no rent because the Venerable Company of St Ursula gives me a small room for the love of God." Margherita and Monicha, twenty-three and twenty, stated: "We have nothing unless we earn our living, and a few pieces of furniture which are worth little or nothing." They claimed a paternal legacy of 700 lire from their brother.

72. This is the case of the Alfanellos (Caterina became an Ursuline in 1560; Francesco Cabrini de Alfianello was confessor of the company in 1559–69); the Astis (Claudia, Cecilia, Antonia, and Durusilla became Ursulines in 1559, Rosana in 1562; Antonia was Matrona and Cecilia mother general in 1592; Irene was mother general in 1616); the Avogadros (Maria was Matrona in 1537; Costanza, her daughter, became an Ursuline in 1561; Hippolita in 1583; Costanza was mother general in 1602, and Mat-

cases Angela's division of status between Ursulines (virgins) and Matrone (widows) appears to have been dropped, since we find a few aristocratic virgins who became Matrone after a couple of decades.[73]

In addition, the properties and credits listed in the patrimonial declarations of this period became quite sizeable.[74] In many respects the assistance provided by the company over the years became more organized. In 1588 legal assistance to the Ursulines was institutionalized, since both in the *Secondo Libro Generale* and in the patrimonial declarations we find an *esattore* who acted for the company in legal matters.[75] Medical assistance appears to have be-

---

teo was protettore); the Bargnani/Pratos (Elisabetta was Matrona in 1537 and mother general in 1572; Hatiruita and Cassandra were Matrone at the end of the century); the Bucci/Buzzis (Veronica was Matrona in the 1530s and mother general in 1555; her daughter Marta became an Ursuline in 1545); the Chizzolas (Caterina was mother general in 1580; in that period Dorothea was Matrona and Giacomo, Hippolito, Antonio were protettori); the Fisognis (Lucrezia and Laura became Ursulines in 1572); the Iseppinis (Laura, Anna, and Barbara became Ursulines in 1559, Theodora in 1561, Cecilia in 1583; Anna was mother general in 1583; Don Giovan Paolo Iseppino was general confessor and father of the company around 1570); the Maggis (Dorotea was an Ursuline and Marta was Matrona; Guerero was protettore at the end of the century); the Manerbas (Julia was an Ursuline in 1580; Camillo and Scipion were protettori in 1573); the Meis (Caterina di Mei was Matrona in 1537, Maddalena di Mei was an Ursuline in 1560, and Domicilla Mey in 1583); the Trussis (Giulia was an Ursuline, Laura was Matrona, and Mario was protettore at the end of the century); and the Ugonis (Aurelia and Aquilea became Ursulines in 1572; Oriana, in 1583; Hippolita was Matrona at the end of the sixteenth century).

73. For example, Antonia and Giulia Asti and Costanza Avogadro.

74. There is also a greater number of polizze available (*PE*, b. 153). The income of the company increased considerably throughout the years, especially between 1568 and 1588. In the patrimonial declaration of the possessions of the company in 1548 we find a total of eight legacies. The company received an annual income of 220 lire, for a capital of 4,400 lire. In the *PE* of 1568 there are a few more legacies (twelve in total). They received 300 lire per year for a capital of 6,000 lire. They declared more *crediti* and *livelli* (livelli from a total of nineteen people for 520 lire per year and for a capital of 10,400 lire; crediti for 470 lire). They had a few debtors who did not want to pay the past livelli (275 lire). In 1548 and 1568 no land or houses were declared. By contrast, in 1588 they claimed ownership of land (they rented out some land worth 360 lire and 18 lire every year). The polizza of 1632 shows a significant increase in properties.

75. The company "pays L. 50 to a Collector to dock the *livelli* and negotiate other affairs of the Company" (*PE,* 1588).

come more organized, too, since the declaration of 1588 states that the company paid two doctors for treatment.[76] Furthermore, the company owned three apartments for the use of the poor virgins[77] and made annual payments to some people for assorted services.[78]

The aristocratization of the Brescian company was not an isolated case. Institutes in other cities also took steps to limit the entrance of lower-class girls. The rule of Bologna, for example, specified that the virgins must give proof that they could support themselves: "possess a patrimony with which to support herself or be able through her own industry to earn her living, or have someone who out of charity wishes to help her, or in some other way, at the discretion of the Congregation."[79] In the chapter on the acceptance of virgins, the 1588 rule of Ferrara specified that women who entered the company must not do so in order to obtain financial support: "Nor shall she enter out of poverty, in the hope of receiving temporal aid, because this Company has been founded to help souls; and so she shall enter only for her salvation, and for the greater glory of God Our Lord."[80]

76. "Pays L.41 a year for two . . . Doctors who take care of the poor of the Company."

77. "In a small house in Brescia . . . for the use of the poor girls of the company . . . without rent"; "in another small house . . . Hospital of the Incurables for use also of the poor girls of the Company who are sheltered in it . . . without rent"; "In another house . . . for use of the poor girls of the Company though not all, nor with full freedom, if not after the death of the lady Antonia di Asti, and two of Mei nephews" (*PE*, b. 152, classified as 1548, but it should be dated 1588). From 1588 we also find that a few Ursulines declared poverty. In 1568 and 1588 they appealed to be relieved from the duty of paying the rent ("and in paying the [following] charges beg for . . . mercy and remission that this work of charity carried out to help so many needy young women be not included for the Taxes," *PE*, 1588).

78. lire for the R.do Padre who takes care of the company; 80 lire the donation for the Church of S. Bernardo, where they had their mass said every day, plus 12 lire for the priest; another 50 lire for various expenses for the maintenance of the church; 40 lire for various expenses (such as little presents for the virgins at Christmas).

79. *Regola della Compagnia di S. Orsola eretta in Bologna*, 18 ("Concerning the condition of those who must be received in the Company").

80. *Regola della Compagnia delle Vergini di Santa Orsola stampate per ordine del molto ill. e R.mo Mons. Paolo Leone vescovo di Ferrara*, f. 13v. This is also the case of Fo-

The involvement of the aristocracy in the company in the second half of the sixteenth century, both in Brescia and in other cities, can be traced to a variety of causes. First is the church's acceptance of Merici's proposal. The number of aristocratic members increased after 1580, the time of Borromeo's pastoral visitation in Brescia and after 1582, when he gave the new rule to the company. Furthermore, there were economic advantages to having a daughter become an Ursuline rather than a nun because the Company of St. Ursula did not require a dowry. This became a significant factor even for the aristocracy given the rising cost of dowries from the end of the sixteenth century.[81] Finally, as Zarri has suggested, the presence of the aristocracy could be explained as part of the new image of the "saint at home," publicized by the church and seen by the aristocracy as a new version of the "saint at court."[82] As we have already noted, the entry of the aristocracy into the company (at least in Brescia) also led to changes in its organization.

Carlo Borromeo's Rules of the Company of St. Ursula

The rules Carlo Borromeo gave the Company of St. Ursula in Brescia[83] and Milan[84] served as models for rules elsewhere. Borromeo's changes placed the Ursulines under male and ecclesiastical

---

ligno, where the daughters of the local elite entered the company founded by Paola di Alessandro and recognized officially in 1600: "fifty virgins among the most noble in the city took this habit and rule without essential vows" (L. Iacobilli, *Vite de' santi e beati dell'Umbria*, 3 [Foligno, 1661], in Sensi, *Storie di Bizzoche*, 28–29).

81. On Brescia, see Ferraro, *Family and Public Life*, 101–30, and on Venice, see Cox, "The Single Self."

82. Zarri, "Orsola e Caterina," 552–54.

83. *Regola della Compagnia di S.Orsola di Brescia di nuovo revista corretta e confirmata da Monsignor illustrissimo Carlo Cardinale di S.Prassede.* I will refer to this rule by citing the name of the city and the chapter of the quotation.

84. *Regola della Compagnia di Santa Orsola fatta per quelle giovani, le quale desiderano servire a Dio nel stato verginale, stando nel secolo.* As for the rule of Brescia, I will refer to the rule of Milan by citing the name of the city and the chapter of the quotation. The Brescian rule was closer to Angela's original because it kept most of her text, although the changes introduced altered it substantially. The Milanese rule was totally different from Angela's original both in its form and content.

control, through a new structure that mediated their relationship with God, controlled their governance, and disciplined the virgins' lives. Furthermore, subsumed into the church's effort to reform moral and religious custom, the Ursuline became a very different figure.

As we have seen, the principal aim of the company became the diffusion of Christian beliefs. Both the Brescian and the Milanese rule specify that the specific duty of the Ursulines was to staff the schools of Christian Doctrine: "Let them remind them [the Ursulines] that all, according to the judgment of their Father confessor, must practice some pious work, and in particular may they be ready and obedient to their Superiors in the work of the Christian Institution, endeavoring in its exercise to teach them good ways as well as doctrine."[85] The *Compendio* introduced in 1603 by Alfonso Paleotti for the company in Bologna explained that its aim was also that to convert whole families: "bring entire families to a more orderly and Christian life, for frequent exhortation might be a stimulus and efficacious means, accompanied by the good odor of virtue and sanctity of one of these virgins, to move and incite the Father, the Mother, the Brothers, the Sisters, the Sisters-in-law, the servants, and sometimes the Masters and the Mistresses, to frequent the holy Sacraments . . . develop affection for pious works and all in all reform their customs according to the law and doctrine of Christ."[86]

Furthermore, Borromeo's rule for the Brescian company introduced a new government that depended on the church and a hierarchical system in which men had power over women. This rule

85. Brescia *Regola*, 19. Similarly, the Milanese rule stated: "On feast days, as well as hearing Mass and the Sermon, may they always seek to be busy with pious exercises, such as reading, meditating and praying, and especially going to the schools of Christian Doctrine, and there practicing teaching, or learning what is taught and learnt in them in Milan" (Milan, XI). In Milan Borromeo appointed the prior-general of the Schools of the Christian Doctrine, Gaspare Belinzaghi, as head of the Company of St. Ursula.

86. *Compendio de gli Instituti della Compagnia di S. Orsola.*

established nine different roles, laid out in fourteen chapters. The bishop of Brescia was the superior of the company *(Padre, Pastore e Superiore)*, a *Vicario particolare* was his substitute, and a *Sostituto e collaboratore del Padre* stood in for the Vicar when necessary. These figures had the final word on all important decisions. Under this male authority there was a complicated female hierarchy. The most important position was that of the *Madre e Superiora della Compagnia,* elected by the daughters but confirmed by the bishop. Then there was the *Vicaria,* who helped the Madre and substituted for her when necessary. The Madre had a circle of advisors, the *Assistenti,* whom she consulted. Eight *Governatrici,* eight *Maestre,* and the *Avvisatrici,* in descending order, were responsible for the life and behavior of the daughters.[87] The company was divided into districts, each consisting of a group of Ursulines (living in a particular area of the city) who were governed by a Governatrice, a Maestra, and an Avvisatrice. The Governatrici reported problems to the Madre Superiore, who made decisions with the Assistenti and reported them for approval to the male superiors (either the Vicario or the Sostituto). In the Milanese rule each district was assigned a male *Priore Particolare* directly responsible for the virgins.

At the same time, the company was given a more institutional outlook, since the Ursulines now underwent a ceremony of acceptance, took the vow of chastity, and wore a distinctive habit, a black veil and the cincture. The spiritual life of the Ursuline changed, too. As already mentioned, Borromeo's rule for Brescia decreed that the advice of the Holy Spirit must be vetted by the spiritual father.[88] In the Milanese rule obedience to God's advice was deleted quite.

In the new rules the spiritual father had full control over the Ursulines' spiritual life. He became the guide to mental prayer and ordained how long to pray in church: "when they have satisfied their

87. It is interesting that in the new rule the *Arricordi* (which appear in an altered version) are directed to the Avvisatrici, who occupied the least important place in the new hierarchy.

88. Brescia *Regola,* 8.

need and their devotion, *according to the judgment of those who sustain their souls,* they must return home."[89] The Ursulines lost their right to chose in which church to pray, and their life became less individual and more communal. According to the 1588 declaration of property of the company, it emerges that they had to hear mass together in the church of St. Bernardo *(per obligo).*

Furthermore, though the new companies retained secularity, the rules imposed a sort of enclosure of the Ursulines in their own houses. The virgins could not leave their house unless pressed by necessity or summoned by a superior's command: "it is not suitable that the virgins be seen frequently outside their homes";[90] "going unnecessarily in the streets is very contrary to their profession; and therefore they must not go around the city unless a necessity requires it or they have been called by their Adviser."[91] The new rules established a new concept of authority. If the virgins did not obey their superiors they could be expelled: "when through not being obedient to her superiors . . . she is cancelled from the Company."[92] The new authority was also manifest in the new pedagogy and in the language of the new rules. The pedagogical principles and ideas that had sustained the Colonelles' role toward their daughters gave way to repressive measures: "Let them hold to account their conversation both outside the house and in it, which they can do by *often visiting them, and when they least expect it.*"[93]

The new rules of the Company of St. Ursula aimed to discipline female behavior through precise prescriptive norms for the Ursulines' secular life. This approach reflected an ideology that saw women as a source of social disorder.[94] Women must be controlled by enforcing chastity, obedience, and modesty to defend their honor, which was the source of their social identity and worth. Inside the house women were carefully protected from the dangers that might compromise their honor: "In their homes they must be obe-

89. Ibid., 19.

90. Ibid.

91. Ibid.

92. Ibid., 2.

93. Ibid., 19.

94. Perry, *Gender and Disorder.*

dient to their Superiors, serve everyone willingly in lawful and honest matters, by which are intended common services: avoiding as far as possible going into the men's rooms, and then only to serve them."[95] In addition, an effort was made to keep the virgins busy in order to avoid their falling into sin, thanks to their female weakness: "always being occupied, either in serving, or in working, or in reading, or in praying, so that the Devil, finding them busy, does not have the time to tempt them."[96] Also there emerged the worry that the Ursulines might promote social chaos by begging and theft: "They must not go begging around the town, or with falsehood or simulations obtain alms, nor must they receive anything from other sisters without permission from their confessor, so that the latter do not rob their own family to give to them."[97]

Conclusions

In conclusion, in northern and central Italy society eventually accepted the new female figure proposed by Angela, as is testified by the company's spread and the entry of aristocrats. As we have seen, the company joined the attempt of the Tridentine church to reform society. The increase of unmarried women and the need to educate the female population promoted growth.[98] The church legitimized the Ursulines as *Terzo Stato* and the company inspired other similar ways of life such as, for example, that of the Dimesse in the Veneto area.[99] From the end of the sixteenth century the Ursulines became teachers within a society in which education was a means of social improvement. Thus women were asked to take part in the construction of a new society in formation. That the church and, later, secular society supported the company shows that the new figure of woman living outside the convent and outside marriage had become more acceptable.

95. Milan, VII.   96. Ibid.
97. Ibid., X.   98. Zarri, "Il terzo Stato," 473–74.
    99. As it was called by the bishop of Verona, Agostino Valier, in 1575 and by the bishop of Ferrara, Paolo Leoni, in 1587; see ibid., 464–66.

The new figure of woman proposed by Angela, however, subsisted under the new controls that emerged from the imposed changes. Italy was entering a new period, which has been defined as the age of confessionalization and social discipline. The Ursulines were disciplined according to a new need to define female identity. Angela's proposal—to give women the responsibility for managing their relationship with God and, consequently, their own existence—became anachronistic. The culture in which Angela lived her religious experience and created the company differed from that in which the Ursulines developed. Angela's ideal of divine union, conceived in a world still open to the action of the living saint, faded with it. Nevertheless, Angela's spirituality remained an inspiration to many later Ursulines, as it offered them a model for individual relationship with God, religious life in the world, human relationships, and personal development.

Bibliography

Primary Sources

Alcune regole cavate da gli ammaestramenti della divina vergine Margherita per la sua unione. In "Serafino da Fermo e le beate Margherita e Gentile e le Regole della Compagnia del Buon Gesù," by Innocenzio Colosio. *La nuova rivista di ascetica e mistica* 2 (1977): 246–58.

Antonio (Meli) da Crema. *Libro de vita Contemplativa: Lectione: Meditatione: oratione: contemplatione. Scala dil paradiso.* Io. Antonio Morandi da Gandino, Brescia, 1527.

Battista (Carioni) da Crema. *Della cognitione et vittoria di se stesso.* Milan, 1531.

———. *Lo specchio interiore.* Milan, 1540.

———. *Via de aperta verità.* Venice, 1532.

Bellintani da Salò, Mattia. *Vita della B.Angela da Desenzano.* Brescia, Biblioteca Queriniana, MS. B.VI.30.

Capitoli della Confraternita del Divino Amore. In *La Riforma Cattolica: Documenti e testimonianze,* by Massimo Marcocchi, 1:221–25. Brescia: Morcelliana, 1967.

Caterina da Bologna. *Sette Armi spirituali.* Edited by Cecilia Foletti. Padua: Editrice Antenore, 1985.

Caterina da Siena. *Dialogo della divina provvidenza.* Edited by Giuliana Cavallini. Rome: Edizioni Cateriniane, 1980.

Compendio de gli Istituti della Compagnia di S.Orsola, che si disegna eriggere nella Città di Bologna. 1603. Biblioteca dell'Archiginnasio di Bologna, A.V.H.VI.5/114.

Constituciones de la Compañia de Jesus. ca. 1556. In *Monumenta Historica Societatis Jesu* (Rome) 64 (1936): 261–727.

Costituzioni dei Barnabiti. In *Storia dei Barnabiti nel Cinquecento,* by Orazio Premoli, 1:422–55. Rome: Desclee & C. Editori, 1913.

Cozzano, Gabriele. *Dichiarazione della Bolla del Papa Paolo III.* Archivio Segreto Vaticano, S. C. Rituum, *Processus* 341, ff. 969r–83v (in MTS, 582–95).

———. *Epistola confortatoria alle Vergini della Compagnia di Sant'Orsola composta per il suo Canceglier Gabriello Cozzano.* Archivio Segreto Vaticano, S. C. Rituum, *Processus* 341, ff. 958v–69r (in MTS, 556–64).

————. *Risposta contro quelli che persuadono la clausura alle Vergini di Sant'Orsola.* Brescia, Biblioteca Queriniana, MS. D.VII.8 (in MTS, 564–82).

Doneda, Carlo. *Vita della B.Angela Merici da Desenzano, Fondatrice della Compagnia di Sant'Orsola.* Brescia (stampe di Giambattista Rossini), 1768.

Erasmus of Rotterdam. *Enchiridion militis Christiani, saluberrimis præceptis refertum autore Des.Erasmo Roterdamo.* Basileae, 1518.

Faino, Bernardino. *Miscellanea.* Biblioteca Queriniana, MS.K.VI.1.

————. *Vita della Serva di Dio di beata memoria la Madre Angela Merici da Desenzano fondatrice della celebre Compagnia di Sant'Orsola di Brescia, il cui Corpo riposa nella Chiesa di Sant'Afra.* Scritta prima, e stampata dal P.Ottavio Gondio Fiorentino; poi riordinata e corretta, et accresciuta dal Superiore Generale d'essa Compagnia. In Bologna, 1672 (per Gio Recaldini).

Fontana, Giovanni Battista. *Lettere spirituali della devota religiosa Angelica Paola Antonia de' Negri Milanese. Vita della medesima raccolta da Gio. Battista Fontana de' Conti.* Roma, 1576.

Gondi, Ottavio. *Vita della Beata Angela Bresciana, prima fondatrice della Compagnia di S.Orsola.* In Brescia, appresso Vincenzo Sabbio, 1600.

Incomincia li capituli delle Ordinationi delli officij de novo riformati, quali s'osservino nel nostro Monastero di Santa Marta. Archivio di Stato di Milano, Fondo di Religione, cartella 4609.

Kempis, Thomas à. *The Imitation of Christ.* London: J. M. Dent & Sons, 1910.

Landini, Francesco. *Estratto d'una lettera del P.Francesco Landini che sta nel Monte vicino a Brescia, scritta al Rev. P. Frate Franceschino Visdomini dell'ordine de Minori adì 21 dicembre 1566.* In *Regola della Compagnia di S.Orsola,* 27–32. Milan, 1569 (in MTS, 531–32).

Lombardi, Girolamo, *Vita della B. Angela Merici Fondatrice della Compagnia di Sant'Orsola.* Venezia, 1778.

Loyola, Ignatius. *Exercicios spirituales.* In *The Spiritual Exercises of St. Ignatius Loyola: Spanish and English with a Continuous Commentary,* edited by Joseph Rickaby, S.J. London: Burns & Oates, 1915.

Merici, Angela. *Arricordi che vanno alli Colonelli.* Archivio Segreto Vaticano, S. C. Rituum, *Processus* 341, ff. 946v–53r (in MTS, 507–12).

————. *Regula della Compagnia de Santa Orsola.* Milan, Biblioteca Trivulziana, codice 367, scaff.le n. 82, palch.to n. 2 (in MTS, 436–58).

————. *Saint Angela Merici, Writings: Rule, Counsels, Testament.* Trans. by a team of Ursulines of the Roman Union, Rome, 1995.

————. *Testamento della Madre suor Angela lassato alle Matrone.* Archivio Segreto Vaticano, S. C. Rituum, *Processus* 341, ff. 953r–58v (in MTS, 512–17).

Nassino, Pandolfo. *Registro di molte cose seguite.* Brescia, Biblioteca Queriniana, MS. C.I.15, 574–75.

Nazari De Sayani, Giovan Battista. *Le justificazioni della vita della Reverenda
Madre suor Angela Terzebita* (also known as *Processo Nazari*). Archivio Segreto Vaticano, S. C. Rituum, *Processus* 341, ff. 936v–45v (in MTS, 533–40).

———. *Libro della Vita della Reverenda et quasi beata Madre suor Angela,
fondatrice della Compagnia di S. Orsola di Brescia, con le justificationi di essa
vita; et anco si contiene il voto delle Vergini di detta Regola.* Archivio Segreto
Vaticano, S. C. Rituum, *Processus* 341, ff. 936v–45v (in MTS, 541–46).

*Ordine et Cerimonie che si fanno con le Vergini che vogliono entrar nella Com-
pagnia di S.Orsola in Brescia.* In Brescia (per Damiano Turlino) s.d., Brescia, Biblioteca Queriniana, Cinq., E.E.I. m.2.

*Polizze d'Estimo in ordine cronologico e in ordine alfabetico dall'anno 1517
all'anno 1687.* Brescia, Archivio di Stato: Archivio Storico Civico.

Quarré, Jean Hughes. *La vie de la Bienheureuse Mère Angèle Premiere Fondatrice de la Compagnie de S.te Ursule. Enrichie de plusierurs remarques et
pratiques de piété, tres-utiles pour la conduite de toutes sortes de personnes
à la Vertu.* Par le R.P.Iean Hugues Quarré Prestre de la Congrégation de
l'Oratoire de Iesus, Docteur en Théologie. A Paris (chez Sébastian Hure,
rue Sainct Iacques au Coeur-Bon), 1648. Brussels, Bibliothèque Royale
Albert I, III, 82784.

*Questo sia el modo che hanno revere quelli del Terzo Ordine del glorioso Sancto
Franceso,* in Pesaro per Hyeronymo Soncino. Nel 1505 adì 12 de Febraro.

Regola dei Teatini. In *La Riforma Cattolica: Documenti e testimonianze,* by
Massimo Marcocchi, 1:263–65. Brescia: Morcelliana, 1967.

*Regola della Compagnia delle Vergini di Santa Orsola stampate per ordine del
molto ill. e R.mo Mons.Paolo Leone vescovo di Ferrara.* In Ferrara (per Vittorio Baldini) 1587. Rome, Archivium Generale Ursulinarum Unionis
Romanae.

*Regola della Compagnia di Santa Orsola fatta per quelle giovani, le quali desid-
erano servire a Dio nel stato verginale, stando nel secolo; e per quelle, le qua-
li nella povertà, o per altri impedimenti non possono entrare in Monasterij.
Agiuntovi i Capitali del Governo, che hanno di havere i Governatori e Gov-
ernatrici di essa Compagnia. Con licentia dell'Illustriss. et Reverendiss. Sig.
Cardinal Borromeo, Arcivescovo di Milano.* In Milano (appresso di Giovan
Battista et fratelli da Ponte alla Dovana) 1567. Milan, Archivio Storico
Diocesano, sez. XII, vol. 145. Rule reprinted in 1569, 1570, 1577, and 1585.

*Regola della Compagnia di S.Orsola di Brescia di nuovo revista corretta e con-
firmata da Monsignor illustrissimo Carlo Cardinale di S.Prassede, arcivescovo di Milano et Visitatore Apostolico.* In Brescia (appresso Pietro Maria
Marchetti), 1582. Brescia, Biblioteca Queriniana, Cinq. I.I.3.

Regola della Compagnia di S. Orsola eretta in Bologna da Mons. Illustriss. e

Reverendiss. Alfonso Paleotti Arcivescovo di detta Città, Confirmata et di molte indulgenze favorita dalla Santità di Nostro Signore Papa Paolo Quinto. Di nuovo reviste, ampliate e ristampate. In Bologna, Per Vittorio Benacci, 1608. Biblioteca dell'Archiginnasio di Bologna, A.V.H.VI.6/22.

Regola della nova Compagnia di Santa Orsola di Brescia per la quale si vede come si habbiano a governar le vergini di detta Compagnia acciocchè vivendo christianamente possino doppo la loro morte fruir i beni de vita eterna. Edizione Turlino, 1569. Brescia, Biblioteca Queriniana, Cinq. EE.1.m.1.

Regola Generale per tutte quelle Vergini della Compagnia di S.Orsola. Le quali si sono retirate à vivere in Congregatione. In Milano (appresso Pacifico Pontio), 1585, con licenza dé Superiori. Milan, Archivio Storico Diocesano, sez. XII, vol. 146.

Sacred Congregation of Rite, *Processus,* 339–44. Archivio Segreto Vaticano.

Secondo Libro Generale della Ven. Compagnia di S.Orsola di Brescia, che finisce l'anno 1632. Brescia, Archivio di Stato, Fondo di Religione, "Cartella Compagnia di S.Orsola," reg. 134.

Serafino (Aceti de' Porti) da Fermo. *Opere spirituali, alla Christiana perfettione utiliss. e necessarie.* In Piacenza appresso Francesco Conti, 1570.

————. *Quarantadue problemi circa l'oratione. La nuova rivista di ascetica e mistica* 2 (1977): 162–72; 259–66.

Serafino (Torresini) da Bologna. *Pharetra divini amoris, tradotto in volgare per Don Serafino da Bologna Canonico regolare.* In Venezia per Paulo Gherardo, 1549.

Statuti della Compagnia dei Battuti di S. Domenico di Bologna. In *La Riforma Cattolica: Documenti e testimonianze,* by Massimo Marcocchi, 1:203–16. Brescia: Morcelliana, 1967.

Tribesco, Giacomo. *Gionta alle cose sopradette circa le meravigliose et divine virtù operate in quella beata serafica Angela, per D.Iacomo [Tribesco] bresciano canonico lateranense.* In *Di vari Santi Bresciani.* Brescia, Biblioteca Queriniana, MS. D.VII.20, ff. 15v–16r.

Secondary Literature

Ahlgren, Gillian T. W., ed. and trans. *The Inquisition of Francisca: A Sixteenth-Century Visionary on Trial.* Chicago: University of Chicago Press, 2005.

Anderson, Bonnie S., and Judith P. Zinsser. *A History of Their Own: Women in Europe from Prehistory to the Present.* Vol. 1. New York: Harper & Row, 1988.

Andreu, Francesco, ed. *Le lettere di San Gaetano da Thiene.* Vatican City: Biblioteca Apostolica Vaticana, 1954.

Ardener, Shirley, ed. *Defining Females: The Nature of Women in Society.* Oxford: Berg, 1993.

Atkinson, Clarissa. *The Oldest Vocation: Christian Motherhood in the Middle Ages.* Ithaca, N.Y.: Cornell University Press, 1991.

Aughterson, Kate, ed. *Renaissance Woman: A Sourcebook. Constructions of Femininity in England.* London and New York: Routledge, 1995.

Baernstein, P. Reneé. *A Convent's Tale: A Century of Sisterhood in Spanish Milan.* London and New York: Routledge, 2002.

Barone, Giulia. "Society and Women's Religiosity (750–1450)." In *Women and Faith: Catholic Religious Life in Italy from Late Antiquity to the Present,* edited by Lucetta Scaraffia and Gabriella Zarri, 62–71. Cambridge, Mass.: Harvard University Press, 1999.

Bartoli, Marco. *Chiara d'Assisi.* Rome: Istituto Storico dei Cappuccini, 1989.

Bell, Rudolph. *The Holy Anorexia.* Chicago: University of Chicago Press, 1985.

Belotti, Gianpiero, ed. *Angela Merici: La società, la vita, le opere, il carisma.* Brescia: Centro Mericiano, 2004.

Bennett, Judith, et al., eds. *Sisters and Workers in the Middle Ages.* Chicago: University of Chicago Press, 1989.

Benton, John. *Culture, Power, and Personality in Medieval France.* London: Hambledon, 1991.

Benvenuti Papi, Anna. "Frati mendicanti e pinzochere in Toscana: Dalla marginalizzazione sociale ai modelli di santità." In *Temi e problemi nella mistica femminile trecentesca,* 109–35. Atti del XX Convegno del Centro di Studi sulla spiritualità medievale, Todi, ottobre 1979. Todi: Accademia Tudertina, 1983.

———. "'Velut in Sepulchro': Cellane e recluse nella tradizione agiografica italiana." In *Culto dei santi, istituzioni e classi sociali in età preindustriale,* edited by Sofia Boesch Gajano and Lucia Sebastiani, 365–455. L'Aquila and Rome: Japadre, 1984.

Beyer, Jean. *Il diritto della vita consacrata.* Milan: Ancora, 1989.

Bilinkoff, Jodi. *The Avila of Saint Teresa: Religious Reform in a Sixteenth-Century City.* Ithaca, N.Y.: Cornell University Press, 1989.

———. "Elite Widows and Religious Expression in Early Modern Spain: The View from Avila." In *Widowhood in Medieval and Early Modern Europe,* edited by Sandra Cavallo and Lyndan Warner, 181–92. London: Longman, 1999.

———. *Related Lives: Confessors and Their Female Penitents, 1450–1750.* Ithaca and New York: Cornell University Press, 2005.

Black, Christopher F. *Italian Confraternities in the Sixteenth Century.* Cambridge: Cambridge University Press, 1989.

Blaisdell, Charmarie J. "Angela Merici and the Ursulines." In *Religious Orders of the Catholic Reformation,* edited by Richard L. DeMolen, 99–137. New York: Fordham University Press, 1994.

Blickle, Peter. *The Revolution of 1525: The German Peasants' War from a New*

Perspective. Translated by T. A. Brady and H. C. E. Midelfort. Baltimore: Johns Hopkins University Press, 1981.

Blok, Anton. "Notes on the Concept of Virginity in Mediterranean Societies." In *Women and Men in Spiritual Culture (XIV–XVII Centuries): A Meeting of South and North,* edited by Elisja Schulte Van Kessel, 27–33. The Hague: Netherlands Government Publishing Office, 1986.

Blumenfeld-Kosinski, Renate, and Timea Szell, eds. *Images of Sainthood in Medieval Europe.* Ithaca, N.Y.: Cornell University Press, 1991.

Boesch Gajano, Sofia, and Lucia Sebastiani, eds. *Culto dei santi, istituzioni e classi sociali in età preindustriale.* L'Aquila and Rome: Japadre, 1984.

Bonora, Elena. *I conflitti della Controriforma: Santità e obbedienza nell'esperienza religiosa dei primi Barnabiti.* Florence: Le Lettere, 1998.

Bornstein, Daniel. "Women and Religion in Late Medieval Italy: History and Historiography." In *Women and Religion in Medieval and Renaissance Italy,* edited by Daniel Bornstein and Roberto Rusconi, 1–27. Chicago: University of Chicago Press, 1996.

Bornstein, Daniel, and Roberto Rusconi, eds. *Women and Religion in Medieval and Renaissance Italy.* Chicago: University of Chicago Press, 1996.

Børresen, Kari. "*Matristics:* Ancient and Medieval Church Mothers." In *Gender and Religion: Genre et religion,* edited by Kari E. Børresen, Sara Cabibbo, and Edith Specht, 203–18. Rome: Carocci, 2001.

Børresen, Kari, Sara Cabibbo, and Edith Specht, eds. *Gender and Religion: Genre et religion.* Rome: Carocci, 2001.

Bossy, John. *Christianity in the West 1400–1700.* Oxford and New York: Oxford University Press, 1985.

———. "The Counter-Reformation and the People of Catholic Europe." *Past and Present* 47 (1970): 51–70.

———. "The Social History of Confession in the Age of the Reformation." *Transactions of the Royal Historical Society* 25 (1975): 21–38.

Brezzi, Paolo. "La spiritualità della 'devotio moderna.'" In *Caratteri e protagonisti della spiritualità cattolica alla fine del Medio Evo,* edited by Paolo Brezzi, 39–61. Naples: Libreria Scientifica Editrice, 1960.

Broadhead, Philip J. "Guildsmen, Religious Reform, and the Search for the Common Good: The Role of the Guilds in the Early Reformation in Augsburg." *Historical Journal* 39, no. 3 (1996): 577–97.

Brown, Judith C. *Immodest Acts: The Life of a Lesbian Nun in Renaissance Italy.* New York: Oxford University Press, 1986.

Brown, Judith C., and Robert C. Davis, eds. *Gender and Society in Renaissance Italy.* London and New York: Longman, 1998.

Burckhardt, Jacob. *Die Kultur der Renaissance in Italien.* Edited by Horst Günther. Frankfurt: Deutscher Klassiker, 1989. English translation: *The*

Civilization of the Renaissance in Italy. 2 vols. Translated by S. G. C. Middlemore. New York: Harper & Row, 1958.

Burke, Peter. "Representation of the Self from Petrarch to Descartes." In *Rewriting the Self: Histories from the Renaissance to the Present,* edited by Roy Porter, 17–28. London and New York: Routledge, 1997.

Bynum, Caroline Walker. *Fragmentation and Redemption: Essays on Gender and the Human Body in Medieval Religion.* New York: Zone, 1991.

———. *Holy Feast and Holy Fast: The Religious Significance of Food to Medieval Women.* Berkeley: University of California Press, 1987.

———. "Introduction: The Complexity of Symbols." In *Gender and Religion: On the Complexity of Symbols,* edited by Caroline Walker Bynum, Stevan Harrell, and Paula Richman, 1–20. Boston: Beacon, 1986.

———. *Jesus as Mother: Studies in the Spirituality of the High Middle Ages.* Berkeley: University of California Press, 1982.

———. "Religious Women in the Later Middle Ages." In *Christian Spirituality II, High Middle Ages and Reformation, World Spirituality: An Encyclopedic History of the Religious Quest,* vol. 17, edited by Jill Raitt, 375–91. New York: Crossroad, 1987.

Cabibbo, Sara. "'Ignoratio Scripturarum, Ignoratio Christi Est': Tradizione e pratica delle scritture nei testi monastici femminili del XVII secolo." *Rivista storica italiana* 101, no. 1 (1989): 85–124.

Cabibbo, Sara, and Marilena Modica. *La santa dei Tomasi: Storia di suor Maria crocifissa (1645–1699).* Turin: Einaudi, 1989.

Caffiero, Marina. "From the Late Baroque Mystical Explosion to the Social Apostolate." In *Women and Faith: Catholic Religious Life in Italy from Late Antiquity to the Present,* edited by Lucetta Scaraffia and Gabriella Zarri. Cambridge, Mass.: Harvard University Press, 1999.

Cairns, Christopher. *Domenico Bollani, Bishop of Brescia: Devotion to Church and State in the Republic of Venice in the Sixteenth Century.* Nieuwkoop: De Graaf, 1976.

Calvi, Giulia, ed. *Innesti: Donne e genere nella storia sociale.* Rome: Viella, 2004.

Cameron, Euan. *The European Reformation.* Oxford: Clarendon, 1991.

Caponetto, Salvatore. *La Riforma protestante nell'Italia del Cinquecento.* Turin: Claudiana, 1992.

Caprioli, Adriano, Antonio Rinoldi, and Luciano Vaccaro. *Diocesi di Brescia.* Brescia: La Scuola, 1992.

Caraman, Philip. *St. Angela: The Life of Angela Merici, Foundress of the Ursulines, 1474–1540.* London and New York: Longman, 1963.

Casagrande, Carla. "The Protected Woman." In *A History of Women in the West,* edited by Georges Duby and Michelle Perrot. Vol. 2, *Silences of the Middle Ages.* Edited by Christiane Klapisch-Zuber, 70–104. Cambridge, Mass.: Harvard University Press, 1992.

Casagrande, Giovanna. "Confraternities and Lay Female Religiosity in Late Medieval and Renaissance Umbria." In *The Politics of Ritual Kinship: Confraternities and Social Order in Early Modern Italy,* edited by Nicholas Terpstra, 48–66. Cambridge: Cambridge University Press, 2000.

Cavallo, Sandra. *Charity and Power in Early Modern Italy: Benefactors and Their Motives in Turin, 1541–1789.* Cambridge: Cambridge University Press, 1995.

Cavallo, Sandra, and Lyndan Warner, eds. *Widowhood in Medieval and Early Modern Europe.* London: Longman, 1999.

Certeau, Michel de. *Mystic Fable.* Vol. 1, *The Sixteenth and Seventeenth Centuries.* Chicago: University of Chicago Press, 1992.

Châtellier, Louis. *The Europe of the Devout: The Catholic Reformation and the Formation of a New Society.* Cambridge: Cambridge University Press, 1987.

Chodorow, Nancy. *The Reproduction of Mothering: Psychoanalysis and the Sociology of Gender.* Berkeley: University of California Press, 1978.

Ciletti, Elena. "The Enactment of Ideal Womanhood in the Judith Paintings of Artemisia Gentileschi." Paper presented at the Renaissance Society of America Annual Meeting, San Francisco, 23–25 March, 2006.

Cistellini, Antonio. *Figure della riforma pretridentina: Stefana Quinzani, Angela Merici, Laura Mignani, Bartolomeo Stella, Francesco Cabrini, Francesco Santabona.* Brescia: Morcelliana, 1948.

———. "La vita religiosa nei secoli XV e XVI." In *Storia di Brescia,* edited by Giovanni Treccani degli Alfieri, 2:399–473. Brescia: Morcelliana, 1963.

Coakley, John. "Friars as Confidants of Holy Women in Medieval Dominican Hagiography." In *Images of Sainthood in Medieval Europe,* edited by Renate Blumenfeld-Kosinski and Timea Szell, 222–46. Ithaca, N.Y.: Cornell University Press, 1991.

———. "Introduction: Women's Creativity in Religious Context." In *Creative Women in Medieval and Early Modern Italy: A Religious and Artistic Renaissance,* edited by E. Ann Matter and John Coakley, 1–16. Philadelphia: University of Pennsylvania Press, 1994.

Cohen, Elizabeth, and Thomas V. Cohen. *Words and Deeds in Renaissance Rome: Trials before the Papal Magistrates.* Toronto: University of Toronto Press, 1993.

Cohen, Sherrill. "Asylums for Women in Counter-Reformation Italy." In *Women in Reformation and Counter-Reformation Europe: Private and Public Worlds,* edited by Sherrin Marshall, 166–88. Bloomington: Indiana University Press, 1989.

———. *The Evolution of Women's Asylums since 1500.* Oxford and New York: Oxford University Press, 1992.

Cohn, Samuel K., Jr. *Women in the Street: Essays on Sex and Power in Renaissance Italy.* Baltimore: Johns Hopkins University Press, 1996.

Colosio, Innocenzio. "Serafino da Fermo e le beate Margherita e Gentile e le Regole della Compagnia del Buon Gesù." *La nuova rivista di ascetica e mistica* 2 (1977): 246–58.

Cousins, Ewert. "The Humanity and the Passion of Christ." In *Christian Spirituality II, High Middle Ages and Reformation, World Spirituality: An Encyclopedic History of the Religious Quest,* vol. 17, edited by Jill Raitt, 375–91. New York: Crossroad, 1987.

Cox, Virginia. "The Single Self: Feminist Thought and the Marriage Market in Early Modern Venice." *Renaissance Quarterly* 48, no. 3 (1995): 513–81.

Craveri, Marcello. *Sante e streghe: Biografie e documenti dal XIV al XVII secolo.* Milan: Feltrinelli, 1980.

Culpepper, Danielle. "'Our Particolar Cloister': Ursulines and Female Education in Seventeenth-Century Parma and Piacenza." *Sixteenth Century Journal* 36, no. 4 (2005): 1017–37.

Dalarun, Jacques. "The Clerical Gaze." In *A History of Women in the West,* edited by Georges Duby and Michelle Perrot. Vol. 2, *Silences of the Middle Ages.* Edited by Christiane Klapisch-Zuber, 15–42. Cambridge, Mass.: Harvard University Press, 1992.

D'Amelia, Marina. "La presenza delle madri nell'Italia Medievale e Moderna." In *Storia della maternità,* edited by Marina D'Amelia, 3–52. Rome and Bari: Laterza, 1997.

Dassa, Battista. *La fondazione di S. Angela Merici come prima forma di vita consacrata a Dio nel mondo.* Milan: Ancora, 1967.

Debongnie, Pierre. "Les thèmes de l'Imitation." *Revue d'histoire ecclésiastique* 36 (1940): 289–344.

De Giorgio, Michela, and Christiane Klapisch-Zuber, eds. *Storia del matrimonio.* Rome and Bari: Laterza, 1996.

Delumeau, Jean. *Sin and Fear: The Emergence of Western Guilt Culture: 13th–18th Centuries.* New York: St. Martin's, 1990.

De Maio, Romeo. *Donna e Rinascimento.* Milan: Il Saggiatore, 1987.

De Molen, Richard L., ed. *Religious Orders of the Catholic Reformation.* New York: Fordham University Press, 1994.

De Rosa, Gabriele, Tullio Gregory, and André Vauchez, eds. *Storia dell'Italia religiosa.* Vol. 2, *L'età moderna.* Rome and Bari: Laterza, 1994.

Diefendorf, Barbara. *From Penitence to Charity: Pious Women and the Catholic Reformation in Paris.* New York: Oxford University Press, 2004.

Di Filippo Bareggi, Claudia. "Una riforma al femminile: La Compagnia di Sant'Orsola fra Angela Merici e Carlo Borromeo." In *Chierici e laici nella Chiesa Tridentina: Educare per riformare,* 60–108. Milan: CUEM, 2003.

Dinzelbacher, Peter. "Mistica e profezia femminile nel Medioevo europeo: Una panoramica." In *Donne, potere e profezia,* edited by Adriana Valerio, 121–38. Naples: M. D'Auria, 1995.

———. "Sante o streghe: Alcuni casi nel tardo medioevo." In *Finzione e santità tra medioevo ed età moderna,* edited by Gabriella Zarri, 52–87. Turin: Rosemberg & Sellier, 1991.

———. *Vision und Visionliteratur im Mittelalter.* Stuttgart: Hiersemann, 1981.

Dizionario degli Istituti di Perfezione. Edited by Guerrino Pelliccia (1962–68) and Giancarlo Rocca (1969–2004). Rome: Edizioni Paoline.

Donati, Claudio. *L'idea di nobiltà in Italia.* Rome and Bari: Laterza, 1988.

Dor, Juliette, Lesley Johnson, and Jocelyn Wogan-Brown, eds. *New Trends in Feminine Spirituality: The Holy Women of Liège and Their Impact.* Turnhout: Brepols, 1999.

Douglas, Mary. *Purity and Danger: An Analysis of the Concepts of Pollution and Taboo.* London: Routledge & Kegan Paul, 1966.

Dronke, Peter. *Women Writers of the Middle Ages: A Critical Study of Texts from Perpetua (203) to Marguerite Porete (1310).* Cambridge: Cambridge University Press, 1984.

Duby, Georges, and Michelle Perrot, eds. *History of Women in the West.* Vol. 2, *Silences of the Middle Ages.* Edited by Christiane Klapisch-Zuber. Cambridge, Mass.: Harvard University Press, 1992.

Dupré, Louis, and Don E. Saliers, in collaboration with John Meyendorff, eds. *Christian Spirituality III, Post-Reformation and Modern, World Spirituality: An Encyclopedic History of the Religious Quest.* Vol. 18. New York: Crossroad, 1990.

Elliott, Dyan. *Proving Woman: Female Spirituality and Inquisitorial Culture in the Later Middle Ages.* Princeton, N.J.: Princeton University Press, 2004.

Erba, Andrea M. *L'umanesimo spirituale: L'enchiridion di Erasmo da Rotterdam.* Rome: Studium, 1994.

Esposito, Anna. "Men and Women in Roman Confraternities in the Fifteenth and Sixteenth Centuries: Roles, Functions, Expectations." In *The Politics of Ritual Kinship: Confraternities and Social Order in Early Modern Italy,* edited by Nicholas Terpstra, 82–97. Cambridge: Cambridge University Press, 2000.

Evangelisti, Silvia. "Wives, Widows, and Brides of Christ: Marriage and the Convent in the Historiography of Early Modern Italy." *Historical Journal* 43, no. 1 (2000): 233–47.

Evenett, H. Outram. *The Spirit of the Counter-Reformation: The Birkbeck Lectures in Ecclesiastical History Given in the University of Cambridge in May 1951.* Edited with a postscript by John Bossy. Cambridge: Cambridge University Press, 1968.

Fabbri, Lorenzo. "Trattatistica e pratica dell'alleanza matrimoniale." In *Storia del matrimonio,* edited by Michela De Giorgio and Christiane Klapisch-Zuber, 91–117. Rome and Bari: Laterza, 1996.

Ferrante, Lucia. "L'onore ritrovato: Donne nella casa del soccorso di San

Paolo a Bologna (sec. XVI–XVII)." *Quaderni storici* 53, no. 2 (1983): 499–527.

Ferraro, Joan. *Family and Public Life in Brescia, 1580–1650: The Foundations of Power in the Venetian State.* Cambridge: Cambridge University Press, 1993.

Filoramo, Giovanni, and Daniele Menozzi, eds. *Storia del cristianesimo: L'età moderna.* Rome and Bari: Laterza, 1997.

Firpo, Massimo. *Riforma protestante ed eresie nell'Italia del Cinquecento.* Rome and Bari: Laterza, 1993.

Foucault, Michel. *Folie et déraison: Histoire de la folie à l'âge classique.* Paris: Plon, 1961.

Fragnito, Gigliola. "Gli ordini religiosi tra Riforma e Controriforma." In *Clero e società nell'Italia moderna,* edited by Mario Rosa, 115–205. Rome and Bari: Laterza, 1992.

Fubini Leuzzi, Maria. "Vita coniugale e vita familiare nei trattati italiani fra XVI e XVII secolo." In *Donna, disciplina, creanza cristiana dal XV al XVII secolo: Studi e testi a stampa,* edited by Gabriella Zarri, 253–67. Rome: Edizioni di Storia e Letteratura.

Fulton, Rachel. *From Judgment to Passion: Devotion to Christ and the Virgin Mary, 800–1200.* New York: Columbia University Press, 2003.

Galloway, Penny. "Neither Miraculous nor Astonishing: The Devotional Practice of Beguine Communities in French Flanders." In *New Trends in Feminine Spirituality: The Holy Women of Liège and Their Impact,* edited by Juliette Dor, Lesley Johnson, and Jocelyn Wogan-Brown, 107–27. Turnhout: Brepols, 1999.

Geertz, Clifford. *The Interpretation of Cultures: Selected Essays.* New York: Basic, 1973.

Gentili, Antonio, and Mauro Regazzoni. *La spiritualità della Riforma Cattolica: La spiritualità italiana dal 1500 al 1650.* Storia della spiritualità 5/C. Bologna: EDB, 1993.

Gill, Katherine. "Open Monasteries for Women in Late Medieval and Early Modern Italy: Two Roman Examples." In *The Crannied Wall: Women, Religion, and the Arts in Early Modern Europe,* edited by Craig A. Monson, 15–47. Ann Arbor: University of Michigan Press, 1992.

———. "Women and the Production of Religious Literature." In *Creative Women in Medieval and Early Modern Italy: A Religious and Artistic Renaissance,* edited by E. Ann Matter and John Coakley, 64–104. Philadelphia: University of Pennsylvania Press, 1994.

Ginzburg, Carlo. *Storia notturna: Una decifrazione del sabba.* Turin: Einaudi, 1989.

Gottlieb, Beatrice. "The Problem of Feminism in the Fifteenth Century." In *Women of the Medieval World,* edited by Julius Kirshner and Suzanne Fonay Wemple, 337–64. Oxford: Blackwell, 1985.

Greenblatt, Stephen. *Renaissance Self-Fashioning: From More to Shakespeare.* Chicago: University of Chicago Press, 1980.

Grendler, Paul F. "Man Is Almost a God: Fra Battista Carioni between Renaissance and Catholic Reformation." In *Humanity and Divinity in Renaissance and Reformation: Essays in Honor of Charles Trinkaus,* edited by John W. O'Malley, Thomas M. Izbicki, and Gerald Christianson, 227–49. Leiden and New York: E. J. Brill, 1993.

Groppi, Angela. *Il lavoro delle donne.* Rome and Bari: Laterza, 1996.

Grundmann, Herbert. *Religious Movements in the Middle Ages: The Historical Links between Heresy, the Mendicant Orders, and the Women's Religious Movement in the Twelfth and Thirteenth Century, with the Historical Foundations of German Mysticism.* Translated by Steven Rowan. Notre Dame, Ind.: University of Notre Dame Press, 1996.

Guarnieri, Romana. "Angela da Foligno, mistica europea." In *Angela da Foligno Terziaria Francescana,* edited by Enrico Menestò, 39–82. Atti del Convegno storico nel VII centenario dell'ingresso della beata Angela da Foligno nell'Ordine Francescano Secolare (1291–1991). Foligno 17–18–19 novembre 1991. Spoleto: Centro Italiano di studi sull'alto medioevo, 1992.

Guerrini, Paolo. "La Compagnia di S. Orsola dalle origini alla soppressione napoleonica (1535–1810)." In *S. Angela Merici e la Compagnia di S. Orsola nel IV centenario della fondazione,* edited by Sigrid Undset et al., 53–247. Brescia: Ancora, 1936.

Hale, John. *Civilization of Europe in the Renaissance.* New York: Simon & Schuster, 1995.

Harline, Craig. "Actives and Contemplatives: The Female Religious of the Low Countries before and after Trent." *Catholic Historical Review* 81, no. 4 (1995): 541–67.

Henderson, John. *Piety and Charity in Late Medieval Florence.* Oxford: Clarendon, 1994.

Herlihy, David. *Opera Muliebria: Women and Work in Medieval Europe.* Philadelphia: Temple University Press, 1990.

Hsia, R. Po-chia, ed. *The German People and the Reformation.* Ithaca, N.Y.: Cornell University Press, 1988.

———. *The World of Catholic Renewal, 1540–1770.* Cambridge: Cambridge University Press, 1998.

Hudon, William. "Religion and Society in Early Modern Italy: Old Questions, New Insights." *American Historical Review* 101 (1996): 783–804.

———. *Theatine Spirituality: Selected Writings.* New York: Paulist, 1996.

Hufton, Olwen. *The Prospect before Her: A History of Women in Western Europe.* Vol. 1. London: Harper Collins, 1995.

Hughes, Diane Owen. "Domestic Ideals and Social Behavior: Evidence from Medieval Genoa." In *Family in History: Lectures Given in Memory of*

Stephen Allen Kaplan under the Auspices of the Department of History at the University of Pennsylvania, edited by Charles E. Rosenberg, 115–43. Philadelphia: University of Pennsylvania Press, 1975.

Jedin, Hubert. *Katholische Reformation oder Gegenreformation? Ein Versuch zur Klärung der Begriffe nebst einer Jubiläumsbetrachtung über das Trienter Konzil.* Lucerne: Josef Stoker, 1946.

Jedin, Hubert, et al., eds. *History of the Church.* Vol. 5, *Reformation and Counter Reformation.* London: Burns & Oates, 1980.

Juan de Valdés. *Alfabeto cristiano. Domande e risposte. Della predestinazione. Catechismo.* Edited by Adriano Prosperi. Turin: Einaudi, 1994.

Jütte, Robert. *Poverty and Deviance in Early Modern Europe.* Cambridge: Cambridge University Press, 1994.

Kelly, Joan. "Did Women Have a Renaissance?" In *Becoming Visible: Women in European History,* edited by Renate Bridenthal and Claudia Koonz, 137–64. Boston: Houghton Mifflin, 1977.

Kieckhefer, Richard. "Holiness and the Culture of Devotion: Remarks on Some Late Medieval Male Saints." In *Images of Sainthood in Medieval Europe,* edited by Renate Blumenfeld-Kosinski and Timea Szell, 288–305. Ithaca, N.Y.: Cornell University Press, 1991.

King, Margaret L. "Book-Lined Cells: Women and Humanism in the Early Italian Renaissance." In *Beyond Their Sex: Learned Women in the European Past,* edited by Patricia H. Labalme, 66–90. New York: New York University Press, 1980.

———. *Women of the Renaissance.* Chicago: University of Chicago Press, 1991.

Klapisch-Zuber, Christiane. "Un salario o l'onore: Come valutare le donne fiorentine del XIV–XV secolo." *Quaderni storici* 79, no. 1 (1992): 41–49.

———. *Women, Family, and Ritual in Renaissance Italy.* Chicago: University of Chicago Press, 1985.

Knox, Dilwyn. "Disciplina: Le origini monastiche e clericali del buon comportamento nell'Europa cattolica del Cinquecento e del primo Seicento." In *Disciplina dell'anima, disciplina del corpo e disciplina della società tra medioevo ed età moderna,* edited by Paolo Prodi, 63–99. Bologna: il Mulino, 1994.

Kraemer, Ross S. "The Conversion of Women to Ascetic Forms of Christianity." In *Sisters and Workers in the Middle Ages,* edited by Judith Bennett et al., 98–207. Chicago: University of Chicago Press, 1989.

Kroeber, Alfred L. *The Nature of Culture.* Chicago: University of Chicago Press, 1956.

Laqueur, Thomas. *Making Sex: Body and Gender from the Greeks to Freud.* Cambridge, Mass.: Harvard University Press, 1990.

Laven, Mary. *Sisters of Venice: Enclosed Lives and Broken Vows in the Renaissance Convent.* London: Penguin, 2003.

Lawrence, Clifford Hugh. *Medieval Monasticism: Forms of Religious Life in Western Europe in the Middle Ages*. London and New York: Longman, 1989.

Leclercq, Jean. *La spiritualité au Moyen Age*. Vol. 1. Paris: Ed. Montaigne-Aubier, 1966.

Ledòchowska, Teresa, OSU. *Angèle Merici et la Compagnie de Ste-Ursule à la lumière des documents*. Rome and Milan: Ancora, 1968.

Le Goff, Jacques. *Pour un autre Moyen Ages*. Paris: Gallimard, 1978.

Leonardi, Claudio. "La santità delle donne." In *Scrittrici mistiche italiane*, edited by Claudio Leonardi and Giovanni Pozzi, 43–57. Genoa: Marietti, 1988.

Leonardi, Claudio, and Giovanni Pozzi, eds. *Scrittrici mistiche italiane*. Genoa: Marietti, 1988.

Lévi-Strauss, Claude. *Les structures élémentaires de la parenté*. Paris: Presses universitaires de France, 1947.

Lévy-Bruhl, Lucien. *Le surnaturel et la nature dans la mèntalité primitive*. Paris: Presses universitaires de France, 1931.

Liebowitz, Ruth P. "Virgins in the Service of Christ: The Dispute over an Active Apostolate for Women during the Counter-Reformation." In *Women of Spirit: Female Leadership in the Jewish and Christian Traditions*, edited by Rosemary Ruether and Eleanor McLaughlin, 131–52. New York: Simon & Schuster, 1974.

Lierheimer, Linda. *The Life of Antoinette Micolon*. Milwaukee: Marquette University Press, 2004.

———. "Preaching or Teaching? Defining the Ursuline Mission in Seventeenth-Century France." In *Women Preachers and Prophets through Two Millennia of Christianity*, edited by Beverly Mayne Kienzle and Pamela J. Walker, 212–26. Berkeley: University of California Press, 1998.

———. "Redefining Convent Space: Ideals of Female Community among Seventeenth-Century Ursuline Nuns." In *Proceedings of the Western Society for French History: Selected Papers of the Annual Meeting*, vol. 24, edited by Barry Rothaus, 211–20. Niwot: University Press of Colorado, 1997.

Lombardi Satriani, Luigi M., and Mariano Meligrana. *Il ponte di San Giacomo: L'ideologia della morte nella società contadina del Sud*. Milan: Rizzoli, 1982.

Lowe, Kate. "Secular Brides and Convent Brides: Wedding Ceremonies in Italy during the Renaissance and Counter-Reformation." In *Marriage in Italy, 1350–1650*, edited by Trevor Dean and Kate Lowe, 41–65. Cambridge: Cambridge University Press, 1997.

MacCormack, Carol P., and Marilyn Strathern, eds. *Nature, Culture, and Gender*. Cambridge: Cambridge University Press, 1980.

Maclean, Ian. *The Renaissance Notion of Woman: A Study in the Fortunes of Scholasticism and Medical Science in European Intellectual Life.* Cambridge: Cambridge University Press, 1980.

Magli, Ida. *La donna un problema aperto, guida alla ricerca antropologica.* Florence: Vallecchi, 1974.

————. *Gli uomini della penitenza: Lineamenti antropologici del medioevo italiano.* Milan: Garzanti, 1977.

Makowski, Elizabeth. *Canon Law and Cloistered Women: Periculoso and Its Commentators, 1298–1545.* Washington, D.C.: Catholic University of America Press, 1997.

Manselli, Raoul. *Il soprannaturale e la religione popolare nel medioevo.* Rome: Studium, 1985.

Marcocchi, Massimo. *La Riforma Cattolica: Documenti e testimonianze.* 2 vols. Brescia: Morcelliana, 1967–70.

Mariani, Luciana, Elisa Tarolli, and Marie Seynaeve. *Angela Merici: Contributo per una biografia.* Milan: Ancora, 1986.

Martin, John J. "Inventing Sincerity, Refashioning Prudence: The Discovery of the Individual in Renaissance Europe." *American Historical Review* 102, no. 5 (1997): 1309–42.

————. *Myths of Renaissance Individualism.* New York: Palgrave Macmillan, 2004.

Martinori, Edoardo. *La moneta: Vocabolario generale.* Rome: Multigrafica editrice, 1977.

Matter, E. Ann. "The Commentary on the Rule of Clare of Assisi by Maria Domitilla Galluzzi." In *Creative Women in Medieval and Early Modern Italy: A Religious and Artistic Renaissance,* edited by E. Ann Matter and John Coakley, 201–11. Philadelphia: University of Pennsylvania Press, 1994.

————. "Mystical Marriage." In *Women and Faith: Catholic Religious Life in Italy from Late Antiquity to the Present,* edited by Lucetta Scaraffia and Gabriella Zarri, 31–41. Cambridge, Mass.: Harvard University Press, 1999.

Matter, E. Ann, and John Coakley, eds. *Creative Women in Medieval and Early Modern Italy: A Religious and Artistic Renaissance.* Philadelphia: University of Pennsylvania Press, 1994.

McLaughlin, Mary Martin. "Creating and Recreating Communities of Women: The Case of Corpus Domini, Ferrara, 1406–1452." In *Sisters and Workers in the Middle Ages,* edited by Judith Bennett et al., 261–88. Chicago: University of Chicago Press, 1989.

McNamara, Jo Ann Kay. *Sisters in Arms: Catholic Nuns through Two Millennia.* Cambridge, Mass.: Harvard University Press, 1996.

Medioli, Francesca. "The Clausura before and after Trent." In *Women in Renaissance and Early Modern Europe,* edited by Christine Meek, 136–52. Dublin: Four Courts, 2000.

Meersseman, Gilles Gérard. *Ordo fraternitatis: Confraternite e pietà dei laici nel Medioevo.* Rome: Herder, 1977.

Moeller, Bernd. *Imperial Cities and the Reformation: Three Essays.* Translated by H. C. E. Midelfort and M. U. Edwards. Philadelphia: Fortress, 1972.

Monica, Mary, OSU. *Angela Merici and Her Teaching Idea (1474–1540).* New York: Longmans, Green, 1927.

Monson, Craig, ed. *The Crannied Wall: Women, Religion, and the Arts in Early Modern Europe.* Ann Arbor: University of Michigan Press, 1992.

Montanari, Daniele. *Disciplinamento in terra veneta: La diocesi di Brescia nella seconda metà del XVI secolo.* Bologna: il Mulino, 1987.

Mooney, Catherine M. "The Auctorial Role of Brother A. in the Composition of Angela da Foligno's Revelations." In *Creative Women in Medieval and Early Modern Italy: A Religious and Artistic Renaissance,* edited by E. Ann Matter and John Coakley, 34–63. Philadelphia: University of Pennsylvania Press, 1994.

———, ed. *Gendered Voices: Medieval Saints and Their Interpreters.* Philadelphia: University of Pennsylvania Press, 1999.

Moore, Henrietta. *Feminism and Anthropology.* Cambridge: Polity, 1988.

Muir, Edward. *Ritual in Early Modern Europe.* Cambridge: Cambridge University Press, 1997.

Naro, Cataldo, ed. *Angela Merici: Vita della Chiesa e spiritualità nella prima metà del Cinquecento.* Convegno di studi storici (Mascalucia 21–22 luglio 1997), Studi del centro "A. Cammarata," 27. Caltanissetta and Rome: Salvatore Sciascia, 1998.

Neel, Carol. "The Origins of the Beguines." In *Sisters and Workers in the Middle Ages,* edited by Judith Bennett et al., 240–60. Chicago: University of Chicago Press, 1989.

Newman, Barbara. *From Virile Woman to WomanChrist: Studies in Medieval Religion and Literature.* Philadelphia: University of Pennsylvania Press, 1995.

Niccoli, Ottavia. *Profeti e popolo nell'Italia del Rinascimento.* Rome and Bari: Laterza, 1987.

O'Malley, John W. "Early Jesuit Spirituality." In *Christian Spirituality II, Post-Reformation and Modern, World Spirituality: An Encyclopedic History of the Religious Quest,* vol. 18, edited by Louis Dupré, Don E. Saliers, and John Meyendorff, 3–27. New York: Crossroad, 1990.

———. Introduction to *Christian Spirituality II, Post-Reformation and Modern, World Spirituality: An Encyclopedic History of the Religious Quest,* vol. 18, edited by Louis Dupré, Don E. Saliers, and John Meyendorff, xiii–xxv. New York: Crossroad, 1990.

———. "The Society of Jesus." In *Religious Orders of the Catholic Reformation,* edited by Richard L. De Molen, 139–63. New York: Fordham University Press, 1994.

————. *Trent and All That: Renaming Catholicism in the Early Modern Era.* Cambridge, Mass.: Harvard University Press, 2000.

————. "Was Ignatius Loyola a Church Reformer? How to Look at Early Modern Catholicism." *Catholic Historical Review* 77, no. 2 (1991): 177–93.

O'Malley, John W., Thomas M. Izbicki, and Gerald Christianson. *Humanity and Divinity in Renaissance and Reformation: Essays in Honor of Charles Trinkaus.* Leiden and New York: E. J. Brill, 1993.

Ortner, Sherry B. "Is Female to Male as Nature Is to Culture?" In *Women, Culture, and Society,* edited by Michelle Zimbalist Rosaldo and Louise Lamphere, 67–87. Stanford, Calif.: Stanford University Press, 1974.

Pasero, Carlo. "Il dominio veneto fino all'incendio della Loggia (1426–1575)." In *Storia di Brescia,* edited by Giovanni Treccani degli Alfieri, 2:3–396. Brescia: Morcelliana, 1963.

Perry, Mary Elizabeth. *Gender and Disorder in Early Modern Seville.* Princeton, N.J.: Princeton University Press, 1991.

Petrocchi, Massimo. *Storia della spiritualità italiana.* Turin: SEI, 1996.

Petroff, Elizabeth A. *Body and Soul: Essays on Medieval Women and Mysticism.* New York and Oxford: Oxford University Press, 1994.

————, ed. *Medieval Women's Visionary Literature.* New York: Oxford University Press, 1986.

Picasso, Giorgio. "L'imitazione di Cristo e l'ambiente di S. Giustina." In *Riforma della Chiesa, cultura e spiritualità nel Quattrocento Veneto,* edited by Giovanni B. Trolese, 263–76. Atti del Convegno per il IV Centenario di Ludovico Barbaro, 1382–1443, Padova-Venezia-Treviso 19–24 settembre 1982. Cesena: Badia di S.Maria del Monte, 1984.

Pomata, Gianna. "Practicing between Earth and Heaven: Women Healers in Seventeenth-Century Bologna." *Dynamis: Acta Hisp. Med. Sci. Hist. Illus.* 19 (1999): 119–43.

Porter, Roy. *Rewriting the Self: Histories from the Renaissance to the Present.* London: Routledge, 1997.

Premoli, Orazio. *Storia dei Barnabiti nel Cinquecento.* Vol. 1. Rome: Desclee & C. Editori, 1913.

Prodi, Paolo, ed. *Disciplina dell'anima, disciplina del corpo e disciplina della società tra medioevo ed età moderna.* Bologna: il Mulino, 1994.

————. "Nel mondo o fuori dal mondo: La vocazione alla perfezione all'inizio dell'età moderna." In *Angela Merici: Vita della Chiesa e spiritualità nella prima metà del Cinquecento,* edited by Cataldo Naro, 13–33. Convegno di studi storici (Mascalucia 21–22 luglio 1997), Studi del centro "A. Cammarata," 27. Caltanissetta and Rome: Salvatore Sciascia, 1998.

————. *Il sacramento del potere: Il giuramento politico nella storia costituzionale dell'Occidente.* Bologna: il Mulino, 1992.

———. "Vita religiosa e crisi sociale nei tempi di Angela Merici." *Humanitas* 19 (1974): 307–18.

Prodi, Paolo, and Peter Johanek, eds. *Strutture ecclesiastiche in Italia e in Germania prima della Riforma.* Bologna: il Mulino, 1984.

Prosperi, Adriano. "Dalle 'divine madri' ai 'padri spirituali.'" In *Women and Men in Spiritual Culture, XIV–XVII Centuries: A Meeting of South and North,* edited by Elisja Schulte van Kessel, 71–90. The Hague: Netherlands Government Publishing Office, 1986.

———. "Riforma cattolica, Controriforma, disciplinamento sociale." In *Storia dell'Italia religiosa.* Vol. 2, *L'età moderna,* edited by Gabriele De Rosa and Tullio Gregory, 3–48. Rome and Bari: Laterza, 1994.

———. *Tribunali della coscienza: Confessori, inquisitori, missionari.* Turin: Einaudi, 1996.

Pullan, Brian. "Support and Redeem: Charity and Poor Relief in Italian Cities from the Fourteenth to the Seventeenth century." *Continuity and Change* 3, no. 2 (1988): 177–208.

Raitt, Jill, ed. *Christian Spirituality II, High Middle Ages and Reformation, World Spirituality: An Encyclopedic History of the Religious Quest.* Vol. 17. New York: Crossroad, 1987.

Rapley, Elizabeth. *The Dévotes: Women and the Church in Seventeenth-Century France.* Montreal and London: McGill-Queen's University Press, 1990.

Reese, Alan W. "Learning Virginity: Erasmus' Ideal of Christian Marriage." *Bibliotheque d'humanisme et Renaissance* 57, no. 3 (1995): 551–67.

Reinhard, Wolfgang. "Disciplinamento sociale, confessionalizzazione, modernizzazione: Un discorso storiografico." In *Disciplina dell'anima, disciplina del corpo e disciplina della società tra medioevo ed età moderna,* edited by Paolo Prodi, 101–23. Bologna: il Mulino, 1994.

———. "Reformation, Counter-Reformation, and the Early Modern State: A Reassessment." *Catholic Historical Review* 75 (1989): 383–404.

Rigon, Antonio. "A Community of Female Penitents in Thirteenth-Century Padua." In *Women and Religion in Medieval and Renaissance Italy,* edited by Daniel Bornstein and Roberto Rusconi, 28–38. Chicago: University of Chicago Press.

Roper, Lyndal. *The Holy Household: Women and Morals in Reformation Augsburg.* Oxford: Clarendon, 1989.

———. *Oedipus and the Devil: Witchcraft, Sexuality, and Religion in Early Modern Europe.* London: Routledge, 1994.

Rosa, Mario. "La religiosa." In *L'uomo barocco,* edited by Rosario Villari, 219–67. Rome and Bari: Laterza, 1991.

———. "Per la storia della vita religiosa e della Chiesa in Italia tra il Cinquecento e il Seicento." In *Religione e società nel Mezzogiorno: Tra Cinque e Seicento,* edited by Mario Rosa, 75–145. Bari: De Donato, 1976.

Rosenwein, Barbara H. "Y avait-il un 'moi' au haut Moyen Âge?" *Revue historique* (2005): 31–52.

Rubin, Miri. *Corpus Christi: The Eucharist in Late Medieval Culture.* Cambridge: Cambridge University Press, 1991.

Sallmann, Jean-Michel. "La sainteté mystique femmine à Naples au tournant des XVIe et XVIIe siècles." In *Culto dei santi, istituzioni e classi sociali in età preindustriale,* edited by Sofia Boesch Gajano and Lucia Sebastiani, 681–702. L'Aquila and Rome: Japadre, 1984.

Sawday, Jonathan. *The Body Emblazoned: Dissection and the Human Body in Renaissance Culture.* London and New York: Routledge, 1995.

Scaraffia, Lucetta, and Gabriella Zarri, eds. *Women and Faith: Catholic Religious Life in Italy from Late Antiquity to the Present.* Cambridge, Mass.: Harvard University Press, 1999.

Scattigno, Anna. "Maria Maddalena de' Pazzi: Tra esperienza e modello." In *Donna, disciplina, creanza cristiana dal XV al XVII secolo: Studi e testi a stampa,* edited by Gabriella Zarri, 85–102. Rome: Edizioni Storia e Letteratura, 1996.

Schulenberg, Jane Tibbetts. "Women's Monastic Communities, 500–1100: Patterns of Expansion and Decline." In *Sisters and Workers in the Middle Ages,* edited by Judith Bennett et al., 208–39. Chicago: University of Chicago Press, 1989.

Schulte van Kessel, Elisja. "Vergini e madri tra cielo e terra: Le cristiane nella prima età moderna." In *Storia delle donne in Occidente,* edited by Georges Duby and Michelle Perrot. *Dal Rinascimento all'età moderna.* Edited by Natalie Zemon Davis and Arlette Farge. Rome-Bari: Laterza, 1991, 156–200.

———. *Women and Men in Spiritual Culture, XIV–XVII Centuries: A Meeting of South and North.* The Hague: Netherlands Government Publishing Office, 1986.

Scribner, Robert. *Popular Culture and Popular Movements in Reformation Germany.* London: Hambledon, 1987.

Seidel Menchi, Silvana. *Erasmo in Italia, 1520–1580.* Turin: Bollati Boringhieri, 1987.

Sensi, Mario. *Storie di Bizzoche tra Umbria e Marche.* Rome: Edizioni di Storia e Letteratura, 1995.

Simoncelli, Paolo. *Evangelismo italiano del Cinquecento: Questione religiosa e Nicodemismo politico.* Rome: Istituto storico italiano per l'età moderna e contemporanea, 1979.

Simons, Walter. *Cities of Ladies: Beguine Communities in the Medieval Low Countries, 1200–1565.* Philadelphia: University of Pennsylvania Press, 2001.

Slade, Carol. "Alterity in Union: The Mystical Experience of Angela of Foligno and Margery Kempe." *Religion and Literature* 23 (1991): 105–20.

Società Internazionale di Studi Francescani. *Movimento religioso femminile e francesanesimo nel secolo XIII*. Atti del VII Convegno Internazionale. Assisi, 11–13 ottobre 1979. Assisi: Tip. Porziuncola, 1981.

Società Italiana Delle Storiche. *Donne sante sante donne: Esperienza religiosa e storia di genere*. Turin: Rosemberg & Sellier, 1996.

Solfaroli Camillocci, Daniela. "Le confraternite del Divino Amore: Interpretazioni storiografiche e proposte attuali di ricerca." *Rivista di storia e letteratura religiosa* 3 (1991): 315–32.

———. *I Devoti della Carità: Le confraternite del Divino Amore nell'Italia del primo Cinquecento*. Naples: La Città del Sole, 2002.

Southern, Richard. *The Making of the Middle Ages*. New Haven: Yale University Press, 1953.

Sowards, J. Kelley. "Erasmus and the Education of Women." *Sixteenth Century Journal* 13, no. 4 (1982): 77–89.

Spearing, Elizabeth, ed. *Medieval Writings on Female Spirituality*. New York: Penguin, 2002.

Strathern, Marilyn. *Women in Between: Female Roles in a Male World, Mount Hagen, New Guinea*. London and New York: Seminar, 1972.

Strocchia, Sharon. "Gender and the Rites of Honour in Italian Renaissance Cities." In *Gender and Society in Renaissance Italy*, edited by Judith C. Brown and Robert C. Davies, 39–60. London and New York: Longman, 1998.

Tarolli, Elisa, ed. *Lettere del segretario, 1540–1546: Testi antichi, traslazione in italiano moderno*. Milan: Ancora, 2000.

Taylor, Charles. *Sources of the Self: The Making of the Modern Identity*. Cambridge: Cambridge University Press, 1989.

Temi e problemi della mistica femminile trecentesca. Atti del XX Convegno del Centro di Studi sulla spiritualità medievale, Todi, ottobre 1979. Todi: Accademia Tudertina, 1983.

Tenenti, Alberto. *Il senso della morte e l'amore della vita nel Rinascimento*. Turin: Einaudi, 1959.

Terpstra, Nicholas, ed. *The Politics of Ritual Kinship: Confraternities and Social Order in Early Modern Italy*. Cambridge: Cambridge University Press, 2000.

———. "Women in Brotherhood: Gender, Class, and Politics in Renaissance Bolognese Confraternities." *Renaissance and Reformation* 26 (1990): 193–211.

Tilatti, Andrea. "La regola delle Terziarie Agostiniane di Udine (sec. XV)." *Analecta Augustiniana* 54 (1991): 65–79.

Tolomio, Ilario. "Il primato dell'etica nella spiritualità della 'devotio moderna.'" In *Riforma della Chiesa, cultura e spiritualità nel Quattrocento Veneto*, edited by Giovanni B. Trolese, 73–90. Atti del Convegno per il IV Centenario di Ludovico Barbaro, 1382–1443, Padova-Venezia-Treviso 19–24 settembre 1982. Cesena: Badia di S.Maria del Monte, 1984.

Trinkaus, Charles. *In Our Image and Likeness: Humanity and Divinity in Italian Humanist Thought.* 2 vols. Chicago: Constable, 1970.

Trolese, Giovanni B., ed. *Riforma della Chiesa, cultura e spiritualità nel Quattrocento Veneto.* Atti del Convegno per il IV Centenario di Ludovico Barbaro, 1382–1443, Padova-Venezia-Treviso 19–24 settembre 1982. Cesena: Badia di S.Maria del Monte, 1984.

Turchini, Angelo. *Sotto l'occhio del padre: Società confessionale e istruzione primaria nello stato di Milano.* Bologna: il Mulino, 1996.

Valerio, Adriana, ed. *Donne, potere e profezia.* Naples: M. D'Auria, 1995.

———. *I sermoni di Domenica da Paradiso.* Spoleto: Centro italiano di studi sull'alto Medioevo, 1999.

Valone, Carolyn. "Roman Matrons as Patrons: Various Views of the Cloister Wall." In *The Crannied Wall: Women, Religion, and the Arts in Early Modern Europe,* edited by Craig Monson, 49–72. Ann Arbor: University of Michigan Press, 1992.

Vandenbroucke, François. *La spiritualité au Moyen Age.* Vol. 2. Paris: Ed. Montaigne-Aubier, 1966.

Vauchez, André. *The Laity in the Middle Ages: Religious Beliefs and Devotional Practices.* Notre Dame: University of Notre Dame Press, 1993.

———. *La sainteté en Occident aux derniers siècles du Moyen Age: D'après les procès de canonisation et les documents hagiographiques.* Rome: Ecole française de Rome, 1981.

Vecchio, Silvana. "The Good Wife." In *A History of Women in the West,* edited by Georges Duby and Michelle Perrot. Vol. 2, *Silences of the Middle Ages.* Edited by Christiane Klapisch-Zuber, 105–35. Cambridge, Mass.: Harvard University Press, 1992.

Verdon, Timothy, and John Henderson, eds. *Christianity and the Renaissance: Image and Religious Imagination in the Quattrocento.* New York: Syracuse University Press, 1990.

Villari, Rosario. *Elogio della dissimulazione: La lotta politica nel Seicento.* Bari: Laterza, 1987.

Vismara, Paola. "Il cattolicesimo dalla 'Riforma Cattolica' all'assolutismo illuminato." In *Storia del cristianesimo: L'età moderna,* edited by Giovanni Filoramo and Daniele Menozzi, 153–98. Rome and Bari: Laterza, 1997.

Wayne, Valerie. "Some Sad Sentence: Vives' *Instruction of a Christian Woman.*" In *Silent but for the Word: Tudor Women as Patrons, Translators, and Writers of Religious Works,* edited by Margaret P. Hannay, 15–29. Kent, Ohio: Kent State University Press, 1985.

Weber, Alison. "Recent Studies on Women and Early Modern Religion in Spanish." *Renaissance Quarterly* 52 (1999): 197–206.

Weiler, Anton G. "Il significato della devotio moderna per la cultura europea." *Cristianesimo nella storia* 15 (1994): 51–69.

Weinstein, Donald, and Rudolph Bell. *Saints and Society: The Two Worlds of Western Christianity, 1000–1700.* Chicago: University of Chicago Press, 1982.

Weissman, Ronald. *Ritual Brotherhood in Renaissance Florence.* New York and London: Academic, 1982.

Winston-Allen, Anne. *Convent Chronicles: Women Writing about Women and Reform in the Late Middle Ages.* University Park: Pennsylvania State University Press, 2004.

Zanelli, Agostino. "La devozione di Brescia a Venezia e il principio della sua decadenza." *Archivio Storico Lombardo* 39 (1912): 23–100.

Zarri, Gabriella. "Ambiente e spiritualità mericiani." In *Angela Merici: Vita della Chiesa e spiritualità nella prima metà del Cinquecento,* edited by Cataldo Naro, 53–76. Convegno di studi storici (Mascalucia 21–22 luglio 1997), Studi del centro "A. Cammarata," 27. Caltanissetta and Rome: Salvatore Sciascia, 1998.

———. "Aspetti dello sviluppo degli ordini religiosi in Italia tra Quattro e Cinquecento: Studi e problemi." In *Strutture ecclesiastiche in Italia e in Germania prima della Riforma,* edited by Paolo Prodi and Peter Johanek, 207–57. Bologna: il Mulino, 1984.

———, ed. *Donna, disciplina, creanza cristiana dal XV al XVII secolo: Studi e testi a stampa.* Rome: Edizioni Storia e Letteratura, 1996.

———, ed. *Finzione e santità tra medioevo ed età moderna.* Turin: Rosemberg & Sellier, 1991.

———. "Gender, Religious Institutions, and Social Discipline: The Reform of the Regulars." In *Gender and Society in Renaissance Italy,* edited by Judith C. Brown and Robert C. Davis, 193–212. London and New York: Longman, 1998.

———. "Monasteri femminili e città (secoli XV–XVIII)." In *Storia d'Italia, Annali IX: La Chiesa e il potere politico dal Medioevo all'età contemporanea,* edited by Giorgio Chittolini and Giovanni Miccoli, 359–429. Turin: Einaudi, 1986.

———. "La nave di S. Orsola." *Annali dell'Istituto storico italo-germanico in Trento* 19 (1993): 527–54.

———. "Orsola e Caterina: Il matrimonio delle vergini nel XVI secolo." *Rivista di storia e letteratura religiosa* 29 (1993): 527–54. English translation: "Ursula and Catherine: The Marriage of Virgins in the Sixteenth Century," in *Creative Women in Medieval and Early Modern Italy: A Religious and Artistic Renaissance,* edited by E. Ann Matter and John Coakley, 237–78. Philadelphia: Pennsylvania University Press, 1994.

———. *Recinti: Donna, clausura e matrimonio nella prima età moderna.* Bologna: il Mulino, 2000.

————. *Le sante vive: Profezie di corte e devozione femminile tra '400 e '500.* Turin: Rosemberg & Sellier, 1990.

Zemon Davis, Natalie. *Society and Culture in Early Modern France.* Stanford, Calif.: Stanford University Press, 1975.

————. *Women on the Margins: Three Seventeenth-Century Lives.* Cambridge, Mass.: Harvard University Press, 1995.

Ziegler, Joanna E. *Sculpture of Compassion: The Pieta and the Beguines in the Southern Low Countries, c. 1300–c. 1600.* Brussels and Rome: Institut historique belge de Rome, 1992.

Index

Spirituality, Gender, and the Self in Renaissance Italy: Angela Merici and the Company of St. Ursula (1474–1540) was designed and typeset in Garamond by Kachergis Book Design of Pittsboro, North Carolina. It was printed on 60-pound Natural Offset and bound by McNaughton & Gunn of Saline, Michigan.